Critical Essays on

WILLIAM CARLOS WILLIAMS

CRITICAL ESSAYS
ON
AMERICAN LITERATURE

James Nagel, General Editor
University of Georgia, Athens

Critical Essays on

WILLIAM CARLOS WILLIAMS

edited by

STEVEN GOULD AXELROD

and

HELEN DEESE

G. K. Hall & Co. / New York
Maxwell Macmillan Canada / Toronto
Maxwell Macmillan International / New York Oxford Singapore Sydney

Acknowledgment for the use of material by William Carlos Williams:
William Carlos Williams: *The Collected Poems of William Carlos Williams,
1909–1939,* vol. 1. Copyright 1938 by New Directions Publishing Corp.
Reprinted by permission of New Directions Publishing Corp.

G. K. Hall & Co.
Macmillan Publishing Company
866 Third Avenue
New York, New York 10022

Maxwell Macmillan Canada, Inc.
1200 Eglinton Avenue East
Suite 200
Don Mills, Ontario M3C 3N1

Library of Congress Cataloging-in-Publication Data

Critical essays on William Carlos Williams / edited by Steven Gould
    Axelrod and Helen Deese.
        p.   cm.
    Includes bibliographical references and index.
    ISBN 0-7838-0015-0
    1. Williams, William Carlos, 1883-1963—Criticism and
interpretation.   I. Axelrod, Steven Gould, 1944–
II. Deese, Helen.
PS3545.I544Z5837   1994
811'.52—dc20   94-32339
                                                           CIP

The paper used in this publication meets the minimum requirements of
American National Standard for Information Sciences—Permanence of
Paper for Printed Library Materials. ANSI Z3948-1984.∞™

10   9   8   7   6   5   4   3   2   1

Printed in the United States of America

Contents

◆

General Editor's Note

◆

This series seeks to anthologize the most important criticism on a wide variety of topics and writers in American literature. Our readers will find in various volumes not only a generous selection of reprinted articles and reviews but original essays, bibliographies, manuscript sections, and other materials brought to public attention for the first time. This volume, *Critical Essays on William Carlos Williams*, is the most comprehensive collection of essays ever published on one of the most important modern writers in the United States. It contains both a sizable gathering of early reviews and a broad selection of more modern scholarship. Among the authors of reprinted articles and reviews are Ezra Pound, D. H. Lawrence, Wallace Stevens, Robert Lowell, Linda Welshimer Wagner, Hugh Kenner, and Cecilia Tischi. In addition to a substantial introduction by Helen Deese on the shape of Williams's career, and a bibliographical essay by Steven Gould Axelrod on the history of Williams scholarship, there are also three original essays commissioned specifically for publication in this volume: new studies by Sheryl A. Mylan on the Stecher trilogy, Sergio Rizzo on *Paterson*, and Elizabeth Klaver on Williams's plays. We are confident that this book will make a permanent and significant contribution to the study of American literature.

JAMES NAGEL
University of Georgia, Athens

Publisher's Note

◆

Producing a volume that contains both newly commissioned and reprinted material presents the publisher with the challenge of balancing the desire to achieve stylistic consistency with the need to preserve the integrity of works first published elsewhere. In the Critical Essays series, essays commissioned especially for a particular volume are edited to be consistent with G. K. Hall's house style; reprinted essays appear in the style in which they were first published, with only typographical errors corrected. Consequently, shifts in style from one essay to another are the result of our efforts to be faithful to each text as it was originally published.

Introduction

HELEN DEESE

> A black black cloud
> flew over the sun
> driven by fierce flying
> rain.

William Carlos Williams tells us in his *Autobiography* that this was his first poem. It came to him "born like a bolt out of the blue . . . unsolicited," breaking "a spell of disillusion and suicidal despondency." It also elicited the first critical response to his poetry, his own quick realization that the image was impossible: "How could clouds be driven by the rain? Stupid."[1]

Neither in his *Autobiography*, nor in his conversations with Edith Heal, recorded in *I Wanted to Write a Poem*, does Williams tell us precisely when those first lines of poetry were written, just that "up to eighteen or even later I had not the slightest intention of writing or of doing anything in the arts." Nor does he confess the details of his nearly "suicidal despondency" whose spell was broken by the "joy I felt, the mysterious, soul-satisfying joy that swept over me at the moment [which] was only mitigated by the critical comment which immediately followed it." That joy in poetic creation, both chastened and fired by his self-fashioned critical theories, pushed him into every genre of verse and prose, inspired him toward an expression of an American life in the American idiom. Because he was so long both unfashionable and out of the traditional grain, that joy had to sustain him in his often lonely wrestle with the whole Euro-American literary establishment.

Not until the publication of *Paterson I* in 1946 did either Williams's poetry or his ideas about poetry receive much positive attention from mainstream reviewers or literary critics. Nevertheless, Williams always read his reviews (however few in number), as well as the commentary of other poets. Usually he responded openly—sometimes ironically or with angry scorn, at other times changing the poems to make them more palatable to editors—

1

and sometimes with assertions of independence that, despite a brash, even defiant, tone, chronicle a developing comprehension of his own individual poetics. This essay will follow the creative interaction, during Williams's lifetime, between his writing and the critical responses it provoked.

Williams never expected to make a living by writing. Even though he wanted be a poet, he also knew that he would go on, as his family had planned, to the University of Pennsylvania to study dentistry—a choice that changed to medicine in his first year at school. Unsentimentally, he knew he needed money to support his independence in writing. He wanted to write like the very best, "like Shakespeare," but he also wanted to "tell people, to tell 'em off, plenty. There would be a bitter pleasure in that, bitter because I instinctively knew no one much would listen." If he could support himself and a family through medicine, then "no one, and I meant no one (for money) was ever (never) going to tell me how or what I was going to write."[2]

During his years in medical school, the young poet wrote two very different kinds of poetry. Keats was then his model for formal poetry, and he copied the romantic young physician's style "religiously." He wrote carefully crafted, Keatsian sonnets and page upon page of a long romance patterned upon *Endymion*. His more spontaneous poems, on the other hand, he reserved for his Whitman-like notebooks; he recorded his "Whitmanesque 'thoughts,' a sort of purgation and confessional, to clear my head and my heart from turgid obsessions." The freer writing in the notebooks (the writing of his inner life) Williams showed to Ezra Pound. He and Pound lived in the same dormitory at the University of Pennsylvania, and they began there a tense, crucial friendship, one that lasted through Williams's life despite their great differences in temperament, poetic practice and theory.

Williams told Edith Heal that "before meeting Ezra Pound is like B.C. and A.D."[3] Pound would come to the young medical student's room to read his own poems aloud to him, some of which were eventually included in Pound's first collection, *A Lume Spento*. In his turn, Williams read Pound his Whitmanesque poems. The result of their mutual reading was a critical and creative independence. According to Williams: "He was impressed with his own poetry; but then I was impressed with my own poetry, too, so we got along all right."[4]

In 1909, while still a resident physician at the Nursery and Child's Hospital in New York City, Williams privately published his first book, a 22-page collection titled simply *Poems*. The poems, sonnets and rhymed couplets in a romantic mode and often expressing a high-minded morality, elicited one review, a short, unsigned courteous notice in the *Rutherford American* that commended Dr. Williams's "open-eyed interest in the things of beauty, the mind and the spirit."[5] Far more important was a letter from Ezra Pound in London. Williams had mailed him a copy of *Poems*, and he received a reply that might have crucially discouraged a lesser ego. Pound admitted that *Poems* had some value "as proof that WCW has poetic instincts," but that was all. He came down on Williams's lack of originality, his imitative voice and form: "Nowhere . . . do you add anything to the poets you have used as models." He included a reading list so that Williams could "learn something about the progress of Eng. poetry in the last century."[6] Undaunted and determined to be a poet, Williams continued to send poems to Pound.

By 1913 Williams had married Florence Herman, settled into his medical practice in Rutherford, New Jersey, and purchased the home at 9 Ridge Road where he and Flossie would live for the rest of their lives. In that same year, Pound arranged for his own publisher in England, Elkin Mathews, to print a collection of 13 of Williams's poems, a volume that Williams titled *The Tempers*. Pound wrote for it not only an Introductory Note but also Williams's first significant public review: "[Mr. Williams] makes a bold effort to express himself directly and convinces one that the emotions expressed are veritably his own. . . . It is this that gives one hope for his future work."[7] Today *The Tempers* represents the beginning of the Williams canon. In later life, Williams told his publisher, James Laughlin of New Directions, that the verses of *Poems* "were not to be reprinted," and the editors of the definitive *Collected Poems of William Carlos Williams* have respected his wishes.[8]

Williams also began to send poems to Harriet Monroe at *Poetry*. Pound particularly recommended one poem to Monroe, "Postlude." She printed that work and three others in the June 1913 issue, but only after asking for some revisions. Williams wrote right back, "Your courteous letter startles me." He had looked, he said, "upon *Poetry* as a forum wherein competent poets might speak freely, uncensored by any standard of rules." It was a good-humored but quite serious letter about the intrusion of officious editors upon poetry that "to be alive must have some tincture of disestablishment." He ended his letter with a flourish of that verbal self-confidence and earnest determination he needed to fashion himself as a poet: "Anyhow, I'm a great poet, and you don't think so, and there we are. And so allow me to send you a revised "Postlude" (when it is done) hoping to gain your good favor in that way—for I must succeed."[9] Williams soon found the more radical forum he needed in *Others*, the magazine founded in 1915 by Alfred Kreymborg and Walter Arensberg. Again, it was Pound who had suggested that Kreymborg look Williams up when Kreymborg moved to New York from London. It was through Williams's association with *Others* that he came to befriend and work with the most vigorous artists and writers in New York City, including Man Ray, Malcolm Cowley, Mina Loy, Marcel Duchamp, Maxwell Bodenheim, Wallace Stevens, and Marianne Moore.[10]

During the four years of the magazine's existence, Williams wrote his poems primarily with *Others* in mind. He worked hard to keep it going, despite his full medical working schedule, making "weekly trips, winter and summer, to help read manuscripts, correct proofs."[11] He edited two issues himself, including the last. In that July 1919 issue, Williams concluded the run of *Others* with an editorial, prose supplement titled "Belly Music." In this angry assessment of American critics, he excoriates their "taste for loveliness." They are "sophomoric, puling, nonsensical." They have no "vision into the desolate PRESENT." Their "criticism is characterised by a deadly fear for the future." Even the best of them, like Amy Lowell and Conrad Aiken, exhibit "little more than an isolated perception of certain values. They pick over dead bones."[12]

This essay was not yet a manifesto of personal poetic theory. Although Williams believed that Ezra Pound, cut off from his locality, "began to die the first time he set foot on a gangplank,"[13] Pound was still a major stimulus to Williams's poetic innovations: "It is the NEW! not one more youthful singer, one more lovely poem. The NEW, the everlasting NEW, the everlasting defiance. Ezra has the smell of it." As part of his own everlasting defiance of the decorous, Williams insisted upon writing poetry in his own language, using his own perceptions of persons and things. "OTHERS saw its inception when I was thirty, when I had already proved a failure time after time. And yet I sing. And if my voice is cracked at least no one can HEAR singing as I can nor put it into the throat so perfectly. Whose throat is yours and which is mine if not the one into which I PUT the music. And I will fight to insist that I am not voiceless. I insist that it is I, I, I who PUTS the music into the throats of those in whom I HEAR my music."[14]

In late 1917, Williams assembled the poems he had written for *Others* and added enough other poems to total the cycle of a year—52 poems, by far his largest collection. This grouping, published by the Four Seasons (William Brown's small press), is the first that is characteristically Williams in voice, subject matter, and form. Williams titled it *Al Que Quiere!* ("To Him Who Wants It"). Beyond its overt meaning, the title was also a pun, a tribute to the publisher of *Others*, Alfred Kreymborg—Al K. Many of *Al Que Quiere!*'s poems, like "Danse Russe," "Tract," "El Hombre," and "The Young Housewife," are now among the most familiar of Williams's poems. Nevertheless, the volume attracted little critical comment and few buyers.

Dorothy Dudley, reviewing for *Poetry*, was offended by William Brown's audacious jacket comments for *Al Que Quiere!* She feared that "the publishers" were trying to intimidate the reader with the "magnificent news that Mr. Williams 'doesn't give a damn for your opinion,' because 'his opinion of you is more important than your opinion of him.' " Despite this external intimidation, Dudley divined "a lovely bloom" as well as "fluid beauty" in at least one poem—"A Prelude."[15] Ironically, her praise discovered the very quality of "loveliness" that Williams had contemptuously dismissed in "Belly Music."

In his review for the *Egoist*, John Gould Fletcher, also concerned with the beauty or loveliness of verbal music, judged that Williams's poems managed to "achieve beauty [only] by accident."[16] He wondered if that meant a poet must be either "definite and pictorial, or indefinite and musical?" Conrad Aiken received a review copy of *Al Que Quiere!*, but not until he published *Scepticisms* in 1919 did he comment, and then without identifying the book by its title. He found the collection "more amiable that beautiful, more entertaining than successful." Aiken's label for Williams was "Puritan." The Puritanism Aiken perceived manifested itself not only in the inhibitions that made Williams ashamed to be "caught crying, exulting, or adoring" but also in his "resolute suppression of beauty" in both sound and "prosodic arrangement."[17] Williams had already said in *Others* what he thought of "loveliness" and, by implication, auditory "beauty," as defining characteristics of poetry.

Ezra Pound reviewed the collection in an essay on four new American writers—T. S. Eliot, Marianne Moore, Mina Loy, and Williams—for the June 1918 issue of *Future*. In this essay (partly reprinted in this volume), Pound recognizes the poetic polarity between Eliot and Williams; the latter's voice is "as distinct and as different as possible from the orderly statements" of Eliot. Far more perceptive than the reviewers looking for beauty and music, Pound notes an essential particularity of Williams: he possesses "the absolute conviction of a man with his feet on the soil, on a soil personally and peculiarly his own. He is rooted."[18]

In 1920, Williams published a volume quite different from anything he had done before—a set of improvisatory prose poems he titled *Kora in Hell*. Three years before publication, Margaret Anderson had printed some of these poems in the *Little Review* (October 1917), and in November Pound had written to Williams about them, terming them "wholly incoherent unAmerican poems." Pound intended both adjectives as praise: "The thing that saves your work is opacity, and don't you forget it. Opacity is NOT an American quality. Fizz, swish, gabble of verbiage, these are echt Amerikanisch."[19] Pound was responding negatively to Williams's obsessive concern about the significance to the American poet of the American place.

Both of Williams's parents had been born outside the United States, his father in England, his mother in Puerto Rico. William George Williams had grown up in the Virgin Islands; Raquel Helene Rose Hoheb (but called Elena) had studied painting for three years in Paris, living with her cousins there. William George Williams had brought Elena from Puerto Rico, first to Brooklyn and then to Rutherford, New Jersey. Although William Carlos Williams lived all his life in Rutherford, his cultural heritages were English, West Indian, Basque, Dutch, Jewish, Spanish, and French. His second and third languages were Spanish and French. According to today's concept of America as both multiethnic and multicultural, Williams was quintessentially American. But in his own day, his claim to an American identity was subject to question. Williams may have written to Pound about their contrary relationships to the United States—Pound fleeing from his American place and Williams trying to claim his. Pound's letter on *Kora* begins by assuring Williams that he is an "Amurkun" author "same as me," and yet taunts him for lacking confidence in his American self, and for rebelling in Freudian fashion against his "Vaterersatz, you have a paternal image at your fireside, and you call it John Bull."[20]

In the remarkable Prologue to *Kora*, Williams acknowledged Pound's letter by reprinting part of it, answering it rather sharply. He metaphorically places Pound in classical Greece and himself among the post-Hellenic, colonial Greeks of Italy and Sicily who "set their backs to Athens": "Hellenism, especially the modern sort, is too staid, too chilly, too little fecundative to impregnate my world."[21] Williams later told Edith Heal that he used the Prologue to "sound off, tell the world—especially my intimate friends—how I felt about them." On the other hand, despite his sometimes impatient reactions, Williams asserted that he nevertheless "paid attention very assiduously to what I was told."[22]

The Prologue to *Kora* also reprinted parts of letters from Hilda Doolittle and Wallace Stevens. H. D.'s letter tells Williams why, as an editor of the *Egoist*, she deleted "all the flippancies" from his poem "March." She wished that nothing "hey-ding-ding" should detract from "the beautiful lines [that] are so very beautiful." She describes writing as "a very sacred thing." In the Prologue Williams retorts that whatever is "sacred is static," and "there is nothing sacred about literature." Literature is change "and change is mockery." He insists that "I'll write whatever I damn please, whenever I damn please and as I damn please and it'll be good if the authentic spirit of change is on it." And this was more than bravado, for the Prologue precedes a radically personal collection of "incoherent unAmerican" improvisations, with comments that do little to clarify them. Nevertheless, in order to be published by H. D. in the *Egoist*, Williams admits that he compromised, as he had earlier with Harriet Monroe; he allowed "March" to be edited to a "purified form."[23]

The excerpts of the letter from Wallace Stevens comment upon *Al Que Quiere!*, suggesting that the collection seems too much like a miscellany: "I am only objecting that a book that contains your particular quality should contain anything else." And Stevens adds "I think your tantrums not half mad enough." Williams quips that perhaps Stevens thinks that he does "not push [his] advantage through to an overwhelming decision."[24] That allusion to "The Love Song of J. Alfred Prufock" echoes the anger Williams was then feeling over the critical enthusiasm for T. S. Eliot. For example, in the September 1918 issue of the *Little Review*, Ezra Pound had reprinted a vitriolic essay, "The Western School," by English classicist Edgar Jepson. The essay damned most current "United States poetry" for being self-consciously American. Jepson asked "What has the fat-headed ruck of the United States or any other country to do with poetry?" He deplored the lack of music in American verse: "I sometimes think that this amazing lack of a sense of the beauty of words comes from the manner in which the language of the United States is spoken—that monotonous drone, generally nasal, or that monotonous nasal whine." On the other hand, Jepson lauded T. S. Eliot for writing in a poetic diction that is "musical with a new music." He asked, "Could anything be more United States, more of the soul of that modern land than 'The Love Song of J. Alfred Prufrock'?" He praised "La Figlia che Piange" as having "delicate, beautiful, intense emotion, with exquisite, beautiful music." This poem he found to be "the very fine flower of the finest spirit of the United States."[25]

In his Prologue, Williams sarcastically refuted Jepson's equation of Prufrock's delicately inept sensibility with the very soul of American modernity. Damning Jepson, and perhaps Pound too, as having the critical sense of an attendant lord, Williams rejected both the perception of Prufrock as a "New World type" and the elevation of Eliot as America's "finest" spirit: "[T]here is always some everlasting Polonius of Kensington forever to rate highly his eternal Eliot. It is because Eliot is a subtle conformist. It tickles the palate of this archbishop of procurers to a lecherous antiquity to hold up Prufrock as a New World type. . . . No. The New World is Montezuma or . . . Guatemozin who had the city of Mexico leveled over him before he was taken."[26] Williams has thus transformed the ideal New World spirit from a would-be English gentleman to that of a proud (even when vanquished) Aztec. A few years later, that native, New World spirit reappeared in Williams's prose work, *In the American Grain* (1926), specifically in the chapter titled "The Destruction of Tenochtitlan."

Kora in Hell received mostly adverse attention. John Gould Fletcher concluded that it was "merely a dodge for wrapping up platitudes in a different kind of statement." The book, he concluded, "should never have been written."[27] Williams retaliated by reprinting in *Contact* a portion of that review, isolated on a page, with Fletcher name's in large bold print— upside down.[28] *Poetry*'s reviewer, Helen Birch-Bartlett, in search of loveliness, thought she had found a soulmate in her wistful reading of Williams's "experiment in delicately insulting, macabre grisaille." "The plainly worded fact I am coming to, slowly enough, and now and then plucking a wayside weed as I travel, is that I find this work sad and beautiful, and very much akin to the rambling but honest way of my own observing sense."[29] In a letter to *Poetry* (reprinted in this volume), Robert McAlmon answered for Williams, refuting any delicate wistfulness in the stressed and discontented mind that had written these improvisations. "There is in this book the spasmodic quality of the active, imaginative, alternately frightened and reckless, consciousness. . . . It is incoherent and unintelligible to those people with lethargy of their sensing organs. . . . To me *Kora in Hell* is immeasurably the most important book of poetry that America has produced."[30] After the demise of *Others*, McAlmon and Williams put together a new journal for the contemporary arts—*Contact*. They published four issues from 1920 to 1921 and one in 1923. On *Contact*'s pages, Williams repeatedly stated his insistence that concrete sensual experience is the first matter of art. He quoted John Dewey: "We are discovering that the locality is the only universal." He quoted the French painter Maurice Vlaminck: "Intelligence is international, stupidity is national, art is local."[31] Williams asserted that "in proportion as a man has bestirred himself to become awake to his own locality he will perceive more and more of what is disclosed and find himself in a position to make the necessary translations."[32]

In the fourth, undated issue, *Contact* published a review of *Kora in Hell* by Marianne Moore. This review delighted and encouraged Williams in a dark time. Immediately, he wrote Moore a letter: "You make the blood to flow in my smallest capillaries again by what you say of my book. . . . Such is the miracle of a friend's good words."[33]

The most unpleasant commentary on *Kora* was a long, personal malediction, written in madly dadaist verse by the woman Williams calls the Baroness in his *Autobiography*—Else von Freytag-Loringhoven. Williams had refused an invitation to the Baroness's bed more than once. Implicitly making fun of his marital status in her title—"Thee I call 'Hamlet of the Wedding-Ring' "—she accuses Williams of indecision, impotency, flippancy, shallowness, and bad art: "W. C. makes practice out of dancing with dead things— has to dance with some things—can not afford palpitating things—."[34] This revenge of a woman scorned against "Carlos Williams—you wobbly-legged business satchel-carrying little louse"[35] might be funny today were it not for her repeated defamation of Williams's Jewish heritage: "W. C. with heavy clumsy brain—atavistically handicapped by Jewish family tradition."[36]

The Baroness's verse critique was published in two issues of New York's *Little Review*. Ezra Pound's fits of anti-Semitism are well known, as is Eliot's more genteel version of the prejudice. That Margaret Anderson was also anti-Semitic is evident in her praise for the Baroness's review. She called it "one of the most intelligent pieces of criticism that has ever come to us."[37] Anderson could say this despite von Freytag's antipathetic observations about Williams, Jews, and Americans—all of whom, von Freytag claims, are clodlike materialists lacking "spirit," incapable of art because incapable of ascending the Christianized Platonic ladder from the physical to the immaterial.

> In materialism callous—brain dense—plebianism—jew—American meet.
> God's goal: body to soul—material to spirit—arriving at Himself.
> In Europe "Kora in Hell" never had chance!
> In Europe W. C. no need do that!—he would not be. Jew mixture—in
> Europe—not a castaway—spirit-deserted.[38]

Williams did not respond in print to the Baroness's crude attack.

Professionally, it was the investiture by Pound and others of the Anglicized Eliot as the Archbishop of American poetry that rankled Williams the most. "I felt that [Eliot] had rejected America and I refused to be rejected and so my reaction was violent. . . . I had envisaged a new form of poetic composition, a form for the future. It was a shock to me that he was so tremendously successful; my contemporaries flocked to him—away from what I wanted. It forced me to be successful."[39] His next two collections of poetry, *Sour Grapes* (1921) and *Spring and All* (1923), are both significant works, bold and explorative in form and subject matter. *Sour Grapes* was reviewed by two men who would soon become major literary critics: Kenneth Burke for *The Dial* and Yvor Winters for *Poetry*. (Burke's review is reprinted in this volume.) Neither writer noted the lack of "music" or "loveliness" in these collections. Indeed, Burke, writing in the *Dial*, revised the charge of a lack of beauty in Williams's texts, accusing them instead of lacking intellectual strength. It is this reading of Williams as unintellectual, as a poet of things rather than ideas, that has plagued Williams's reputation, leading to critical and scholarly condescension. Burke defined Williams as "the master of the glimpse" with a simple *ars poetica*: "There is the eye, and there is the thing upon which that eye alights; while the relationship existing between the two is a poem." For Burke, Williams's directness mistakenly displaced "Culture" as poetry's genesis. Williams had written in *Contact* that "sensual values" derived from "contact" with the world "are the only realities in writing." Burke reponded in this review that "contact" resolves "into the counterpart of Culture, and Williams becomes thereby one of the most distinguished Neanderthal men. His poetry deals with the coercions of nature—and by nature I mean iron rails as well as iron ore—rather than with the laborious structure of ideas man has erected above nature. His hatred of the idea in art is consequently pronounced, and very rightly brings in its train a complete disinterest in form."[40]

Burke exaggerated. Williams was no Neanderthal nor was he so opposed to form, only to the privileging of form over sensuous experience. In the final issue of *Contact*, published 16 months after Burke's review, Williams implicitly answered him by defining the relationship of sense and form in his own poetic practice: "The sense is not carried as an extraneous 'meaning,' but is constituted by the work itself. One does not write a poem to say something, but to write a poem. . . . By 'form' is meant everything in a work which relates to structural unity rather than to 'meanings' dragged over from former associations."[41]

Yvor Winters, unlike Burke, found evidence in *Sour Grapes* of both an intelligence at work and a knowledge of the English poetic tradition. He pointed out that Williams, as a means to structural unity, frequently used the Jacobean metaphysical conceit, which is "an intellectual relationship between two objects physically unrelated." Even in poems that use "the simple physical image," Williams "looks for relations and the sharpest way to get them down."[42] Winters later changed his mind about Williams, but here he discovered cerebral elements that allowed him to praise the poems he liked.

In *Spring and All* (1923), a prose poetry matrix, Williams formally recognized that the intellectual quality primary to his poetry—and perhaps his life—was the force and scope of his imagination, that power of the mind that invited the ontology of observed "things" into an empathetic correlation with itself. "In the composition, the artist does exactly what every eye must do with life, fix the particular with the universality of his own personality—Taught by the largeness of his imagination to feel every form which he sees moving within himself, he must prove the truth of this by expression."[43] He proposed that poems and paintings are not representations of reality, but are themselves present actualities: "The only realism in art is of the imagination. It is only thus that the work escapes plagiarism after nature and becomes a creation."[44]

In hindsight today, we know how crucial *Spring and All* was as a declaration of Williams's evolving poetic practice. In 1923, however, the small book was virtually ignored. *Poetry* published the only comment of any length and that was a modestly favorable review by Marjorie Allen Seiffert, a poet herself and a friend of Williams. She liked the prose, saying it "achieves its object, clarity, by swiftness and flight, by gleeful gusto," but then she admitted that she could not "intelligently experience" many of the poems because "after all we like to see works of the imagination 'looking like nature.' "[45] Perhaps because of the near silence that attended *Spring and All*, Williams did not publish another collection of poems until *Collected Poems* in 1931.

The truth is that not only Seiffert but most reviewers understood Williams's prose long before they could comprehend his poetry. Although Williams considered himself to be foremost a poet, he had been writing prose all along—doctor stories, reflective pieces, dramatic pieces—publishing some of them in *Others* and *Contact*. In the spring of 1923, at the instigation of Ezra Pound, a small private press in Paris published a short (81-page) novel that Williams had completed some time before and put aside. He called it *The Great American Novel*, a semi-satiric lament on the harsh conditions of American life and culture as well as a trying out of new possibilites in prose effects. Matthew Josephson, who had ignored Williams's poetry and whom Williams did not like, responded to *The Great American Novel* with pleasure, comparing it to Laurence Sterne's *Tristram Shandy*. Williams, he wrote, demonstrates that "to make words play . . . is the only reality the artist in literature knows." Williams's "disassociations," when sharp, "have a necessity about them that is more satisfying than causality."[46] Paul Rosenfeld, in the first overview of Williams's work, recognized in *The Great American Novel* the freeing influence of James Joyce and praised the novel's "crass, unvoluptuous, vitriolic language."[47] Unlike others, Rosenfeld also felt he understood Williams's poems; they have, he wrote, "a truthfulness wanting [in] those of certain of his fellows; . . . his poems give the relationship of things more justly than do those of [Eliot]."[48]

In June 1923, Bill and Flossie Williams embarked upon a year-long break from his medical practice, staying first in New York City, where he and Flossie did much of the research for *In the American Grain*, and then in Europe where most of the book was written. This set of imaginative prose pieces on figures in North American history, ranging from Eric the Red to a hermaphroditic Abraham Lincoln, produced a significant broadening in Williams's public reception. For the first time, Williams's work was reviewed in the mainstream press. Kenneth Burke, however, wrote two negative reviews. In the *New York Times*, he concluded that Williams's "style, at its worse, is meaninglessly inchoate—a sacrifice to experimentation, perhaps, and highly unfortunate."[49] In the *Herald Tribune*, he reported that Williams's method of reimagining the true character of the New World heroes "tends toward the maximum of 'interpretation' and a mimimum of research."[50]

Lola Ridge's more positive review for the *New Republic* (reprinted in this volume) responded to that problematic relationship of "interpretation" to "facts." "There is in Williams a higher fealty than that demanded by mere factual truth. He has in him the truth that can only be proven by emotional recognition." She recognizes that "he has achieved here as searching an analysis of Puritanism as was possible to one not yet quite convalescent from its effects." On the other hand, astutely and unconventionally for her time, she faults Williams on two subjects—the African-American and the woman. Ridge notes that Williams's "treatment of the Negroes, a people who have given so much to America's spiritual and aesthetic life, is singularly inadequate. He is not unsympathetic—far from it. But he approaches them as a spectator. . . ." As for women, she perceives with some regret that "he joins foreigners, who have not the knowledge that contact gives, in regarding New England women as sexless. But they are no more sexless than any other women, merely encased in congealed opinion." She finds in Williams "signs of sex-antagonism. There seems to be in him a streak of what is not so much commonness as a desire, almost a hunger, to share its contacts."[51]

D. H. Lawrence, not surprisingly, also perceived a desire by Williams for heterosexual "contact." In his review of *In the American Grain* for the *Nation* (reprinted in this volume), Lawrence perceives Williams as trying "to bring into his consciousness America itself, the still-unravished bride of silences." Williams's America is not the public "national" America which is "bastardardized European" but the "unravished *local* America," a spirit of the physical place. Whereas Ridge resented Williams's sensual "sex-antagonism," Lawrence presumed that men create themselves against women and rejoiced in the antagonistic, male response to an alluring America, seeing it as a challenge to develop a new un-European masculinity. "[Williams] sees the genius of the continent as a woman with exquisite, super-subtle tenderness and recoiling cruelty. It is a myth-woman who will demand of men a sensitive awareness, a supreme sensuous delicacy, and at the same time an infinitely tempered resistance, a power of endurance and of resistance."[52] Unfortunately, despite the contending insights of Ridge and Lawrence, *In the American Grain* did not sell well.

In 1927, Williams arranged for his two sons to spend a year at the same school in Switzerland that he and his brother had once attended. Just as his own mother had stayed in Switzerland to be near her sons, so too did Flossie stay in Switzerland to be near hers. To contain his loneliness, Williams worked hard throughout that year at both medicine and writing. He began and completed *A Voyage to Pagany*, a romantic novel about three women a young doctor loves during a year of living in France, Italy, and Austria. The novel is a disturbing revision of the Williams's trip to Europe in 1923.

A Voyage to Pagany, which came out in 1928, sold little better than *In the American Grain*, although it was reviewed even more widely. Nevertheless, the novel did put Williams in touch with younger poets and publishers. It furnished Richard Johns with a title for his new literary magazine, *Pagany*, a journal for which Williams did much of the early editorial work. A young New York poet, Louis Zukofsky, who had been referred to Williams by Pound, reviewed *A Voyage to Pagany* for *Hound and Horn*. Zukofsky perceived a parallel between Williams's reimagined experience of Europe and an earlier reimagining by Henry Adams in his *Mont St. Michel and Chartres*: "Two minds . . . have reacted as Americans, though along different lines, towards what might be termed the European unchanging."[53] More significant to Williams was Zukofsky's essay, "American Poetry 1920–1930," which Zukofsky conceived of as a sequel to René Taupin's *L'Influence du symbolisme français sur la poésie américaine (de 1910 à 1920)*, in which Taupin names Williams as one of the three most significant contemporary American poets, the other two being Pound and Eliot. Zukofsky concluded his essay with a section focusing on Williams alone, a writer of "rare importance . . . , for whatever he has written the direction of it has been poetry." He praised Williams as noting and recording shifting experience in "swiftly trained deliberations of the mind."[54] Williams read this essay in manuscript at a time when he was in both a depressed mood and a difficult writing slump. The essay's praise, when so little of his work was selling, raised his spirits and broke a writer's block that had bedeviled him for months.

In 1932, Williams published his first book of short stories: *The Knife of the Times*. It received only two reviews, one in *Books* and one in *Saturday Review*, both anonymous and negative. In the same year, Zukofsky, Charles Reznikoff, and other objectivists created TO Publishers and published Williams's *A Novelette and Other Prose*, which no one seems to have reviewed. Then Carl Rakosi and George Oppen took over TO, renamed it The Objectivist Press, and published Williams's *Collected Poems, 1921–1931*. Williams asked Wallace Stevens to write the preface, but what Stevens wrote annoyed

Williams. In his preface, reprinted here, Stevens describes Williams as essentially a romantic poet, one who counterpoints his emotions with the "anti-poetic": "The anti-poetic is his spirit's cure. He needs it as a naked man needs shelter or an animal needs salt. To a man with a sentimental side the anti-poetic is that truth, that reality to which all of us are forever fleeing."[55] Williams disliked Stevens's perception of duality in his work. The phrase "anti-poetic" especially irritated him: "It's all one to me—the antipoetic is not something to enhance the poetic—it's all one piece. . . . I have never been satisfied that the anti-poetic had any validity or even existed."[56]

Collected Poems, 1921–1931 appeared in early 1934. For the first time, Williams's poetry received attention from the mainstream press—a modestly favorable review by Babette Deutsch in the *New York Herald Tribune* and some faint praise from G. Poore in the *New York Times*. For Williams, the most personally meaningful review was that of Marianne Moore for *Poetry*. She noted that "with an abandon born of inner security, Dr. Williams nicknames the chain of incontrovertibly logical apparent nonsequiturs, rigmarole."[57] Williams wrote to thank her for the acuteness of her reading. His inner security and sense of a whole derived, he explained, from a youthful moment of despair: "The inner security . . . is an overwhelmingly important observation. . . . It is something which occurred once when I was about twenty, a sudden resignation to existence, a despair . . . which made everything a unit and at the same time a part of myself. I suppose it might be called a sort of nameless religious experience."[58] Williams felt that finally, in Moore, he had found a reader sympathetic to his poetry's heart.

Williams's next publications, slim volumes titled *An Early Martyr and Other Poems* (1935) and *Adam and Eve & the City* (1936), were elegantly printed, limited editions of 165 copies each. Ironically, these rather expensive Alcestis Press editions, selling at $7.50 per copy, attracted favorable attention for their proletarian quality. Ruth Lechlitner, writing for the *New York Herald Tribune*, especially liked Williams's "poems of realistic social content," such as "To a Poor Old Woman," "The Dead Baby," and "Proletarian Portrait," works in which "clear observation and unconfused sympathetic understanding combine with an almost flawless perfection of form." And she astutely complained that Williams "has gone too long without honor in critical circles."[59]

At least some honor in critical circles came to Williams with his next novel, *White Mule*, published in June 1937 by James Laughlin, who had recently begun a new publishing house, New Directions. *White Mule*, the first part of a projected trilogy based upon Flossie's family, not only received highly favorable reviews from Philip Rahv in the *Nation* and Alfred Kazin in the *New York Times Book Review*, but also sold out its first printing of 500 copies. Rahv asserted that for Williams "the conflict of classes might seem to be interfering, and perhaps gratuitously so, with the clean functioning of the written word." He went on to apply Stevens's diagnosis of Williams's poetry to his prose, using a somewhat different trope. Rahv found "plain and humble subject matter" to be "characteristic of Williams, who has a passion for the anti-poetic, which he sees as the solvent of the unreal in art."[60] Stevens's comment continued to show up in reviews of Williams's work through the next two decades, usually, as in Rahv's case, with its source unacknowledged.

Laughlin's New Directions followed *White Mule*, in 1938, with a volume of short stories, *Life Along the Passaic River*. The reviews were good. The *New Republic* took the stories as an indication that Williams's "social awareness has grown considerably since 'The Knife of the Times.'"[61] Eda Lou Walton, writing for the *Nation* (the review is included in this volume), discovered a sympathy for the "straight Communist ticket" but concluded that "despite the evidence in his writings of a clear political position . . . Williams is never a propagandist."[62]

In 1938, New Directions also published a major book of Williams's poetry: *The Complete Collected Poems 1906–1938*. For the most part, however, critics continued to misunderstand Williams's form and tone. R. P. Blackmur did not use the word "anti-poetic," but that is what he meant: "Dr. Williams's poetry, including the rendition, is unexpanded notation."[63] Yvor Winters's review is significant in that it demonstrates just what it is about Williams's poetry that has offended many critics—its Deweyan distrust of ideas ungrounded in experienced reality. Winters assumed, wrongly, that because Williams distrusted metaphysical ideas, he distrusted "all ideas" and consequently, "the entire range of feeling which is immediately motivated by ideas." Winters termed Williams "an uncompromising romantic." Yet, despite Winters's skeptical misgivings about the romanticism he perceived in Williams's poetry, he anticipated the place that Williams would eventually occupy in the poetic canon: "The end of the present century will see him securely established, along with Stevens, as one of the two best poets of his generation."[64]

One reviewer did not regard Williams as anti-poetic or anti-intellectual or socially unconcerned. Ruth Lechlitner's review for *Poetry* noted "the incisive development not only of Williams's technique, but his growth, through choice of subject, as a poet whose deepening social perceptions have kept his poems alive." Lechlitner perceived in his tropes "the expansion of the image, as contemporary object-incident, to become (through historical focus) a voiced comment on a natural or a human order." Finally she looks forward to *Paterson*, his work in progress, as "a possible fusion or cohesion of those factual, though disassociated and separately represented facets of the American social scene into something completely observed."[65]

The first part of *Paterson* did not appear until 1946. While thinking out the problem of form, while striving for the right means to achieve his enormous aspirations for a pastoral epic using American language, images, and objects, while gestating that difficult first book of *Paterson*, Williams continued to write other poems as well as prose and plays. In 1940, New Directions published *In the Money*, the second part of his trilogy fictionalizing Flossie's family. *In the Money* was widely praised, even by *Time* magazine (on 2 December 1940).

Through the theatrically self-reflexive device of the play within the play, Williams joined three prose pieces he had originally written for the Rutherford Little Theatre into a single three-act play plus six scenes in verse. The six scenes constituted the framing play that initiated and commented upon the inner plays. New Directions published the text in its *1942 Year Book* as "Trial Horse No. 1: Many Loves." *Many Loves* was eventually produced off Broadway in 1959 by the Living Theatre and ran in repertory there for almost a year. Brooks Atkinson for the *New York Times* judged it to be "original in form, exhilarating in content and alive with knowledge about human beings."[66] It was produced again off Broadway in 1961 "with marked success" and then in Europe in repertory with Jack Gelber's *The Connection* and Bertold Brecht's *In the Jungle of the Cities*.

In 1944, The Cumington Press published a handsome, limited edition of another book of Williams's poems, *The Wedge*. Williams meant this collection to be, like *Spring and All*, "an explanation of my poetic creed."[67] In its introduction, he implicitly denied that his poetry was "anti-poetic," formless, or sentimental because "there is nothing sentimental about a machine," and "a poem is a small (or large) machine made of words." When someone "makes" a poem, "it isn't what he *says* that counts as a work of art, it's what he makes, with such an intensity of perception that it lives with an intrinsic movement of its own to verify its authenticity."[68]

When *The Wedge* appeared in 1944, Williams was 61 years old. He had become a poetic elder statesman, whose poetry had finally begun to be recognized as a new generation of poets responded to his poems and his poetic creed. Perhaps the most influential of these younger poets was Randall Jarrell. Unfortunately, Jarrell's review of *The Wedge*, despite Williams's introduction, repeated the banal imputations of Williams's anti-intellectualiy and sentimentality. "The rather astonishing limitations of his work" are "neither technical nor moral but intellectual." He added that "even his good critical remarks sound as if they had been made by Henry Ford." Finally he transformed Stevens's insight—that Williams is an empathetic poet, off-setting his "sentimental side" with the "anti-poetic," into a condescending image: "The tough responsible doctor-half that says and does, the violent and delicate free-Freudian half that feels and senses, have their precarious connection in one of the great mythological attitudes of our country: in Brooklyn, the truck-driver looking shyly at the flower."[69] A year later, Jarrell wrote in a decidedly different tone. The occasion was the publication of *Paterson* (Book I), and Jarrell's brilliant analysis for *Partisan Review* (reprinted in this volume) marks a watershed in the critical reception of Williams's poetry. Williams, at least for Jarrell, is no longer either anti-intellectual or formless. Jarrell read *Paterson* as a work of "beauty, delicacy, and intelligence." Every part of the poem "is interwoven with everything else, just as the strands of the Falls interlace." And, he concluded, if the promised three additional books that will continue the epic "are as good as this one, the whole poem will be far and away the best long poem any American has written."[70]

The significance for American poetry of Jarrell's praise was perceived immediately by another young poet, Robert Lowell, whose *Lord Weary's Castle* had just won the 1946 Pulitzer Prize for poetry. Lowell called Jarrell's comments "a review that I imagine will become famous as an example of 'the shock of recognition.' " He could think, he said, of "no book published in 1946 that is as important" as *Paterson I*, or "of any living English or American poet who has written anything better or more ambitious" than Williams. Lowell, conscious of Williams's ongoing critque of Pound and Eliot, noted that Williams had effectively demonstrated his case: "In *Paterson* his position has paid off, when compared with Pound's. It is a sort of anti-Cantos rooted in America, in one city, and in what Williams has known long and seen often."[71]

New Directions brought out *Paterson II* in 1948. In his review for the *Nation* (reprinted in this volume), Lowell refuted charges of both anti-intellectualism and sentimentality, arguing that Williams's line from *Paterson I*—"no ideas but in things"—is "misleading." In so far as Williams locates ideas in things, he is a Platonist, for *Paterson's* "symbolic man and woman are Hegel's thesis and antithesis. They struggle toward synthesis—marriage." All the things in the poem are symbols, "not allegorical, but loose, intuitive, and Protean." Because Williams is "with the raw and the universal, his 'Paterson' is not the tragedy of the outcast but the tragedy of our civilization."[72]

Edward Honig, in his *Poetry* review, percieved the two books of *Paterson* as already "a major achievement in contemporary literature" and quite possibly, when complete, the "master work of our age." He was concerned, however, that the "obtrusive autobiographic turn" of *Paterson II* is beginning "to disrupt the objective symbolic relationships set up in Book One."[73]

Although Williams was 64 in 1948, he was writing and publishing at a prodigious rate, perhaps spurred by the positive reviews his work was now receiving. In that year, besides *Paterson II*, New Directions published his play *A Dream of Love*, and two small presses printed, each in booklet form, *The Clouds* and *The Pink Church*. In 1949, New Directions brought out both *Paterson III* and *Selected Poems*. The scholarly press now was attentive to Williams. Richard Ellmann, for the *Yale Review*, finally put to rest the adjective "anti-poetic": he called *Paterson* in its three books "the most pro-poetic of poems."[74]

Williams asked Randall Jarrell to write an introduction for *Selected*

Poems, encouraged by the young poet's review of *Paterson I*. This choice eventually caused Williams almost as many misgivings as his earlier choice of Stevens for the preface to the *Collected Poems*. Jarrell's enthusiasm for *Paterson* had been waning with each successive book, but Williams was not to know that until Jarrell's review of *Paterson IV*. Jarrell's introduction to Williams's *Selected Poems* is a variation of the *ad hominem* fallacy in argument: he lauds the man while slighting the poetry. First he identifies Williams with the American philosophic pragmatists William James and Charles Peirce, praising their character while reducing the philosophy to a common phrase about facts. He said that, like James and Peirce, Williams is "outspoken, good-hearted, and generous." No one is more American: "There is always on his lips the familiar, pragmatic, American *These are the facts.*" Williams becomes a kindly poet—not a rebel against European domination of American culture, not an angry iconoclast forcing a radical revision of language and poetry, but a nice doctor writing poetry "remarkable for its empathy. . . . When you have read *Paterson* you know for the rest of your life what it is like to be a waterfall."[75]

Williams thanked Jarrell by letter but he "secretly . . . chafed at Jarrell's giving with his right hand what his left hand kept taking away." Because *Selected Poems* is compendious and inexpensive, it has been the volume readers, especially students, have usually picked up when first they begin a study of Williams. The introduction informs their first response to his poetry. That, as Paul Mariani observes, "was an irony that would hardly have escaped Williams."[76]

Paterson III appeared in late 1949, and in early 1950 the committee for the National Book Awards bestowed upon Williams and *Paterson* its first annual Gold Medal for Poetry. Random House published another collection of his short stories, *Make Light of It*, and New Directions brought out the *Collected Later Poems*, both volumes appearing in 1950. Finally, in 1951 New Directions published *Paterson IV*, which Williams intended to be the final book.

After his review of *Paterson I*, Jarrell had waited for the next three books to be published before writing again, so that he could come to some conclusions about *Paterson* as a whole. His conclusions were bluntly negative: "*Paterson* has been getting rather steadily worse." He returned to the familiar allegation that "[Williams] is a *very* good but very *limited* poet. . . . not, of course, an intellectual at all." In a final, ironic touch he noted that Williams comes off "surprisingly badly . . . when we compare the whole of *Paterson* with the *Four Quartets*," Eliot's long poem.[77] Williams came to believe that Jarrell was offended by the subject matter of Book IV. He "couldn't take the identification of the filthy river with the perversion of the characters at the close of the fourth section of the poem."[78]

Marianne Moore privately but forcefully wrote to Williams of her own adverse reactions to Book IV, especially to the sexual scenes. Williams answered with two affectionate letters in June of 1951 explaining the pastoral genesis of both the lesbian Corydon, who "represents the 'great world,' " the Old World, and Phyllis, the young nurse who typefies "the impact of Paterson in 'his young female phase' with a world beyond his own." "To me," he wrote, "the normal world is something which to you must seem foreign. I won't defend my world. I live in it. . . . I rather like my old gal who appears in the first pages of *Paterson* IV." To Lowell, Williams wrote, "It is cheering to me to hear that you enjoyed the fourth book of *Paterson*. . . . Marianne Moore went berserk over it, taking me to task in no uncertain terms."[79]

Other significant critics responded far more positively than Jarrell or Moore to *Paterson* as a whole. M. L. Rosenthal discovered in the epic "a kind of human-ecological mysticism," an attempt "to see what meaning, if any, can be read into a given cultural unit, in its way symbolic of life in America." Williams, says Rosenthal, seeks a "language commensurate with the terrible need of individuals to communicate the nature of their love."[80] Richard Eberhart thought the exchanges between Corydon and Phyllis to be "delightful . . . in the usual elliptical glance-style." Williams "has . . . humanized the imagination and has given us a philosophy of probability and use."[81]

In March 1951, Williams suffered a stroke. Nevertheless, his writing continued to be prodigious. As he recovered, he finished his *Autobiography*. For a reading at Harvard, he composed "The Desert Music," a poem inspired by his trip in 1950 across the desert from California to El Paso. In early 1952, he finished *The Build Up*, thus completing the trilogy of the Stecher family. And then, still shaky from his stroke, he began both *Paterson* V and "Asphodel, That Greeny Flower." In August of that year, however, he had a second, more serious stroke that left him unable to use his right hand for writing.

Williams, at 70, was now a famous man, reviewed in the mainstream press as well as in the literary journals. And yet his honors remained few: the Dial Award in 1926, the Russell Loines Award in 1948, and the National Book Award in 1950. Finally, in 1952, came the possiblity of meaningful recognition. He was nominated to be Consultant in Poetry at the Library of Congress. His duties were to begin in September. Although the appointment would require the presence of the poet at the Library, it had few prescribed duties; rather the consultantship was a means by which the nation could, with an official and prestigious appointment, honor its poets. In this instance, however, a national bureaucracy, made paranoid during the frantic anti-Communist era, dishonored itself by suspecting its most devotedly American poet of disloyalty. And, in effect, it punished him. As soon as the announcement of Williams's appointment was made public in the press, "patriotic" zealots denounced him as a Communist sympathizer. An FBI investigation followed and dragged on. In official letters and interviews, Williams was treated with coldness and condescenion by both Luther Evans, the Librarian, and Verner Clapp, the Chairman of the Library's Loyalty Board. Not until June 1953 did the FBI report exonerating him reach Evans, who could have acted upon its findings but did not. If he had, Williams, who had recovered sufficently to come to Washington, could have been the Library's Consultant in Poetry for at least a few months. Instead, Evans flew to Europe to assume a new post with UNESCO without evaluating the report; Williams was left with a handful of nothing.[82]

It was probably the darkest year of Williams's life. Just a week before the announcement in the press of his appointment, he had had his second stroke. Although he went on writing during the months that followed, the physical paralysis of his right side as well as the Communist hunters in Washington pushed him into a progressively deeper depression. He was hospitalized in February 1953 and stayed there for eight weeks.[83] One honor did come to him during this dark night of the soul and body—the 1953 Bollingen Award for Poetry, a felicitous testament from his fellow poets.

Despite Williams's disappointment over the Consultantship, his stroke, his inability to use his right hand to type, and the depression that put him in the hospital, he did manage to write two poems while there: an imitation of Theocritus's first idyll and "The Mental Hospital Garden." He went on writing after he came home, typing with one finger. Soon he had 11 poems as well as "The Desert Music" and a section of "Asphodel, that Greeny Flower" that he titled for the occasion "Work in Progress." All these became a new volume of verse, *The Desert Music*, published by Random House in 1954.

Except for the title poem itself, the poems of *The Desert Music* are written in Williams's three line, step-down measure, a measure he described in a letter to John C. Thirlwall as "my solution to the problem of modern verse (which I have long sought)."[84] He writes that he first used this triadic measure in Book II of *Paterson* in the passage beginning with "The descent beckons . . . ,"[85] and he calls that passage "the lines that have most influenced my life." Williams tells Thirlwall that "as far as I know, as my forthcoming book makes clear, I shall use no other form for the rest of my life, for it represents the culmination of all my striving after an escape from the restrictions of the verse of the past."[86]

In his review of *The Desert Music*, Robert Creeley suggested that for Williams what poetry or "the poem is . . . comes again and again to the fact of women." He ends with admiration: "It is fantastic, to me, that Williams at such a time as now confronts him should be so incredibly clear."[87] Kenneth Rexroth went beyond even that: Williams "is the living poet who looks most like a classic. . . . his poetic line is organically welded to American speech like muscle to bone, like the choruses of Euripides were welded to the speech of the Athenians in the market place." Williams, he prophesied, "will rise as far above his contemporaries as Yeats did above his."[88] In her review for *Imagi*, Sister M. Bernetta Quinn notes Williams's imagistic use of flowers throughout the collection as emblems standing for love.[89]

Williams completed his "Work in Progress," titled it "Asphodel, that Greeny Flower," and published it in 1955 as the long poem that anchors his next volume of verse, *Journey to Love*. Strangely, this poem and collection received little immediate critical attention. Randall Jarrell wrote a paragraph of modest praise for the *Yale Review*, terming the book a "reflective, very personal revery" that "anyone who likes Williams's poetry will want to read."[90] Edwin Honig, in a longer paragraph, recognized that beginning with *The Desert Music*, Williams "has burst into a new greenness, a poetry of clarity, luminosity and personal affirmation."[91] Richard Eberhart, in a short review essay, wrote that Williams has exercised "his whole personality to unlock a remarkable lyical lore of love. . . . It is a mature man speaking direct truth."[92]

After the publication of *Paterson IV* in 1951, Williams had contemplated the need for a fifth book: "I have come to understand not only that many changes have occurred in me and the world, but I have been forced to recognize that there can be no end to such a story I have envisioned with the terms which I had laid down for myself. I had to take the world of Paterson into a new dimension if I wanted to give it imaginative validity."[93] New Directions published *Paterson V* in 1958. In form, the new book proved that Williams's commitment to the three line, step-down measure as the one "escape from the restrictions of the verse of the past" had been overly confining. Other routes of escape, which also maintained a discipline in writing, were possible. No single verse pattern, not even of his own conception, could absolutely prescribe either the measure or the visual conditions for Williams's next poem or even the next part of his poem. In *Paterson V*, the verse structures vary from page to page.

In his essay for *Saturday Review*, John Ciardi pointed out that, of the epic's various male figures, the Paterson of Part V is "the most intimately" Williams himself: "The first four books have . . . found the place. It is himself the poet must now find." And to do so "it is finally to that woman of the life-bearing virtues the poet comes, the virgin-and-whore, the whole woman." In perhaps his most significant comment, Ciardi pointed to the "central characteristic" of *Paterson*: "The statement is never complete at any one point. . . . There is never any one statement on which one may put his finger and say 'this is the meaning.' The meaning is a constant process."[94]

Richard Eberhart perceived this characteristic of endless process as a subversion of the tragic mode: "Since there is a touch of the comic in the fact of *Book Five*, a denial of the work of art as inevitable, an insistence on its flowing, protean, ever-changing nature, Dr. Williams should continue with this breath-taking work. A tragedy has an end, but history does not."[95]

In October of 1958, Williams suffered a third stroke that left him in progressively deteriorating health. Yet he continued to write. He began composing poems based on the paintings of Brueghel. On 13 January 1959, he was delighted that his play *Many Loves* opened off Broadway. He wrote a poem about the event, ruefully titled "15 Years Later," and subtitled "On seeing my own play / *Many Loves* / on the stage for the first time."[96] In 1959 New Directions published *Yes, Mrs. Williams*, a reminiscence of his mother's voice and stories. Both *Many Loves* and *The Farmers' Daughters*, a collection of his short stories, appeared in 1961. But by that year, Williams could no longer read and could barely type.

In the late summer of 1962, New Directions published *Pictures from Brueghel and Other Poems*, a volume subtitled *Collected Poems 1950–1962* because it also reprinted *The Desert Music* and *Journey to Love*. In the Fiftieth Anniversary number of *Poetry* (October–November 1962) appeared "the last poem Floss was sure her husband had written." It is about the Williams's young Shetland puppy and is titled "Stormy."[97] On 4 March 1963 Williams died at his home, 9 Ridge Road, in Rutherford, N. J. A few months later, his *Pictures from Brueghel* was awarded the Pulitzer Prize for poetry.

In Denise Levertov's memorial to Williams, she tells us that Williams's "tremendous outpouring" of writing in every form has the interior unity of purpose "that is one of the marks of a great writer." She speaks of "Asphodel, that Greeny Flower" and *Journey to Love* as the culmination of his work, followed not, despite the poet's age and illness, by a deterioration but rather, in the last book of *Paterson*, by the movement of a wave withdrawing, a part of the same rhythm. And at the very last—in the poems collected last year as *Pictures from Brueghel*—he gave us, when he could hardly speak and could no longer read to himself, typed with one hand with great difficulty, a sheaf of flowers, fresh flowers of a new, ancient spring."[98]

Notes

1. *The Autobiography of William Carlos Williams* (New York: New Directions, 1951), 47.

2. *Autobiography*, 48–49.

3. *I Wanted to Write a Poem: The Autobiography of the Works of a Poet*; Edith Heal, reporter and ed. (New York: New Directions, 1978; first published in 1958, rev. 1967), 5.

4. *I Wanted to Write a Poem*, 5.

5. Emily Mitchell Wallace, *A Bibliography of William Carlos Williams* (Middletown, Conn.: Wesleyan University Press, 1968), 8–9.

6. *The Letters of Ezra Pound 1907–1941*, ed. D. D. Paige (New York: Haskell House, 1974), 7–8.

7. Ezra Pound, "Reviews: *The Tempers*," *New Freewoman* 1 (1 December 1913): 227.

8. Walton Litz and Christopher MacGowan, eds., "Preface" to *The Collected Poems of William Carlos Williams*, vol. 1 (New York: New Directions, 1986), xviii.

9. Harriet Monroe, *A Poet's Life* (New York: Macmillan, 1938), 269, 270–71.

10. Paul Mariani, *William Carlos Williams: A New World Naked* (New York: McGraw-

Hill, 1981), 123 ff. I am indebted to Paul Mariani's brilliant biography of Williams for much of the information that I use throughout this essay.

11. *I Wanted to Write a Poem*, 19.

12. "Belly Music," *Others* 5 (July 1919): 26–31.

13. "Belly Music," 31.

14. "Belly Music," 28.

15. Dorothy Dudley, " 'To Whom It May Concern,' " *Poetry* 12 (April 1918): 41.

16. John Gould Fletcher, "Two American Poets," *Egoist* 4 (April 1918): 60.

17. Conrad Aiken, "Reed, Powys, Kilmer," *Scepticisms: Notes on Contemporary Poetry* (New York: Alfred A. Knopf, 1919), 184–86.

18. "Books Current," *Future* (June 1918): 188–90.

19. *Letters of Ezra Pound*, 180–81.

20. *Letters of Ezra Pound*, 181.

21. William Carlos Williams, *Imaginations*, ed. Webster Shott (New York: New Directions, 1970), 11–12.

22. *I Wanted to Write a Poem*, 30.

23. *Imaginations*, 12–13.

24. *Imaginations*, 15–16.

25. Edgar Jepson, "The Western School," *Little Review* 4 (September 1918): 8–9.

26. *Imaginations*, 24.

27. Fletcher, review of *Kora in Hell, Freeman* 3 (18 May 1921): 238.

28. "The Italics are God's," *Contact* 4 (1921): 15.

29. Birch-Bartlett, "Koral Grisaille," *Poetry* 17 (March 1921): 331.

30. McAlmon, "Concerning 'Kora in Hell,' " *Poetry* 17 (April 1921): 57–58.

31. "A Matisse," *Contact* 2 (January 1921): 7.

32. "Comment," *Contact* 2 (January 1921): 11–12.

33. "To Marianne Moore, March 23, 1921," *The Selected Letters of William Carlos Williams*, ed. John C. Thirlwall (New York: McDowell, Obolensky, 1957), 52.

34. Freytag-Loringhoven, "Thee I call 'Hamlet of Wedding-Ring': Criticism of William Carlos William's [sic] 'Kora in Hell' and why," *Little Review* 7 (September 1920): 52.

35. Freytag-Loringhoven, *Little Review* 7 (January 1921): 110.

36. Freytag-Loringhoven, *Little Review* 7 (September 1920): 54.

37. Margaret Anderson, *Little Review* 7 (June 1920): 59.

38. Freytag-Loringhoven, *Little Review* 7 (September–December 1920): 60.

39. *I Wanted to Write a Poem*, 30.

40. Kenneth Burke, "Heaven's First Law," *Dial* 72 (February 1922): 197, 199–200.

41. "Glorious Weather," *Contact* 5 (June 1923): 2.

42. Yvor Winters, "Carlos Williams's New Book," *Poetry* 20 (July 1922): 217–18.

43. *"Spring and All," Imaginations*, 105.

44. *Imaginations*, 111.

45. M. A. Seiffert, "Against the Middle-Aged Mind," *Poetry* 24 (April 1924): 46, 50.

46. Matthew Josephson, "Great American Novels," *Broom* 5 (October 1923): 178.

47. Paul Rosenfeld, "William Carlos Williams," *Port of New York: Essays on Fourteen American Moderns* (1924; reprint, Urbana: University of Illinois Press, 1961), 110–11.

48. Rosenfeld, 109.

49. Kenneth Burke, "American Pot-Pourri," *New York Times Book Review* (7 February 1926): 21.

50. Burke, "Subjective History," *New York Herald Tribune Books* (14 March 1926): 7.

51. Lola Ridge, "American Sagas," *New Republic* 46 (24 March 1926): 149.

52. D. H. Lawrence, "American Heroes," *Nation* 122 (14 April 1926): 413.

53. Louis Zukofsky, "Beginning Again with William Carlos Williams," *Hound and Horn* 4 (January–March 1931): 261.

54. Zukofsky, "American Poetry 1920–1930," *Symposium* 2 (January 1931): 79, 81.

55. Wallace Stevens, "Preface" to *Collected Poems, 1921–1931*. Reprinted as "Williams" in Stevens's *Opus Posthumous* (New York: Alfred A. Knopf, 1966), 252.

56. *I Wanted to Write a Poem*, 52.

57. M. Moore, "Things Others Never Notice," *Poetry* 44 (May 1934): 103.

58. *The Selected Letters of William Carlos Williams*, 147.

59. Ruth Lechlitner, "An Early Martyr," *New York Herald Tribune Books* (19 January 1936): 13.

60. Philip Rahv, "Torrents of Spring," *Nation* 144 (24 June 1937): 733.

61. Fred Miller, "Passaic River Stories," *New Republic* 94 (20 April 1938): 341.

62. Eda Lou Walton, "X-Ray Realism," *Nation* 146 (19 March 1938): 334, 335.

63. R. P. Blackmur, "Nine Poets," *Partisan Review* 6 (Winter 1939): 114.

64. Yvor Winters, "Poetry of Feeling," *Kenyon Review* 1 (Winter 1939): 104, 106.

65. Ruth Lechlitner, "The Poetry of William Carlos Williams," *Poetry* 54 (September 1938), 332, 334.

66. Quoted in Mariani, 745.

67. *I Wanted to Write a Poem*, 70.

68. "Author's Introduction" to *The Collected Poems of William Carlos Williams, Vol. II, 1939–1962*, ed. Christopher MacGowan (New York: New Directions, 1988), 54.

69. R. Jarrell, "Poetry in Peace and War," *Partisan Review* 12 (Winter 1945): 122–23.

70. R. Jarrell, "The Poet and His Public," *Partisan Review* 13 (September–October, 1946): 493, 499.

71. R. Lowell, "Thomas, Bishop, and Williams," *Sewanee Review* 55 (Summer 1947): 500, 503.

72. R. Lowell, "*Paterson II*," *Nation* 166 (19 April 1948): 693, 694.

73. E. Honig, "The Paterson Impasse," *Poetry* 74 (April 1949): 41, 38.

74. Richard Ellmann, "From Reneshaw to Paterson," *Yale Review* 39 (Spring 1950): 545.

75. R. Jarrell, "Introduction" to *The Selected Poems of William Carlos Williams*, paperback edition (New Directions: New York, 1963), ix, xi, xii.

76. Paul Mariani, 586.

77. R. Jarrell, "A View of Three Poets," *Partisan Review* 18 (November–December 1951): 698, 700.

78. *I Wanted to Write a Poem*, 79.

79. *Selected Letters*, 304, 305, 301–2.

80. M. L. Rosenthal, "In the Roar of the Present," *New Republic* 125 (27 August 1951): 18.

81. R. Eberhart, "A Vision Welded to the World," *New York Times Book Review* (17 June 1951): 5.

82. Mariani, 651–55, 658–59, 666–67.

83. Mariani, 660–62.

84. *Selected Letters*, 334.

85. *Paterson* (New York: New Directions, 1963; paperback edition), 77–79.

86. *Selected Letters*, 324.

87. R. Creeley, "A Character for Love," *Black Mountain Review* 1 (Summer 1952): 45–48.

88. K. Rexroth, "A Poet Sums Up," *New York Times Book Review* (28 March 1954): 5.

89. M. B. Quinn, review of *The Desert Music and Other Poems*, *Imagi* 6, #4 (1955): 10–12.

90. R. Jarrell, *Yale Review* 45 (Spring 1956): 478.

91. E. Honig, *Partisan Review* 23 (Winter 1956): 117.

92. R. Eberhart, "American Passion," *Saturday Review* 19 (18 February 1956): 49.

93. "A Statement by William Carlos Williams About the Poem Paterson," *Paterson*, ed. Christopher MacGowan (New York: New Directions, 1992), xiv.

94. J. Ciardi, "The Epic of a Place," *Saturday Review* 41 (11 October 1958): 533.

95. R. Eberhart, "A Vision of Life and Man that Drives the Poet On," *New York Times Book Review* (14 September 1958): 4.

96. *Collected Poems of William Carlos Williams*, Vol. II, ed. Christopher MacGowan (New York: New Directions, 1988): 424.

97. Mariani, 766.

98. D. Levertov, "William Carlos Williams," *Nation* 196 (16 March 1963): 230.

The Critical Reception of
William Carlos Williams

◆

STEVEN GOULD AXELROD

From the 1920s through the mid-1960s, when a Eurocentric conception of literary culture held sway, T. S. Eliot and Ezra Pound occupied the central position in American poetry. This was ironic given the fact that, as William Carlos Williams complained in *Paterson*, both those poets had (geographically, at least) "run off / toward the peripheries" (35).[1] They had reduced American Eurocentrism to its absurd endpoint by physically relocating themselves in Europe, renouncing American citizenship in Eliot's case, and committing acts that could plausibly be construed as treasonous in Pound's. Although Williams remained physically and spiritually rooted in a version of Hometown, U. S. A.—Rutherford, New Jersey—*he* was deemed culturally peripheral by critics. Reflecting the Eurocentric viewpoint, William Empson wrote that Williams had "renounced all the pleasures of the English language"—presumably with an emphasis on "English."[2] Williams troped on his situation in "El Hombre":

> It's a strange courage
> you give me ancient star:
>
> Shine alone in the sunrise
> toward which you lend no part!
> (*Poems I*, 76)

From the mid-1960s through the mid-1980s, however, successive waves of phenomenology, structuralism, and poststructuralism flowed across American literary studies. Although the waves of theory originated in Europe, they had the ironic effect of reversing American Europhilia and raising Wallace Stevens to prominence as the new "genius of the sea" of poetry. Stevens thereby repatriated the American laurels from London and Rapallo to New Haven, Connecticut. The rising tide of theory helped raise the reputation of Williams as well, since those methods worked almost as well on his texts as they did on Stevens's. Whereas Eliot—now weighed down by his outdated persona and associations—foundered on the rocks, Williams cruised buoyantly ahead, a dinghy pulled by Stevens's yacht. Although it probably would not have occurred to Williams that he would one day be viewed as second to Stevens, he would not have been surprised to learn that his reputation seemed to wax and wane in inverse relation to that of Eliot, his nemesis.

Predicting the future is difficult, like eating peas with a knife. Nevertheless, we might hazard the guess that in coming years a growing interest in cultural studies, together with a sophisticated awareness of the problematics of language, will continue to work in Williams's favor. Indeed, Williams has already begun to look less like the barely visible star of "El Hombre" than like a sun.

1950–1963

Although book reviews provided the primary critical discourse about Williams until his death in 1963, by 1950 the rain of academic criticism had already begun. The first big drop in the bucket was Vivienne Koch's introductory *William Carlos Williams* (1950).[3] This book, which has generally been ignored, is intelligent and opinionated. It argues that Williams imbued his poems with a fresh vision and addressed them to present-day concerns: "It was the present, the thick, living flux of the present he wished to fix or 'raise to the imagination' " (16). Koch's book surveys the entire course of Williams's writing up until 1950: poems, plays, fiction, and essays. That conscientious inclusiveness results in the book's severest limitation. Koch treats all texts, major and minor, with the same briskness. Her method is to quote, comment, and move on. She does not give herself enough time to penetrate very deeply or enduringly into Williams's oeuvre.

A second introductory study appeared about a dozen years later, in the year of Williams's death: John Malcolm Brinnin's Minnesota pamphlet, *William Carlos Williams* (1963).[4] Portraying Williams as "the man on the margin" (5), this study too contains some helpful introductory commentary but has largely been superseded.

During the early period of criticism, a number of essays and book chapters appeared that continue to shed light on Williams's accomplishment today. Perhaps most significant is Roy Harvey Pearce's intellectually lively discussion of *Paterson* and the shorter poems in *The Continuity of American Poetry* (1961).[5] Pearce's analysis places Williams in the American Adamic and epic traditions as well as in the modernist tradition of the new. Sister Bernetta Quinn's *PMLA* article "William Carlos Williams" (1955) and especially her chapter on *Paterson* in *The Metamorphic Tradition in Modern Poetry* (1955) were also important in establishing Williams as a figure to be reckoned with by academic criticism.[6] Ralph Nash's "The Uses of Prose in *Paterson*" (1953) had a major impact too, as did essays by Louis Martz, Norman Holmes Pearson, M. L. Rosenthal, John Thirlwall, and George Zabriski.[7] As most of the titles indicate, *Paterson* served as the basis for Williams's reputation during these years.

Randall Jarrell, however, a contrarian and the best poetry critic of his time, famously complained in his review of *Paterson IV* (1951) that the poem "has been getting rather steadily worse" and that Williams has been "organizing a long dreary imaginary war in which America and the Present are fighting against Europe and the Past."[8] Nevertheless, when Jarrell placed that review together with a second, positive review and two generally positive essays in *Poetry and the Age* (1953), Williams came to dominate the latter third of his landmark book.[9] Indeed, in Jarrell's newly minted concluding lines, he seemed to be joining Williams's "imaginary war" almost against his will: "If you want to know how the Muse, 'install'd here amid the kitchenware' of a New World, already half recovered from the nausea of departure, already swearing soberly (in a voice with hardly a trace of accent) that she will uphold the laws of this republic—if you want to know how the Muse sounds in such a situation, here is one good place to find out" (271). Jarrell, with uncanny foresight concerning later literary judgment, seemed to be preparing Williams for a prominent position in the pantheon of the future.

1964–1980

The years following Williams's death in 1963 witnessed the publication of two foundational critical works: Linda Wagner's *The Poems of William Carlos Williams* (1964) and J. Hillis Miller's *Poets of Reality* (1965).[10] Wagner's book-length study and Miller's long chapter on Williams are basic in a double sense. As the first intensive analyses of Williams's poetry, they established him as a major creator of American culture, worthy of the company of Eliot, Pound, and Stevens. Moreover, these studies put two main approaches to Williams's work in place.

Wagner, writing in a liberal humanist tradition, employed a combination of manuscript research, literary history, and close reading to interpret Williams's poems in terms of his developing ideas about poetry. Miller, conversely, represented Williams's poetic accomplishment with reference to phenomenological theory. Thus, Wagner adopted a time-honored reading strategy in American criticism, whereas Miller adapted a strategy highly innovative for its time and place. Each strategy succeeded in its own way, opening up Williams's poems to different orders of appropriation and insight. As Wagner herself was ultimately to observe, her book appealed to those Americanists who already admired Williams, whereas Miller's book introduced Williams to a wider audience for poetry and theory.[11] Nevertheless, if Miller's brilliant, philosophically oriented book established Williams as a major international figure, Wagner's meticulous scholarship and explications set the stage for most of the Williams criticism to be written over the next 30 years. Both books have therefore proved highly influential. Their methods, far from mutually exclusive, remain in dialogue with each other to the present day.

Wagner's *The Poems of William Carlos Williams*, part of which is reprinted here, proposed to demonstrate the reasons for Williams's poetic excellence and to disprove the disparaging assumption that he wrote "instinctively" (3). The book provided detailed analysis of the language and thematics of specific poems along with a sophisticated discussion of Williams's poetics. Wagner divided her topic into seven categories: poetic theory, imagery, technique, figuration, measure, formal experiment in *Paterson*, and communitarian concerns in his late poems. Each of the first five chapters proceeded through Williams's oeuvre chronologically, emphasizing stylistic changes and constants. For example, the chapter on figuration demonstrated that although Williams's use of metaphor developed through several distinct stages, he always employed metaphor as a structural feature rather than as an ornament. Wagner's last two chapters focused on specific volumes. The chapter on *Paterson* exposed the poem's symphonic interplay of dispersive and convergent verbal forces, positing an underlying drama of the individual's search for a relationship with his local culture. The last chapter—on *The Desert Music, Journey to Love*, and *Pictures from Brueghel*—similarly pointed to human concerns emerging from Williams's technical innovations. Wagner's study provided an image of Williams as a brilliant and complex artist, concerned with both language and society, highly self-aware and tirelessly inventive.

In his long chapter on Williams in *Poets of Reality*, part of which is reprinted here, J. Hillis Miller also represented the poet as a prodigious creator. Miller focused on the philosophical dimension of Williams's texts— the way they compose a verbal field different from, yet curiously congruent with, the physical world of things, events, and people. Perhaps the most powerful example of phenomenological criticism applied to an American writer, Miller's chapter was revolutionary in method and theory. Miller treated all of Williams's writing as a single unit, from which the critic could pick illustrations regardless of textual or chronological boundaries. He also argued that Williams's work marks a fundamental shift in human sensibility: a movement beyond the subject / object dichotomy at the core of classical, Renaissance, and romantic epistemology. According to Miller, Williams resigned himself to existence and thereby escaped the isolated ego with its nostalgias, tensions, and despairs. Rather than the romantic "dramas of interchange" between subject and object, Williams's texts enact an "interpenetration of consciousness and the world" (287). Inhabiting a space both subjective and objective, they "leap into things," achieving what Williams himself called an "approximate co-extension with the universe" (288–89).

Some of Miller's theorizing may seem limited 30 years later. For example, his discussion of such categories as "self" and "reality" failed to recognize the way language constructs such categories for us—the very point Miller's subsequent work helped bring home. Using British romanticism as his frame of reference, he minimized Williams's debts to American originators. And Miller's assertion that Williams's texts provide "no basis for metaphor" and "no symbolic meanings" (306–7) surely requires qualification in light of Wagner's analysis. In its theorizing, *Poets of Reality* seems to occupy a phenomenological way station between liberal humanism and poststructuralism, situated just before the linguistic turn in the road. Some years later, Miller was to relocate his Williams commentary further on down that road (see notes 24, 54). In spite of its limits, *Poets of Reality* enacted a critical revolution whose effects are still being felt. A surprising amount of Williams criticism over the last 30 years implicitly derives from one of two phrases: "as Miller says" or "contrary to what Miller says." With its astonishing intelligence, its novel fusion of philosophical and literary discourse, and its difficulty and good humor, this chapter certified a place for Williams in the front rank of American poets.

In the decade and a half following the publication of Wagner's and Miller's books, 20 full-length studies of Williams appeared, along with hundreds of articles and chapters. Of the books, a dozen have been especially influential. Perhaps to compensate for Miller's placement of Williams in a version of intellectual history emanating from Great Britain and continental Europe, many of these books have emphasized the poet's peculiarly American qualities.

James Breslin, for example, focused on Williams's evolving identity as an American writer. In *William Carlos Williams: An American Artist* (1970), a portion of which is reprinted here, Breslin indicated both the unity and the range of Williams's writing.[12] He traced Williams's career from his early debt to Whitman through his major achievements to his final "celebration of the light." Williams repeatedly sought to enter the present moment and to find the "new forms required for its expression" (3). Seeking a poetics of immersion rather than transcendence, he looked to his roots—his locality—for sources of creativity. Williams's poetic theory ultimately depended on a theory of consciousness. Modern individuals, having become abstracted from immediate experience, needed to restore their psychic fluidity and their fertile contact with reality.

According to Breslin, Williams started to produce ground-breaking works in the 1920s. The serial poem *Spring and All* employs conflicting forces, hard edges, and an "intense, ego-shattering concentration upon physical objects" (54) to discover plenty amid apparent barrenness. The historical study *In the American Grain* perceives a split between instinct and will in its major characters, who become archetypal as well as real. Fictional works of the 1930s such as "Old Doc Rivers," "Jean Beicke," "A Face of Stone," and *The White Mule* gain a tough-minded yet sympathetic access to the ordinary life of working-class Americans. Williams's "pre-epic" of the 1940s, *Paterson I–IV*, is an experimental poem of assembled fragments, accidental matter, and multiple voices. Concerned with its own creation, the poem deliberately keeps the relation of its parts ambiguous. Finally, poems of the 1950s such as *Paterson V* and "Asphodel, That Greeny Flower" establish a more personal, harmonious, and accessible mode. After a lifetime of formal experimentation that banished the ego from his texts, Williams ultimately returns to himself—emotionally open, willing to universalize his experience. In this voyage through Williams's career as an American artist, Breslin provided a coherent, insightful, and influential account of the poet's achievement.

Although Mike Weaver's *William Carlos Williams: The American Background* (1971) resembled Breslin's book in emphasizing American culture and biography, it differed in offering no sustained readings of any of Williams's texts.[13] Rather, as the subtitle indicates, it highlighted the American artistic, intellectual, and political milieu out of which the texts arose. This strategy resulted in a kind of fragmentary literary history, almost a collage. The shards of information Weaver assembled are indubitably fascinating. Some of them ultimately may not add up to much: Otto Weininger's sexual philosophy; Dora Marsden's feminism; the impact of alchemy on *Paterson*. But others really do affect the reader's understanding of Williams in crucial ways: Thomas Ward's dreadful nineteenth-century poem *Passaic* as an ironic precursor of *Paterson*; the manic informational flow of David Lyle's letters as another catalyst for *Paterson*; the way 1920s localism shaped Williams's aesthetics; and the influence of objectivism, surrealism, jazz, avant-garde painting, photography, and visual arts theory on Williams's development. Perhaps most illuminating was Weaver's sympathetic account of the poet's politics. Williams, a liberal Democrat who repudiated communism and fascism, was at times suspected of both (because of his involvement with leftist reform movements and social credit theory). For all of Weaver's interest in cultural contexts, however, he concluded on a surprisingly individualistic note: Williams used "the gestures and figures of his poetry for self-revelation" (163).

James Guimond's *The Art of William Carlos Williams: A Discovery and Possession of America* (1968), published a few years before Breslin's and Weaver's studies, lacked the critical incisiveness of the former and the historical detail of the latter.[14] Nevertheless, it was a solid and often perceptive introduction to Williams's work. Guimond took a generally chronological path through Williams's texts. A beginning chapter discussed the poet's conception of literature as redemptive and his trope of poetic immersion and renewal. Subsequent chapters analyzed his imagistic poems of the 1910s and 1920s; his stylistic debt to the painters Charles Demuth and Charles Sheeler; the theme of America in *In the American Grain* and other works of the 1920s; the objectivist texts of the 1930s such as *White Mule*; and Williams's use of nontraditional materials in his poetry and his focus on the poor in his stories. Guimond's final three chapters concentrated on *Paterson* and later poems. Although he had many valuable things to say about Williams's epic, he unfortunately cemented into place a view of the poem as unwittingly sexist and homophobic. His approach was imprinted by the poem's early lines about "innumerable women, each like a flower" (*Paterson* 7). Despite such eloquent and powerful female figures in the poem as Cress, Mme Curie, and Corydon and Phyllis, Guimond contuinued to posit the women of *Paterson* as passive, interchangeable, and valuable only in their relations with men. At one point, he acknowledged that the presence of Mme Curie "indicates that invention and discovery will no longer be purely male prerogatives" (196). But that isolated insight is not allowed to modify the general terms of his argument. Otherwise a well-researched, thoughtful, and humane study, Guimond's book highlights Williams's allegiance to traditional sex roles while obscuring the ways in which Williams subverts and problematizes such sex roles.

Four specialized books written during this period also took an approach indebted to American or cultural studies. Two of them focused on Williams's debt to the visual arts in the first half of his career, whereas the other two highlighted developments in the second half of his career.

Dijkstra's *The Hieroglyphics of a New Speech: Cubism, Stieglitz, and the Early Poetry of William Carlos Williams* (1969) demonstrated that innovations in the visual arts between 1910 and 1930 had an immediate and lasting influence on Williams's poetry.[15] In a fascinating and illuminating narrative, Dijkstra showed how the photographer and influential cultural figure Alfred Stieglitz helped make European art of the 1910s available to New York artists and intellectuals. Williams discovered his poetic voice by translating into the language of *Kora in Hell* and *Sour Grapes* Cézanne's interest in "sheer paint" and the Cubists' concern for objectivity, simultaneity, spacial materialization, and the fracturing of form. In the 1920s, Stieglitz and his circle rejected the European move toward abstraction, preferring instead to find universal significance in the visually precise and immediate object and in the American locality. The writing of Paul Rosenfeld, Waldo Frank, and Marsden Hartley—together with the art of Charles Demuth, Charles Sheeler, John Marin, and Stieglitz himself—contributed to the style and concerns of *In the American Grain, Spring and All*, and other works of the 1920s and beyond.

Dickran Tashjian's *William Carlos Williams and the American Scene, 1920–1940* (1978), an elegantly written text with beautiful illustrations, was set in a slightly later time frame than Dijkstra's study, but covered much the same ground: Stieglitz, Hartley, Demuth, Sheeler, visual objects, and American localism.[16] It did add some territory of its own: Matisse, Dada, and ethnic and proletarian art. Furthermore, the book's reproductions gave the reader a glorious view of the art works that stimulated and influenced Williams during this period.

Jerome Mazzaro's *William Carlos Williams: The Later Poems* (1973) analyzed Williams's texts written after World War II in terms of their literary, artistic, and scientific influences.[17] Admirably learned, this study was also somewhat inchoate—and it occasionally repeated material already discussed by Weaver and Dijkstra. After discussing the cultural and aesthetic schema within which Williams wrote, Mazzaro analyzed some key poems. He interpreted *Paterson I–IV* as a failed attempt to translate the techniques of synthetic cubism into poetry; "Asphodel, That Greeny Flower" as a retreat from the vivid detail of "The Red Wheelbarrow" into a world of memory and imagination (a movement reversed in the more vital *Paterson V*); the "Cress" letters of *Paterson I–II* as a successful effort to balance the poem's otherwise masculine struggle; and *Paterson V* and "Pictures from Brueghel" as studies of the artist digesting the objective world in the process of creating a verbal one.

Narrower and more lucid than Mazzaro's book, Sherman Paul's *The Music of Survival* (1968) focused on a single poem from Williams's late phase: "The Desert Music."[18] Paul judged this poem to be one of Williams's great achievements—a recovery from crisis and a new beginning. In 1951, just after completing his *Autobiography*, Williams suffered a massive stroke. In writing "The Desert Music," a poem about a remembered visit to Juarez, he demonstrated that he could restore himself to creative life by applying his imagination to the materials of memory. A poem about the making of poems, "The Desert Music" helped Williams master chaos, defeat despair, and rebuild his poetic world.

Of the formalist studies published during this period, Thomas Whitaker's *William Carlos Williams* (1968, 1989) had the widest range.[19] This book provided concise and elegant readings of virtually all of Williams's substantial texts. After an introductory chapter on Williams's poetics (and, in the revised edition, a chapter on his biography), Whitaker nimbly guided the reader through the poems and improvisations, plays and nonfiction prose, novels and short stories. He found *Spring and All, In the American Grain, Paterson*, and "Asphodel, That Greeny Flower" to be the high points in an oeuvre termed "tremendously uneven" in the first edition (163) and simply "uneven" in the second (127). Yet despite the unevenness, Whitaker found that Williams qualified as one of the century's great writers because of his attention to actuality, his honest grappling with the limits of language and awareness, and the very diversity of his work.

If Whitaker's study emphasized the variety of Williams's work, Linda Wagner's *The Prose of William Carlos Williams* (1970) made a case for its "amazing unity" (3).[20] In this book, her second on Williams, Wagner focused on the interplay between his prose and poetry, and between different texts. Thus, she had much to say about the poetry as well as the prose—and about the distinctions between the two genres that Williams drew and erased. Wagner proceeded chronologically through Williams's oeuvre. Early chapters analyzed *Kora in Hell* as a not wholly successful improvisation; *Spring and All* as Williams's first prose poem matrix; *The Great American Novel* as an initial attempt to redefine the American novel; *In the American Grain* as a search for meaning that succeeds in its central arc of De Soto through Boone; *Voyage to Pagany* as a second attempt at a novel; and "The Descent of Winter" as a second prose poem matrix. Later chapters explicated Williams's short stories such as "The Colored Girls of Passenack—Old and New," "A Face of Stone," and "The Farmer's Daughters"; the novels *White Mule, In the Money,* and *The Build Up;* the plays *Many Loves, A Dream of Love,* and *Tituba's Children; Paterson* as the culmination of Williams's struggle to convey his world; Williams's late poetry about the people he loved; and finally the prose of *Paterson* and *Yes, Mrs. Williams.* Wagner found that Williams's most powerful prose appears in the best of his stories. More importantly, she showed that Williams regarded art as a constant process of development in which each text fructifies the others.

In *Paterson: Language and Landscape* (1970), Joel Conarroe acted as a tour guide through *Paterson*, which he regarded as Williams's "major achievement" (4).[21] He focused on the poet's commitment to the American locale and his search for a redemptive language. Introductory chapters provided an overview of *Paterson's* organization; its relation to epic; its debt to poems by Whitman, Pound, Eliot, and Crane; its prose poetry form; its sources in Williams's earlier work; and its "Preface." Subsequent chapters proceeded through the poem thematically. An illuminating chapter traced the progress of Paterson, the protagonist, through the five books of the poem. Another helpful chapter studied the flow of the Passaic River as a unifying textual feature. A now-dated chapter on Williams's female characters found only Mme Curie admirable or powerful, referring to the challenging, if admittedly disturbed, letters of Cress as "hysterical" (102). A chapter on economics seemed less informed than the one in Weaver's study. A final chapter on Williams's quest for a language commensurate with the contemporary world contained valuable insights. In the critical style of its time, this book tried to discover the essential truth of *Paterson*—an aim that sometimes made the poem appear simple and unitary where a later critical style would construct it as complex and self-divided. Nevertheless, decades after its composition, Conarroe's book remains a useful entry point to Williams's text.

Benjamin Sankey's *A Companion to William Carlos Williams's Paterson* (1971) offered a valuable complement to Conarroe's book and indeed to all other studies of *Paterson*.[22] It explained many of the poem's allusions, and it identified the main reference texts from which Williams worked: Nelson's

History of the City of Paterson and the County of Passaic, New Jersey, Nelson and Shriner's *History of Paterson and Its Environs*, Barber and Howe's *Historical Collections of the State of New Jersey*, the Federal Writing Project's *New Jersey: A Guide to Its Present and Past*, and the historical newspaper the *Prospector*. Sankey began by discussing the overall design of *Paterson*—its relation to language, the past, and local geography; its symbology and form; its style. He then moved through the poem, providing detailed commentary and identifying sources. Although Sankey slighted book V, this study is otherwise just what it aspires to be: a trustworthy companion on an adventurous journey.

Joseph Riddel's *The Inverted Bell: Modernism and the Counterpoetics of William Carlos Williams* (1974) was the first and only full-length poststructuralist account of the poet's achievement.[23] Along with J. Hillis Miller's *Poets of Reality* and *The Linguistic Moment* and Riddel's own subsequent articles on Williams, this book is a key document in continental philosophy's encounter with Williams.[24] Rather than analyze Williams's poems per se, *The Inverted Bell* expounded on Williams's poetics: the interpretable but not wholly recoverable deep structure that informs all of Williams's individual texts. According to Riddel, Williams's poetry functions as an "inverted bell" (*Paterson*, 124), resounding but empty, characterized by free play and pointing to no hidden presence. Furthermore, Williams's texts thematize this poetics, reflecting on their own processes and contradictions, their problematic of language and desire.

Riddel's introduction, relying on Martin Heidegger and Jacques Derrida, argued that interpretation never rests and the hermeneutic circle never closes. Similarly, Williams's poems, as interpretations themselves, are a locus of differences, a gathering of dissonant meanings. In subsequent chapters, Riddel studied the underlying structures, linguistic theory, sense of history, and destructive and creative vectors in Williams's poems, particularly *Paterson*. If in his analysis Conarroe tended to fix *Paterson*'s meanings in place, Riddel set them free in a sometimes bewildering flow of meditation, insight, speculation, and discursive play. According to Riddel, *Paterson* incorporates multiple beginnings, wanderings, and dispersals. Its language flowers in the fictional space of the poem, not in the revelation of truth. Even in its treatment of history, *Paterson* moves outside "the tyranny of the center" (165), subverting received beliefs and principles of order. In a final chapter, Riddel argued that book V moves the entire poem to a higher metapoetic plane. The unicorn tapestries are metaphors for the poem's inability to recover pure origin or to tell all. Riddel portrayed *Paterson* as an early, major example of postmodernism. His analysis was complex and powerful, if occasionally opaque and even mistaken. Two decades after its publication, this book remains central in the canon of Williams commentary.

Of the other books written about Williams during this period, Rod Townley's *The Early Poetry of William Carlos Williams* (1975) had perceptive things to say about *Kora in Hell, Sour Grapes*, and *Spring and All*, though it also spent a great deal of time on poems best forgotten.[25] Margaret Lloyd's *William Carlos Williams's "Paterson": A Critical Reappraisal* (1980) provided a useful overview of Williams's epic, with some especially penetrating analyses of its mosaic structure.[26] Robert Coles's *William Carlos Williams: The Knack of Survival in America* (1975) reflected its author's perspectives as child psychiatrist and cultural critic and focused on Williams's sympathetic portayal of the working poor in narratives such as "Face of Stone," "Jean Beicke," *White Mule*, and *In the Money*.[27] Reed Whittemore's *William Carlos Williams: Poet from Jersey* (1975) was an interesting first biography, though its breezy style irritated some scholars and the book has, in any case, been superseded by Paul Mariani's more informative life story (discussed below).[28] Three other critical books published during these years were introductory in nature: Hélène Dupeyron-Marchesson's *William Carlos Williams et le renouveau du lyrisme* (1967); Alan Ostrom's *The Poetic World of William Carlos Williams* (1966); and Walter Scott Peterson's *An Approach to "Paterson"* (1967).[29]

This period saw an efflorescence of valuable articles and chapters on Williams by Charles Altieri, Diane Ashton, Paul Bové, Kurt Heinzelman, Hugh Kenner, Cary Nelson, and others.[30] It also witnessed the publication of four major bibliographies: Emily Wallace's indispensible guide to primary materials, *A Bibliography of William Carlos Williams* (1968); Paul Mariani's sometimes harsh but generally discerning survey of secondary materials though 1973, *William Carlos Williams: The Poet and His Critics* (1975); Linda' Wagner's *Reference Guide* to secondary materials through 1976; and Wagner's invaluable discussion of editions and commentary, "William Carlos Williams," in *Sixteen Modern American Authors* (1973, 1990).[31] Finally, during this period a vital source of information and interpretation first appeared: the *William Carlos Williams Newsletter*, soon renamed the *William Carlos Williams Review* (1975–present).

1981–PRESENT

As the 1980s commenced, a grand monument of Williams scholarship appeared: Paul Mariani's beautifully researched, sympathetic biography, *William Carlos Williams: A New World Naked* (1981), part of which is reprinted here.[32] For the first time, readers wishing to know what was happening in Williams's life at any particular time, how his texts grew out of his life, or the meaning his texts acquired in a biographical context, could find the answer. The book exhaustively detailed the circumstances and movements of Williams's life, yet it was also attentive to its inner dimensions: Williams's creative drive (which would never let go of him) and his commitment to a "revolution in the word" (769). Mariani's book was as good on this interior drama as it was on exterior developments; his interpretations of Williams's writing and life were equally powerful.

This biography gave the reader a front row seat to the dramas of Williams's life: his repeated failure to find an audience or even, until James Laughlin rescued him, a publisher; his sense of isolation from the literary community as well as his need to feel a part of it; his troubled but in many ways triumphant marriage to Floss; his ambivalence about his ethnically mixed background and his celebration of ethnic diversity in his texts; his lifelong struggle with depression and with his sexual drive; his fascination with, and misunderstanding of, women; his intense and often anguished relations with Pound, Eliot, Crane, H. D., Moore, and "the real contender," Stevens (479); his remarkable generosity to friends and younger poets; his recurrent involvement with and flight from politics, culminating in his elation at the election of John Kennedy; the incredible sadness of his final years; and always, until the very end, his signature—the creative quest, the search for a new measure, the urge to begin again. Writing with insight and passion, Mariani constructed Williams as a figure of complex tragedy and brilliance, as finally, indisputably, one of the great writers of his age.

In the years following Mariani's outstanding achievement, Williams criticism changed discernably. If it became increasingly knowing, it also lost the sense of excited discovery that marked the work of the heroic generation of Williams scholars such as Wagner, Miller, Breslin, Weaver, Guimond, Dijkstra, Riddel, and Mariani himself. To borrow a metaphor from Pound's "A Pact," those earlier critics broke the new wood. Now was a time for carving.

A number of the new studies focused on Williams and the visual arts, a topic first broached by Dijkstra, Tashjian, and Mazzaro. Of these works, Peter Schmidt's *William Carlos Williams, the Arts, and Literary Tradition* (1988), part of which is reprinted here, represented the most inclusive and authoritative synthesis.[33] Employing an interdisciplinary method indebted to art history and American studies as well as to literary history, Schmidt showed how Williams combined the influence of twentieth-century painting, photography, and collage with his knowledge of poetic traditions. From the precisionist theory and practice of Demuth and Stieglitz, Williams devised a poetry in which focused depiction suggests a psychological and cultural drama. Visual objects became the equivalents for feelings in poems like "Queen-Anne's-Lace" and "Burning the Christmas Greens." From cubist theory and practice, Williams developed an art of fragmentation, juxtaposition, and polyphony—a style appearing in such poems as "The Rose" and "Overture to a Dance of Locomotives" and later critiqued in "The Desert Music." From dada, Williams appropriated the nihilist, irrationalist mode evident in *Kora in Hell* and parts of *Spring and All*. In *Paterson*, Williams adapted elements of both cubist (coherent) collage and dadaist (incoherent) collage in order to refresh the classic and romantic traditions of epic. In late odes such as "The Sparrow" and "Asphodel, That Greeny Flower," Williams developed a new, casual, and digressive personal voice, whereas in his very last poems, he moved back toward a taut, ironic, avant-garde style. Throughout his career, Williams used the visual arts to renew literary tradition, expressing his "tortured constancy" to that tradition through a series of rebellions (249).

In *William Carlos Williams and the Ethics of Painting* (1991), Terence Diggory used Williams's texts about paintings to explore questions first raised by Miller and Riddel.[34] Diggory wished to resist the interpretive violence inherent in deconstruction and to establish instead an ethic based on intimacy and tolerance—between reader and text as well as between text and things. Considering depictions of the Epiphany in Breughel's *The Adoration of the Kings* and Williams's late poems "The Gift," *Paterson V*, and "Pictures from Breughel," Diggory focused in turn on the infant Jesus, the wise men, the soldiers, Joseph, and Mary. In the process, he illuminated what he saw as Williams's radical poetics, and posed an alternative to the views of Miller, Riddel, Whitaker, Charles Altieri, and Sandra Gilbert. According to Diggory, Williams attempts to defeat the threat of "alien mastery" by undermining the traditional foundation of knowledge and by attending to the new blossoming that occurs in its place (28). Giving up his wish for conquest, Williams achieves relationships based on a form of identification that includes both equality and difference. Diggory recommended that we replace Jacques Derrida's deconstruction and Hans-Georg Gadamer's hermeneutics with an analogous model of reading based on Julia Kristeva's psychoanalytic discourse. This model of communion as well as separation assumes a place beyond interpretation or knowing. Mounting a critique of Miller and Riddel, Diggory is also their worthy successor. His study, philosophically informed though perhaps idealized in its portrayal of human feeling, suggested that the intellectual work of the 1990s has carried on the legacy of the 1960s.

Henry Sayre's *The Visual Text of William Carlos Williams* (1983) was yet another work that studied Williams in terms of the visual arts.[35] Sayre argued that the poet based his late "variable foot" on a visual rather than an auditory sense of form. Reflecting the influence of dada, cubism, and surrealism, these poems resemble concrete poetry in their emphasis on linguistic materiality. Disputing both Miller's idea of a leap into things and Dijkstra's identification of sources, Sayre asserted that Williams conceived of form as arbitrary rather than organic. He believed—though it is not always clear why—that this form allowed Williams to expose conflicts between mind and world. Sayre argued that Williams's effort to create a visual text appeared as early as "The Red Wheelbarrow," became centrally important in *Paterson I–IV* and "Asphodel," and reached its apex in *Paterson V* and *Pictures from Breughel*. These latter texts, properly seen as postmodern, achieve a powerful visual form while using visual art as their subject matter.

Two of the more valuable book-length studies published in this period concentrated on genres of autobiography or history. Ann Fisher-Wirth's *Williams and Autobiography: The Woods of His Own Nature* (1989) focused on autobiography.[36] Fisher-Wirth began by usefully distinguishing between two sorts of autobiography: the public and the private. The public mode presents an exemplary self worthy of social imitation, whereas the private mode enacts an individual self's quest for "inner standing" (5). Fisher-Wirth found that Williams's *Autobiography* functions as public autobiography. Because it obeys generic conventions and masks Williams's complexities with a myth of innocence, it cannot help him confront and redeem his interior life. Almost everything else Williams wrote belongs in the category of private autobiography. In his play *A Dream of Love*, for example, he candidly enters the wilderness of his own experience, revealing his transgressions and achieving self-discovery. Although his early autobiographical poem, "Philip and Oradie," was hopelessly derivative, such later poems as "Queen-Anne's-Lace" and "The Crimson Cyclamen" complexly evoke his yearnings for love and creativity. Fisher-Wirth showed that "Asphodel, That Greeny Flower," Williams's most beautiful autobiographical poem, even comes close to bridging the gap between private and public.

Bryce Conrad's *Refiguring America* (1990) considered Williams as historiographer.[37] Whereas most previous commentators defended *In the American Grain* for its poetic qualities, Conrad took it seriously as historiography. Influenced by Arthur Danto and Hayden White's conceptions of history as discourse, Conrad presented Williams's book as open to the language of the past while aware of itself as linguistic artifact. Thus Williams exposes his struggle over narration even as he mounts a passionate cultural critique. He quarrels with the Puritan and Spanish epistemologies of conquest, celebrates Father Rasles's responsiveness to native peoples, and laments the gradual Europeanization of the land. Unfortunately, Williams also demonstrates an unconscious fear of the voices of women. Finally, according to Conrad, *In the American Grain* is a book founded on the author's interactions with the historical narratives he variously quotes, excerpts, edits, reinterprets, and even plagiarizes. Conrad's analysis, which challenged its predecessors, will undoubtedly be challenged in turn. Nevertheless, it stunningly resituated debate about a book that it argued is both flawed and great.

Two important books published during this period took up the topic of Williams's poetic relations with women. The more wide-ranging of these was Kerry Driscoll's *William Carlos Williams and the Maternal Muse* (1987), part of which is reprinted here.[38] This book contained some of the most accomplished biographical criticism of Williams to date. Driscoll showed that throughout Williams's life he was dependent on and fascinated by his mother. Elena Hoheb Williams served as his muse and the basis of his identity. Driscoll analyzed Williams's memoir, *Yes, Mrs. Williams*, as a dialogic assemblage in which Elena Williams is allowed to speak in her own words, providing unmediated glimpses of her relationship to her son. Although several short poems written at the same time reveal a failure of mother and son to make contact, *Yes, Mrs. Williams* emphasizes their "aesthetic kinship" and even symbiosis (15). In both poems and memoir, Williams encodes himself in Elena, turning his representations of her into a species of autobiography. But in *Paterson*, he reverses the procedure, subtly encoding Elena in himself, revealing the extent to which she lived in him and shared responsibility for his texts. In perhaps her most brilliant analysis, Driscoll described how Ezra Pound—always careless with facts and too interested in race and ancestry—tried to deny Williams an American identity. Williams successfully repelled this assault by using his immigrant mother as his poetic model, founding his identity on a multicultural basis and refiguring the United States as ethnically heterogenous. Driscoll's study proved that despite the patriarchal bias that may appear in individual texts, Williams's oeuvre is bound together by a continuous female presence. As a result, it frequently negotiates gender relations with complexity and power.

Marilyn Kallet's *Honest Simplicity in William Carlos Williams's "Asphodel, That Greeny Flower"* (1985), part of which is reproduced here, described Williams's late poem as a triumphant effort to regain the love of his wife Flossie and, at the same time, to renew his creativity after a period of illness.[39] "Asphodel" enacts Williams's grief of emotional separation from Flossie and his determination to achieve closeness through the language of memory. Emphasizing the poem's music rather than its visuality, Kallet analyzed its diction, line, tempo, rhythm, and patterns of stress. She found the poem to be staccato yet steady, flowing in gently ascending and descending waves. Making connections to Homer, Virgil, Proust, and communal song, Kallet saw the poem as an inner journey to hell and back, an archetypal pattern of descent and return. She also found that Williams carefully revised the poem to make it more focused, dramatic, and laden with emotion. Despite an occasionally impressionistic method, this book provided the most sustained and richly contextualized reading "Asphodel" has yet received.

Two books bear on Williams's relationship to his American Romantic forebears. Stephen Tapscott's *American Beauty: William Carlos Williams and the Modernist Whitman* (1984) analyzed Williams's efforts to learn from and rewrite Walt Whitman.[40] Tapscott supplemented Breslin's work on Whitman's early influence by showing that Whitman's impact reached its apex in *Paterson I–IV*. Rejecting Harold Bloom and ignoring other theorists of language and influence, Tapscott treated authors as imperial agents whose debts to prior texts are both conscious and welcome. Despite this theoretical weakness, and despite an uncritical repetition of gender clichés common in Williams's era but dubious in our own, Tapscott's book became genuinely illuminating when it got more specific. It described two distinct Walt Whitmans—the visionary giant and the local citizen—and showed how both of those selves contribute to William Carlos Williams's poetic project.

Whitman tacitly appears twice in *Paterson*: as the city-giant-dreamer of book I and as the lone man heading inland at the end of book IV. According to Tapscott, Williams recognizes the incompatibility of the polarities yoked in Whitman's presentation—the many and the one, exteriority and interiority—and self-consciously makes a poem about that very incompatibility. Whereas Whitman's romantic poet essentially grows large though incorporating smallness, Williams's modern poet speaks from a position of smallness while struggling toward a larger synthesis.

Carl Rapp's *William Carlos Williams and Romantic Idealism* (1984) argued that, far from being a modernist or postmodernist, the poet was actually a romantic in the manner of Hegel and Emerson.[41] Rapp, a former student of J. Hillis Miller, attempted to refute everything Miller ever wrote about Williams. Certainly Rapp (like Hyatt Waggoner before him and Ron Callan after) was right to insist on Emerson's centrality. But Rapp unfortunately made both Emerson and Williams into static, single-minded figures. Taming both writers' talent for surprise, he portrayed them as egotists who believed in the transcendence of the mind and in a universal force directing the mind. Rapp founded his argument on "Love and Service" and other jottings unpublished during Williams's lifetime. Nevertheless, Williams said many things in a life of writing; by selective quotation, one could probably prove he was a Branch Davidian. Rapp quoted few poems published between 1914 and 1950 because they simply do not sustain his argument. In Rapp's chapter on the late poems, Williams's work actually does support his case. Still, it would be more convincing to say that in old age Williams fell back into an idealism he had previously qualified or rejected than to argue, as Rapp did, that he adhered to it all along.

Brian Bremen's *William Carlos Williams and the Diagnostics of Culture* (1993), part of which is reprinted here, posed a more complex and probing challenge to Miller's foundational work.[42] Questioning Miller's rigorous textualism, Bremen argued that Williams regarded literature and history as inseparable. Bremen, following Kenneth Burke, understood Williams as a medicine man who diagnosed culture in his writing just as he diagnosed patients in his medical practice. Bremen detected a dialectic between prose and poetry running throughout much of Williams's oeuvre. The imaginative language of poetry undercuts the more static language of prose, but it also helps reveal the poetry hidden in the prose. According to Bremen, Williams does not seek apprehension of an *a priori* truth but uses writing to produce unforeseen discoveries, to initiate a process in which subjects both empathize and retain identity and in which cultural objects both change and remain themselves.

Bremen replaced Freud's Oedipal model of human development, which renders the mother passive and the son competitive, with Kohut and Benjamin's mother-based model, which emphasizes the child's identity with and difference from the mother. Bremen then described how Williams experienced the tensions of sameness and difference, gradually rejecting gender polarities and moving from modes of domination toward a mutuality that includes the voice of the other. Just as Williams the physician diagnosed the whole patient rather than the symptom, so Williams the writer (in such texts as "The Use of Force" and *In the American Grain*) employs strategies of involvement and self-questioning to achieve a dialogue between self and other, individual and community. The influence of Burke and Louis Zukovsky led him to a politics designed to empower the dispossessed and to show that "we are, too, the others" (144). Bremen focused at last on *Paterson I–IV*, arguing that Williams's poetic grammar of discovery is analogous to the empathic identifications of his cultural critique and medical practice. All of Williams's acts were intended to create a democratic, intersubjective space in which conversation might take place. Bremen's book—difficult, opaquely written, intellectually rich, subtly interweaving literary and social concerns, and daringly transforming the questions usually asked about texts—pointed to a new horizon in the study of Williams.

Among the other critical books published during this period, six considered the whole range of Williams's career. Stephen Cushman's illuminating *William Carlos Williams and the Meanings of Measure* (1985) explored Williams's use of "measure" both as a prosodic term involving issues of freedom and limitation and as a trope for mimesis, expressivity, social reality, intertextuality, and, again, freedom and limitation.[43] Like earlier studies by Tapscott and Rapp, Ron Callan's insightful *William Carlos Williams and Transcendentalism* (1992) placed Williams's work in the context of American Romanticism—not simply Rapp's Emerson and Tapscott's Whitman but Thoreau as well.[44] Employing Kenneth Burke's "pentad" as an organizing system, Bernard Duffey's *A Poetry of Presence* (1986) studied Williams's texts as an interdependent web of writing that evokes a poet at home amid the world's rubble.[45] Three other studies are not likely to have much impact on the critical conversation about Williams: Neil Baldwin's biography for young people, *To All Gentleness: William Carlos Williams, the Doctor-Poet* (1984); Charles Doyle's introductory *William Carlos Williams and the American Poem* (1982); and Audrey Rodgers's formulaic *Virgin and Whore: The Image of Women in the Poetry of William Carlos Williams* (1986).[46]

Eight additional books offered more specialized views. Four of these examined Williams's early career, dating from about 1909 to the mid–1920s. David Frail's *The Early Politics and Poetics of William Carlos Williams* (1987) provided detailed information and balanced judgment about the young Williams as a political writer—fervent, progressive, individualistic, nostalgic, and above all transfixed and confused by the social transformations of modernity.[47] Roy Miki's *The Prepoetics of William Carlos Williams: "Kora in Hell"* (1983) studied the way the poet negotiates contraries in his improvisations.[48] Christopher MacGowan's *William Carlos Williams's Early Poetry: The Visual Arts Background* (1984) documented the impact of Marcel Duchamp, Charles

Demuth, Wassily Kandinsky, Ezra Pound, Marsden Hartley, Juan Gris, dada, localism, and precisionism on the volumes through *Spring and All*.[49] Taking a more biographical approach, William Marling's *William Carlos Williams and the Painters, 1909–1923* (1982) focused on most of the same artists and movements while discussing precisely the same set of books.[50] Two other specialized books provided helpful commentary on Williams's dramaturgy. David Fedo's *William Carlos Williams: A Poet in the American Theatre* (1983) discerningly surveyed Williams's entire dramatic oeuvre, whereas Stephen Ross Loevy's *William Carlos Williams's "A Dream of Love"* (1983) briefly explicated Williams's most personal play.[51] T. Hugh Crawford's *Modernism, Medicine, & William Carlos Williams* (1993) studied the intersection of medical discourse with Williams's writing practices.[52] The last specialized book, Robert Gish's *William Carlos Williams: A Study of the Short Fiction* (1989), was an introductory analysis.[53]

In these years, the two initiating theorists in Williams criticism, J. Hillis Miller and Joseph Riddel, produced their culminating essays, each apparently influenced by the critique of the other.[54] Cultural theorists such as Sandra Gilbert, Theodora Graham, and Aldon Nielsen published groundbreaking studies of Williams's representation of women and African-Americans.[55] Lisa Steinman and Cecilia Tischi simultaneously published major studies of Williams, science, and technology—both partially reprinted here.[56] New editions of Williams's poetry by Christopher MacGowan and A. Walton Litz and a volume of correspondence edited by Hugh Witemeyer also contained valuable commentary.[57] Finally, innumerable book chapters and scholarly articles appeared, by Barbara Bell, Gerald Bruns, James Clifford, Paul Christensen, Margaret Dickie, Philip Furia, Marjorie Perloff, Wendy Steiner, David Walker, and many others.[58]

Williams, internalizing the condescension with which he was often received, once described himself as "a stupid, uninfluential poet, excluded / from anthologies" (*Poems II*, 473). For once, Williams was not right—or at least did not remain right. "The scene / indeed has changed" (*Poems II*, 266). As the proliferating commentaries testify, William Carlos Williams has taken his place in the spiral of literary history as one of the most brilliant, influential, and pleasure-giving poets of his century.

Notes

1.   Parenthetical references in this essay are to the following volumes by Williams: *Collected Poems of William Carlos Williams, Volume I, 1909–1939*, ed. A. Walton Litz and Christopher MacGowan (New York: New Directions, 1986); *Collected Poems of William Carlos Williams, Volume II, 1939–1962*, ed. Christopher MacGowan (New York: New Directions, 1988); *Paterson*, ed. Christopher MacGowan (New York: New Directions, 1992); *Selected Essays* (New York: New Directions, 1954; rpt. 1969).

2.   William Empson, "Rhythm and Imagery in English Poetry," *Journal of the British*

Society of Aesthetics 2 (January 1962); rpt. *William Carlos Williams: A Critical Anthology*, ed. Charles Tomlinson (London: Penguin, 1972), 365.

3. Vivienne Koch, *William Carlos Williams* (Norfolk, Conn.: New Directions, 1950).

4. John Malcolm Brinnin, *William Carlos Williams* (Minneapolis: University of Minnesota Press, 1963).

5. Roy Harvey Pearce, *The Continuity of American Poetry* (Princeton: Princeton University Press, 1961), 111–29, 335–48.

6. M. Bernetta Quinn, "William Carlos Williams: A Testament of Perpetual Change," *PMLA* 70 (June 1955): 292–322; M. Bernetta Quinn, *The Metamorphic Tradition in Modern Poetry* (New Brunswick: Rutgers University Press), 89–129.

7. Ralph Nash, "The Use of Prose in *Paterson*," *Perspective* 6 (1953): 191–99; Louis Martz, "William Carlos Williams: On the Road to *Paterson*," *Poetry New York* no. 4 (1951): 18–32; Norman Holmes Pearson, "Williams, New Jersey," *Literary Review* 1 (Autumn 1957): 29–36; M. L. Rosenthal, "Williams and Stevens," in *The Modern Poets: A Critical Introduction* (New York: Oxford University Press, 1960), 113–31; John C. Thirlwall, "William Carlos Williams' *Paterson*: The Search for a Redeeming Language," *New Directions in Prose and Poetry* 17 (1961): 252–310; George Zabriskie, "The Geography of *Paterson*," *Perspective* 6 (1954): 201–16.

8. Randall Jarrell, "A View of Three Poets," *Partisan Review* 18 (1951): 691–700.

9. Randall Jarrell, *Poetry and the Age* (New York: Alfred A. Knopf, 1953), 220–71.

10. Linda Welshimer Wagner, *The Poems of William Carlos Williams: A Critical Study* (Middletown, Conn.: Wesleyan University Press, 1964); J. Hillis Miller, "William Carlos Williams," in *Poets of Reality: Six Twentieth-Century Writers* (Harvard University Press, 1965), 285–359.

11. Linda W. Wagner, "William Carlos Williams," in *Sixteen Modern American Authors: A Survey of Research and Criticism*, ed. Jackson R. Bryer (Durham: Duke University Press, 1969; rpt. New York: Norton, 1973), 580.

12. James E. Breslin, *William Carlos Williams: An American Artist* (New York: Oxford University Press, 1970).

13. Mike Weaver, *William Carlos Williams: The American Background* (Cambridge: Cambridge University Press, 1971).

14. James Guimond, *The Art of William Carlos Williams: A Discovery and Possession of America* (Urbana: University of Illinois Press, 1968).

15. Bram Dijkstra, *The Hieroglyphics of a New Speech: Cubism, Stieglitz, and the Early Poetry of William Carlos Williams* (Princeton: Princeton University Press, 1969); rpt. as *Cubism, Stieglitz, and the Early Poetry of William Carlos Williams* (Princeton: Princeton University Press, 1978).

16. Dickran Tashjian, *William Carlos Williams and the American Scene, 1920–1940* (New York: Whitney Museum of American Art / Berkeley: University of California Press, 1978).

17. Jerome Mazzaro, *William Carlos Williams: The Later Poems* (Ithaca: Cornell University Press, 1973).

18. Sherman Paul, *The Music of Survival: A Biography of a Poem by William Carlos Williams* (Urbana: University of Illinois Press, 1968).

19. Thomas R. Whitaker, *William Carlos Williams* (New York: Twayne, 1968; rev. ed. Boston: Twayne, 1989).

20. Linda Welshimer Wagner, *The Prose of William Carlos Williams* (Middletown, Conn.: Wesleyan University Press, 1970).

21. Joel Conarroe, *William Carlos Williams' Paterson: Language and Landscape* (Philadelphia: University of Pennsylvania Press, 1970).

22. Benjamin Sankey, *A Companion to Williams's Paterson* (Berkeley: University of California Press, 1971).

23. Joseph N. Riddel, *The Inverted Bell: Modernism and the Counterpoetics of William Carlos Williams* (Baton Rouge: Louisiana State University Press, 1974).

24. Miller and Riddel, the twin deconstructors of Williams's poetry, maintained a cool cordiality toward each other in the pages of their books: see Riddel's *The Inverted Bell*, 25, 63, 211; Miller's *Poets of Reality*, 236, 239; and Miller's *The Linguistic Moment*, 351–52, note 54. In the scholarly journals, however, they battled. They were fighting for the same critical and theoretical territory, and their argument helped define the poststructuralist enterprise in the United States. See Riddel's review of Miller's anthology of essays (*Modern Language Journal* [January 1968]: 44–46) and especially Miller's review of Riddel's *The Inverted Bell* ("Deconstructing the Deconstructors," *Diacritics* 5 [Summer 1975]: 24–31) and Riddel's reply ("A Miller's Tale," *Diacritics* 5.2 [Autumn 1975]: 56–61). For their similar positions at the forefront of Wallace Stevens criticism, see Steven Gould Axelrod and Helen Deese, "Wallace Stevens: The Critical Reception," *Critical Essays on Wallace Stevens*, ed. Axelrod and Deese (Boston: G. K. Hall, 1988), 13–15. For other philosophical engagements with Williams's texts, see work by Altieri, Bové, Bremen, Bruns, Clifford, Diggory, and Duffey in notes below.

25. Rod Townley, *The Early Poetry of William Carlos Williams* (Ithaca: Cornell University Press, 1975).

26. Margaret Glynne Lloyd, *William Carlos Williams's "Paterson": A Critical Reappraisal* (Rutherford: Fairleigh Dickinson University Press, 1980).

27. Robert Coles, *William Carlos Williams: The Knack of Survival in America* (New Brunswick: Rutgers University Press, 1975).

28. Reed Whittemore, *William Carlos Williams: Poet from Jersey* (Boston: Houghton Mifflin, 1975).

29. Hélène Dupeyron-Marchesson, *William Carlos Williams et le renouveau du lyrisme* (Paris: Presses Universitaires de France, 1967); Alan Ostrom, *The Poetic World of William Carlos Williams* (Carbondale: Southern Illinois University Press, 1966); Walter Scott Peterson, *An Approach to "Paterson"* (New Haven: Yale University Press, 1967).

30. One of these is partially reprinted here: Hugh Kenner, *A Homemade World: The American Modernist Writers* (New York: Alfred A. Knopf, 1975), 54–67, 85–90. Other notable book chapters include: Steven Gould Axelrod, *Robert Lowell: Life and Art* (Princeton: Princeton University Press, 1978), 84–101, 154–56; Michael André Bernstein, *The Tale of the Tribe: Ezra Pound and the Modern Verse Epic* (Princeton: Princeton University Press, 1980); L. S. Dembo, *Conceptions of Reality in Modern American Poetry* (Berkeley: University of California Press, 1966), 48–80; Edwin Fussell, *Lucifer in Harness: American Meter, Metaphor, and Diction* (Princeton: Princeton University Press, 1973), 166–76; Suzanne Juhasz, *Metaphor and the Poetry of Williams, Pound, and Stevens* (Lewisburg, Pa.: Bucknell University Press, 1974), 32–74, 162–260; Harry Levin, *Grounds for Comparison* (Cambridge: Harvard University Press, 1972), 278–88; Todd M. Lieber, *Endless Experiments: Essays on the Heroic Experience in American Romanticism* (Columbus: Ohio State University Press, 1973), 191–241; James E. Miller, *The American Quest for a Supreme Fiction* (Chicago: University of Chicago Press, 1979), 126–60; Cary Nelson, *The Incarnate Word: Literature as Verbal Space* (Urbana: University of Illinois Press), 185–204; Dickran Tashjian, *Skyscraper Primitives: Dada and the American Avant-Garde 1910–1925* (Middletown, Conn.: Wesleyan University Press, 1975), 91–115; Hyatt Waggoner, *American Poets, From the Puritans to the Present* (Boston: Houghton Mifflin, 1968), 369–86; and A. Kingsley Weatherhead, *The Edge of the Image: Marianne Moore, William Carlos Williams, and Some Other Poets* (Seattle: University of Washington Press, 1967), 96–169.

Notable articles on Williams's early and middle poetry include: Charles Altieri, "Presence and Reference in a Literary Text: The Example of Williams's 'This Is Just to Say,' " *Critical Inquiry* 5 (1979): 489–510; David Antin, "Modernism and Postmodernism: Approaching the Present in American Poetry," *Boundary 2* 1 (1972): 98–146; James E. Breslin, "Whitman and the Early Development of William Carlos Williams," *PMLA* 82 (December 1967):

613–21; James E. Breslin, "William Carlos Williams and Charles Demuth: Cross-Fertilization in the Arts," *Journal of Modern Literature* 6 (1977): 248–63; Robert von Hallberg, "The Politics of Description: W. C. Williams in the 'Thirties," *ELH* 45 (1978): 131–58; Thomas P. Joswick, "Beginning with Loss: The Poetics of William Carlos Williams's *Kora in Hell*," *Texas Studies in Literature and Language* 19 (Spring 1977): 98–119; Richard A. Macksey, " 'A Certainty of Music': Williams' Changes," in *William Carlos Williams: A Collection of Critical Essays*, ed. J. Hillis Miller (Englewood Cliffs, N. J.: Prentice-Hall, 1966), 132–47; Norma Procopiow, "William Carlos Williams and the Origins of the Confessional Poem," *Ariel* (Canada) 7 (April 1976): 63–75; and Joseph Evans Slate, "*Kora* in Opacity: Williams's Improvisations," *Journal of Modern Literature* 1 (May 1971): 463–76.

Articles on *Paterson* and the later poetry include: Diane Ward Ashton, "The Virgin-Whore Motif in William Carlos Williams' *Paterson*," *Modern Poetry Studies* 4 (Autumn 1973): 193–209; Paul Bové, "The World and Earth of William Carlos Williams: *Paterson* as a 'Long Poem,' " *Genre* 11 (1978): 575–96; F. Douglass Fiero, "Williams Creates the First Book of *Paterson*," *Journal of Modern Literature* 3 (April 1974): 965–86; Neil Myers, "Decreation in Williams' 'The Descent,' " *Criticism* 14 (Fall 1972): 315–27; Christine Rabin, "Williams' Autobiographeme: The Inscriptional I in 'Asphodel,' " *Modern Poetry Studies* 6 (Autumn 1975): 157–74; and Stephen Tapscott, "Paterson A'Bloom: Williams, Joyce, and the Virtue of ABCedmindedness," *Arizona Quarterly* 33 (1977): 348–66.

Articles on Williams's drama, fiction, and nonfictional prose include: Kurt Heinzelman, "Staging the Poem: William Carlos Williams' *A Dream of Love*," *Contemporary Literature* 18 (Autumn 1977): 491–508; Alan Holder, "In the American Grain: William Carlos Williams on the American Past," *American Quarterly* 19 (Fall 1967): 499–515; Ron Loewinsohn, "Introduction" to *The Embodiment of Knowledge*, William Carlos Williams (New York: New Directions, 1974), ix–xxv; Marjorie Perloff, "The Man Who Loved Women: The Medical Fictions of William Carlos Williams," *Georgia Review* 34 (Winter 1980): 840–53; and Joseph Evans Slate, "William Carlos Williams, Hart Crane, and 'The Virtue of History,' " *TSLL* 6 (1965): 496–511.

31. Emily Mitchell Wallace, *A Bibliography of William Carlos Williams* (Middletown, Conn.: Wesleyan University Press, 1968); Paul L. Mariani, *William Carlos Williams: The Poet and His Critics* (Chicago: American Library Association, 1975); Linda W. Wagner, *William Carlos Williams: A Reference Guide* (Boston: G. K. Hall, 1978); Linda W. Wagner, "William Carlos Williams," in *Sixteen Modern American Authors: A Survey of Research and Criticism*, ed. Jackson R. Bryer (New York: Norton, 1973), 573–86; Linda W. Wagner-Martin, "William Carlos Williams," in *Sixteen Modern American Authors: A Survey of Research and Criticism*, vol. 2, ed. Jackson R. Bryer (Durham: Duke University Press, 1990), 675–715.

32. Paul Mariani, *William Carlos Williams: A New World Naked* (New York: McGraw-Hill, 1981).

33. Peter Schmidt, *William Carlos Williams, the Arts, and Literary Tradition* (Baton Rouge: Louisiana State University Press, 1988).

34. Terence Diggory, *William Carlos Williams and the Ethics of Painting* (Princeton: Princeton University Press, 1991).

35. Henry M. Sayre, *The Visual Text of William Carlos Williams* (Urbana: University of Illinois Press, 1983).

36. Ann W. Fisher-Wirth, *William Carlos Williams and Autobiography: The Woods of His Own Nature* (University Park: Pennsylvania State University Press, 1989).

37. Bryce Conrad, *Refiguring America: A Study of William Carlos Williams' "In the American Grain"* (Urbana: University of Illinois Press, 1990).

38. Kerry Driscoll, *William Carlos Williams and the Maternal Muse* (Ann Arbor: UMI Research Press, 1987).

39. Marilyn Kallet, *Honest Simplicity in William Carlos Williams' "Asphodel, That Greeny Flower"* (Baton Rouge: Louisiana University Press, 1985).

40. Stephen Tapscott, *American Beauty: William Carlos Williams and the Modernist Whitman* (New York: Columbia University Press, 1984).

41. Carl Rapp, *William Carlos Williams and Romantic Idealism* (Hanover, N.H.: University Press of New England, 1984).

42. Brian A. Bremen, *William Carlos Williams and the Diagnostics of Culture* (New York: Oxford University Press, 1993).

43. Stephen Cushman, *William Carlos Williams and the Meanings of Measure* (New Haven: Yale University Press, 1985).

44. Ron Callan, *William Carlos Williams and Transcendentalism: Fitting the Crab in a Box* (London: Macmillan, 1992).

45. Bernard Duffey, *A Poetry of Presence: The Writing of William Carlos Williams* (Madison: University of Wisconsin Press, 1986).

46. Neil Baldwin, *To All Gentleness: William Carlos Williams, the Doctor-Poet* (New York: Atheneum, 1984); Charles Doyle, *William Carlos Williams and the American Poem* (New York: St. Martin's Press, 1982); Audrey T. Rodgers, *Virgin and Whore: The Image of Women in the Poetry of William Carlos Williams* (Jefferson, N.C.: McFarland, 1986).

47. David Frail, *The Early Politics and Poetics of William Carlos Williams* (Ann Arbor: UMI Research Press, 1987).

48. Roy Miki, *The Prepoetics of William Carlos Williams: "Kora in Hell"* (Ann Arbor: UMI Research Press, 1983).

49. Christopher J. MacGowan, *William Carlos Williams's Early Poetry: The Visual Arts Background* (Ann Arbor: UMI Research Press, 1984).

50. William Marling, *William Carlos Williams and the Painters, 1909–1923* (Athens: Ohio University Press, 1982).

51. David A. Fedo, *William Carlos Williams: A Poet in the American Theatre* (Ann Arbor: UMI Research Press, 1983); Steven Ross Loevy, *William Carlos Williams's "A Dream of Love"* (Ann Arbor: UMI Research Press, 1983).

52. T. Hugh Crawford, *Modernism, Medicine, & William Carlos Williams* (Norman: University of Oklahoma Press, 1993).

53. Robert F. Gish, *William Carlos Williams: A Study of the Short Fiction* (Boston: Twayne, 1989).

54. J. Hillis Miller, *The Linguistic Moment: From Wordsworth to Stevens* (Princeton: Princeton University Press, 1985), 349–89; Joseph N. Riddel, " 'Keep Your Pecker Up'— *Paterson Five* and the Question of Metapoetry," *Glyph* 8 (1981): 203–31.

55. Rachel Blau Du Plessis, *The Pink Guitar: Writing as Feminist Practice* (New York: Routledge, 1990), 41–67; Sandra M. Gilbert, "Purloined Letters: William Carlos Williams and 'Cress,' " *William Carlos Williams Review* 11 (Fall 1985): 5–15; Theodora R. Graham, " 'Her Heigh Compleynte': The Cress Letters of William Carlos Williams' *Paterson*," in *Ezra Pound & William Carlos Williams*, ed. Daniel Hoffman (Philadelphia: University of Pennsylvania Press, 1983), 164–93; Theodora R. Graham, "Williams, Flossie, and the Others: The Aesthetics of Sexuality," *Contemporary Literature* 28 (Summer 1987): 163–86; Joan Nay, "William Carlos Williams and the Singular Woman," *William Carlos Williams Review* 11 (Fall 1985): 45–54; Aldon L. Nielsen, *Reading Race: White American Poets and the Racial Discourse in the Twentieth Century* (Athens: University of Georgia Press, 1988), 72–84; Aldon L. Nielsen, "Whose Blues?," *William Carlos Williams Review* 15 (Fall 1989): 1–8; Sergio Rizzo, "Can 'Beautiful Thing' Speak?: Race and Gender in *Paterson*" (included in the present volume); Linda W. Wagner, "The Outrage of *Many Loves*," *Sagetrieb* 3 (Fall 1984): 63–70.

56. Lisa M. Steinman, *Made in America: Science, Technology, and American Modernist Poets* (New Haven: Yale University Press, 1987), 78–112; Cecilia Tischi, *Shifting Gears: Technology, Literature, Culture in Modernist America* (Chapel Hill: University of North Carolina Press, 1987), 230–88.

57.   A. Walton Litz and Christopher MacGowan, eds., *Collected Poems of William Carlos Williams: Volume I, 1909–1939* (New York: New Directions, 1986), 467–548; Christopher MacGowan, ed., *Collected Poems of William Carlos Williams: Volume II, 1939–1962* (New York: New Directions, 1988), 439–516; Christopher MacGowan, ed., *Paterson* (New York: New Directions, 1992), 241–307; Hugh Witemeyer, ed., *William Carlos Williams and James Laughlin: Selected Letters* (New York: Norton, 1989), vii–xxiii.

58.   One of these is partially reprinted here: Marjorie Perloff, *The Poetics of Indeterminacy: Rimbaud to Cage* (Princeton: Princeton University Press, 1981), 109–54. Other significant book chapters include: Charles Altieri, *Painterly Abstraction in Modernist American Poetry* (Cambridge: Cambridge University Press, 1989), 223–42; James E. B. Breslin, *From Modern to Contemporary: American Poetry, 1945–1965* (Chicago: University of Chicago Press, 1984), 88–159; Gerald L. Bruns, *Inventions: Writing, Textuality and Understanding in Literary History* (New Haven: Yale University Press, 1982), 145–59; James Clifford, *The Predicament of Culture: Twentieth Century Ethnography, Literature, and Art* (Cambridge: Harvard University Press, 1988), 1–17; Margaret Dickie, *On the Modernist Long Poem* (Iowa City: University of Iowa Press, 1986), 77–105; Stephen Fredman, *Poet's Prose: The Crisis in American Verse* (Cambridge: Cambridge University Press, 1983), 12–54; Albert Gelpi, *A Coherent Splendor: The American Poetic Renaissance, 1910–1950* (Cambridge: Cambridge University Press, 1987), 321–72; Joseph G. Kronick, *American Poetics of History: From Emerson to the Moderns* (Baton Rouge: Louisiana State University Press, 1984), 196–227; Vera M. Kutzinski, *Against the American Grain: Myth and History in William Carlos Williams, Jay Wright, and Nicolas Guillen* (Baltimore: Johns Hopkins University Press, 1987), 1–46; Herbert Leibowitz, *Fabricating Lives: Explorations in American Autobiography* (New York: Knopf, 1989), 229–68; Margueritte S. Murphy, *A Tradition of Subversion: The Prose Poem in English from Wilde to Ashbery* (Amherst: University of Massachusetts Press, 1992); Sherman Paul, *Hewing to Experience: Essays and Reviews* (Iowa City: University of Iowa Press, 1989), 87–141; Marjorie Perloff, *The Dance of the Intellect: Studies in the Poetry of the Pound Tradition* (Cambridge: Cambridge University Press, 1985), 88–118; M. L. Rosenthal and Sally M. Gall, *The Modern Poetic Sequence: The Genius of Modern Poetry* (New York: Oxford University Press, 1983), 233–88; William Chapman Sharpe, *Unreal Cities: Urban Figuration in Wordsworth, Baudelaire, Whitman, Eliot, and Williams* (Baltimore: Johns Hopkins University Press, 1990), 134–74; Wendy Steiner, *The Colors of Rhetoric: Problems in the Relation between Modern Literature and Painting* (Chicago: University of Chicago Press, 1982), 71–90; David Walker, *The Transparent Lyric: Reading and Meaning in the Poetry of Stevens and Williams* (Princeton: Princeton University Press, 1984), 117–77; and Jeffrey Walker, *Bardic Ethos and the American Epic Poem: Whitman, Pound, Crane, Williams, Olson* (Baton Rouge: Louisiana State University Press, 1989), 154–202.

Articles on Williams's early and middle poetry include: Marie Borroff, "Questions of Design in William Carlos Williams and Marianne Moore," *William Carlos Williams Review* 14 (Spring 1988): 104–15; Allen Dunn, "Williams's Liberating Need," *Journal of Modern Literature* 16 (Summer 1989): 49–59; James Paul Gee, "The Structure of Perception in the Poetry of William Carlos Williams: A Stylistic Analysis," *Poetics Today* 6 (1985): 375–97; Christopher J. Knight, "William Carlos Williams, Paul Cézanne and the 'Technique of Originality,'" *Mosaic* 20 (Winter 1987): 83–96; Patrick Moore, "Cubist Prosody: William Carlos Williams and the Conventions of Verse Lineation," *Philological Quarterly* 65 (Fall 1986): 515–36; Michael North, "The Sign of Five: Williams's 'The Great Figure' and Its Background," *Criticism* 30 (Summer 1988): 325–48; Michel Orens, "Williams and Gris: A Borrowed Aesthetic," *Contemporary Literature* 26 (Summer 1985): 197–211; Michael Riffaterre, "Intertextual Representation: On Mimesis as Interpretive Discourse," *Critical Inquiry* 11 (September 1984): 141–62; and Linda Arbaugh Taylor, "Lines of Contact: Mina Loy and William Carlos Williams," *William Carlos Williams Review* 16 (Fall 1990): 26–47.

Articles on *Paterson* and the later poetry include: Nancy K. Barry, "The Fading Beautiful Thing of *Paterson*," *Twentieth Century Literature* 35 (Fall 1989): 343–63; Eleanor Berry,

"Williams' Development of a New Prosodic Form—*Not* the 'Variable Foot,' but the 'Sight-Stanza,' " *William Carlos Williams Review* 7 (Fall 1981): 21–30; Joan Burbick, "Grimaces of a New Age: The Postwar Poetry and Painting of William Carlos Williams and Jackson Pollock," *Boundary 2* 10 (Spring 1982): 109–23; Paul Christensen, "William Carlos Williams in the Forties: Prelude to Postmodernism," in *Ezra Pound and William Carlos Williams*, ed. Daniel Hoffman (Philadelphia: University of Pennsylvania Press, 1983), 143–63; Philip Furia, "*Paterson*'s Progress," *Boundary 2* 9 (Winter 1981): 31–49; Jay Grover-Rogoff, "Hart Crane's Presence in *Paterson*," *William Carlos Williams Review* 11 (Spring 1985): 20–29; Paul Mariani, "The Hard Core of Beauty," *Sagetrieb* 3 (Spring 1984): 7–26; Kathleen Matthews, "Competitive Giants: Satiric Bedrock in Book One of William Carlos Williams' *Paterson*," *Journal of Modern Literature* 12 (July 1985): 237–60; Jay Rogoff, "Pound-Foolishness in *Paterson*," *Journal of Modern Literature* 14 (Summer 1987): 35–44; Peter Schmidt, " 'These': Williams' Deepest Descent," *William Carlos Williams Review* 9 (Fall 1983): 74–90; Gay Sibley, "Documents of Presumption: The Satiric Use of the Ginsberg Letters in William Carlos Williams' *Paterson*," *American Literature* 55 (March 1983): 1–23; Maria Anita Stefanelli, "A Stylistic Analysis of Williams' 'The Descent,' " *Language and Style* 16 (Spring 1983): 187–210; and Dawn Trouard, "Perceiving Gestalt in 'The Clouds,' " *Contemporary Literature* 22 (Spring 1981): 205–17.

Articles on the fiction, drama, and prose include: Barbara Currier Bell, "Williams' 'The Use of Force' and First Principles in Medical Ethics," *Literature and Medicine* 3 (1984): 143–51; Elizabeth Klaver, "Williams's Drama: From Expressionism to Postmodernism in *Many Loves, A Dream of Love*, and *Paterson IV*" (included in the present volume); David B. Morris, "Williams's Force," *Literature and Medicine* 5 (1986): 122–40; Sheryl A. Mylan, " 'Witness the Words Being Born': The Miscarriage of Language in Williams's Stecher Trilogy" (included in the present volume); Linda Ray Pratt, "Williams's Stecher Trilogy: 'The Pure Products of America,' " *Studies in American Fiction* 10 (Spring 1982): 41–54; and Peter Schmidt, "Introduction to Williams' 'Letter to an Australian Editor' (1946): Williams' Manifesto for Multiculturalism," *William Carlos Williams Review* 17 (Fall 1991): 4–12.

General assessments include: Harold Bloom, "Introduction," *William Carlos Williams* (New York: Chelsea House, 1986), 1–9; Bonnie Costello, " 'Polished Garlands of Agreeing Difference': William Carlos Williams and Marianne Moore, An Exchange," in *The Motive for Metaphor*, ed. Francis C. Blessington and Guy Rotella (Boston: Northeastern University Press, 1983), 64–81; and Julio Marzan, "Mrs. Williams's William Carlos," in *Reinventing the Americas*, ed. Bell Chevigny and Gari Laguardia (Cambridge: Cambridge University Press, 1986), 106–21.

REVIEWS

Al Que Quiere!

♦

The New Poetry

Ezra Pound

Distinct and as different as possible from the orderly statements of Eliot, and from the slightly acid whimsicalities of these ladies, are the poems of Carlos Williams. If the sinuosities and mental quirks of Misses Moore and Loy are difficult to follow I do not know what is to be said for some of Mr. Williams' ramifications and abruptnesses. I do not pretend to follow all of his volts, jerks, sulks, balks, outblurts and jump-overs; but for all his roughness there remains with me the conviction that there is nothing meaningless in his book, "Al que quiere," not a line. There is whimsicality as we found it in his earlier poems. "The Tempers" (published by Elkin Mathews), in the verse to "The Coroner's Children," for example. There is distinctness and color, as was shown in his "Postlude," in "Des Imagistes"; but there is beyond these qualities the absolute conviction of a man with his feet on the soil, on a soil personally and peculiarly his own. He is rooted. He is at times almost inarticulate, but he is never dry, never without sap in abundance. His course may be well indicated by the change of the last few years; we found him six years ago in "The Postlude," full of a thick and opaque color, full of emotional richness, with a maximum of subjective reality:

Reprinted from *Future* (June 1918): 189–90. Copyright © 1993 by The Ezra Pound Literary Property Trust. Reprinted by permission of New Directions.

POSTLUDE

Now that I have cooled to you
Let there be gold of tarnished masonry,
Temples soothed by the sun to ruin
That sleep utterly.
Give me hand for the dances,
Ripples at Philae, in and out,
And lips, my Lesbian,
Wall flowers that once were flame.

Your hair is my Carthage
And my arms the bow,
And our words the arrows
To shoot the stars,
Who from that misty sea
Swarm to destroy us.

But you there beside me—
Oh! how shall I defy you,
Who wound me in the night
With breasts shining like Venus and like Mars?
The night that is shouting Jason
When the loud eaves rattle
As with waves above me,
Blue at the prow of my desire.

O prayers in the dark!
O incense to Poseidon!
Calm in Atlantis.

From this he has, as some would say, "turned" to a sort of maximum objective reality in

THE OLD MEN

Old men who have studied
every leg show
in the city
Old men cut from touch
by the perfumed music—
polished or fleeced skulls
that stand before
the whole theatre
in silent attitudes
of attention,—
old men who have taken precedence

over young men
and even over dark-faced
husbands whose minds
are a street with arc-lights.
Solitary old men
for whom we find no excuses . . .

This is less savage than "Les Assis." His "Portrait of a Woman in Bed" incites me to a comparison with Rimbaud's picture of an old actress in her "loge." Not to Rimbaud's disadvantage. I don't know that any, save the wholly initiated into the cult of anti-exoticism, would take Williams' poem for an exotic, but there is no accounting for what may occur in such cases.

PORTRAIT OF A WOMAN IN BED

There's my things
drying in the corner;
that blue skirt
joined to the gray shirt—

I'm sick of trouble!
Lift the covers
if you want me
and you'll see
the rest of my clothes—
though it would be cold
lying with nothing on!

I won't work
and I've got no cash.
What are you going to do
about it?
—and no jewelry
(the crazy fools).

But I've my two eyes
and a smooth face
and here's this! look!
it's high!
There's brains and blood
in there—
my name's Robitza!
Corsets
can go to the devil—
and drawers along with them!
What do I care!

My two boys?
—they're keen!
Let the rich lady
care for them—
they'll beat the school
or
let them go to the gutter—
that ends trouble.

This house is empty
isn't it?
Then it's mine
because I need it.
Oh, I won't starve
while there's the Bible
to make them feed me.

Try to help me
if you want trouble
or leave me alone—
that ends trouble.

The county physician
is a damned fool
and you
can go to hell!

You could have closed the door
when you came in;
do it when you go out.
I'm tired.

This is not a little sermon on slums. It conveys more than two dozen
or two hundred magazine stories about the comedy of slum-work. As the
memoir of a physician, it is keener than Spiess' notes of an advocate in the
Genevan law courts. It is more compact than Vildrac's "Auberge," and has
not Vildrac's tendency to sentiment. It is a poem that could be translated into
French or any other modern language and hold its own with the contemporary
product of whatever country one chose.

Kora in Hell

◆

Concerning "Kora in Hell"

ROBERT McALMON

*D*ear POETRY:—Writers, quite as much in the countries of older art tradition as in America, may be divided into two classes: one the professionals, whose concern is style, technique, finished achievement; the other, those who attempt at least to explore and develop new experience. The former class restrict themselves generally to quite conventional themes; or, if they are very daring, develop for themselves new themes—about which they write "verses"—ultimately hardening into a manner, inherited or their own, and softening in so far as ability to penetrate deeply goes. Limiting ourselves strictly to America, we may mention such poets of the first class as Masters, Sandburg, Aiken—the list need stop short of only a very few names. Particularly with Sandburg may one be sure that he will take an image, and consciously sustain and develop it, long after he has lost poignant feeling for the validity of the image. He is a professional writer. He has learned, in his own manner to be sure, how to use the image, the metaphor, the brutal truth, and the sentimental humanitarianism. So, starting out with the statement that the moon is a pot of gold mud, he must have that gold mud spread over worldly possessions, and of course at last a love-woman. He, and many others, seem to feel that it is necessary to write—if not an authentic poem, to write anyway. Unless from an impulse to say something keenly felt, writing is without justification.

Reprinted with permission from **Poetry**, 18 (April 1921): 54–59.

Of this first group few pass from their adolescent rebellions and miseries into a more spiritual type of searching. Their discovery of experience is limited to material environment—the corn-fields, the marching men, small-town viciousness, the hog-butchers of industrialism. Outside, and perhaps controlling the forces back of these externalities, are more fundamental forces which they do not sense, forces which have a universal application, while retaining also a strictly local significance. The experience of the locality is after all that of the universe. The history of any individual relates itself with startling similarity to that of the age.

Today is a time of the breakdown of faiths amongst the so-called "sensitized" and "intellectuals." With the coming of the theory of evolution the more sublime metaphysical theories were gradually abandoned; pragmatism, with its doctrines concerning the usable realities, followed on to lubricate the joints of a mechanistic universe. However, where a few began to doubt the value of these "practical" answers before the war, literally thousands now doubt. Why should we believe in evolution which does not explain involution, or the quite evident lack of progress? Have we anything to prove that physically and spiritually the human species is not on the retrograde? What is morality?—is non-morality a possibility? Dogmatized, it becomes at last a degenerate morality—must all ethics be individualized then? Many questionings, cynicisms, scoffings and doubtings attack all former judgments, and demand that their defenders prove their basis, and indicate clearly that it is something other than blind faith, or inward hunger rhapsodized into a proclamatory religion made out of dream-stuff. Ecstatic faith and prophetic exaltation are too primitive to be explainable in the religious instinct—for, say Whitman—to satisfy the diagnostic mind, and the psychologist.

Whatever certain groups or individuals may think or feel, the civilized peoples of the world are groping for some basis of faith: a faith in the mere value of living out their lives rather than a religious explanation of existence. But there is a new difficulty in their groping: they no longer trust logic, sequence, order—the intelligible, rational, deducible.

It is writers who are sensitive to this baseless way of accepting life, or rather tolerating it because life is what we have, who are developing the so-called "modern forms." Both *modern* and *form* are words that signify too much traditionally, and too little actually. To qualify, let me say I mean by modern that which is of the quality of today, displaying sensitive consciousness of the age's attitudes and philosophies. By form I mean method of expression and conveyance, and I have no concern with any structural form—metrical, rhythmic, or geometric.

James Joyce with his prose first indicated the modern form. Possibly his style could be traced back to the oftentimes incoherent Rimbaud; the likeness here is purely a mode—the texture, quality of perception, attitude, and substance are quite different: the one has the mature detached mind;

the other tossed himself with the seething of adolescence into the field of sophisticated discovery, and perhaps when adolescence and its ragings were over he would have relapsed into quite conventional or mediocre writing.

In America William Carlos Williams, and he beginning only with his improvisations entitled *Kora in Hell*, is conscious of the new form in relation to the dubiety of the day. Not agnosticism, for the agnostic will say "I can't know" decisively; we are simply doubting, and doubting whether we are right in doubting. There is in this book the spasmodic quality of the active, imaginative, alternately frightened and reckless, consciousness. One will search in vain for sequential outline; it is incoherent and unintelligible to— may I say the ordinary mind, though I dislike the superior implication of self which the phrase carries with it? (Since minds are so elusive, none is actually ordinary.) It is incoherent and unintelligible to those people with lethargy of their sensing organs. They look for the order and neatness of precise, developed thought. It is not there. *Kora in Hell* is accepted as a portrait of Williams' consciousness—a sort of retouched photograph. He is not distinctly located to himself—it's a "Should I, or shouldn't I, and what if I don't?" It's a conscientious sensitive mind, or life organism; trained in childhood to staid and tried acceptances and moralities, trying to be open, and to think, sense, or leap to a footing which more acceptably justifies the life-process than any of the traditional footings seem to.

To me *Kora in Hell* is immeasurably the most important book of poetry that America has produced. I find in Whitman a hardened exaltation, which proclaims rhapsodic dogmatism—the result of physical well-being, of the freedom of open air, space, and green fields. Admirable in its day, but the day is by for those of us who live in cities such as New York and Chicago, and who perhaps have never seen a real prairie or the mountains of the Great Divide, and who sleep in tenement-house bedrooms several stories up from the soil which flavors Indian imagism and produces sweep-of-the-corn-sap-flowing rhythms. And we will not accept the statement that "it is regrettable we have never had these things." Our situation is our situation, and by the artist can be utilized as substance for art. There can be no turning back to the soil, to the Indians—literature is not thus consciously developed. We are here, in the cities of smoke, subways, tired faces, industrialism; here with the movies and their over-gorgeousness, and the revues and follies which gradually inject their ultra-coloration into vaudeville; here where it is deemed necessary to applaud "art things"—Mozart and Schumann music, established classics which fall dully upon our hyper-neurotic senses. Be the conditions hectic, heated, artificial (are economic, political and social forces then "not natural"?) they are the conditions of a great portion of the country.

For those who wish poetry to create some sublime beauty, which to others grows irksome since it is necessary to turn from its sublimity to the reality of existence, William Carlos Williams' *Kora in Hell* will mean little. To those however who rather like to have the record of somebody else's conscious states by which to check their own, with which to respond and commune, it will mean a great deal. The writer, not caring for literature as literature; not knowing what function it performs in life other than that of a mental decoration if it does not get into, reveal, and sensitize people to, new experience; believes, however, that no book previously produced in this country has been so keenly, vividly aware of age conceptions, qualities, colors, noises, and philosophies as *Kora in Hell*. It is a break-away from poetry written by poets who set out to be poets. It is adventurous exploration.

Sour Grapes

◆

Heaven's First Law

KENNETH BURKE

It had once been my privilege to see a page written by William Carlos Williams on which he undertook to reproduce nine times the lovely sunshine thought, "Order is Heaven's first law." Now, by the fifth time, the poet became noticeably impatient, and from the seventh on the copy was completely unreadable. The ninth version was a mere wavy line, broken in four places. At first I took this to be quite damning; but on second thought, what use could Williams make of order? He thinks in an entirely different set of terms. To add organization to his poetry would have no more meaning than to insist that his lines begin in alphabetical rotation.

What Williams sees, he sees in a flash. And if there is any correlation whatsoever, it is a certain determined joyousness in a poet who would find it awkward to weep. For as his arch-enemy has noted, Williams is a bad Freudian case whose poetry is certainly not allowed to come out the way it came in. But beyond this very reasonable pudency, which he shares with no less an artist than Flaubert, consistency falls away.

No, Williams is the master of the glimpse. A line of his, suddenly leaping up out of the text, will throw the reader into an unexpected intimacy with his subject, like pushing open a door and advancing one's nose into some foreign face. Given a subject, he will attack it with verve, striking where he can break through its defense, and expecting applause whenever a

Reprinted from the *Dial* 72 (February 1922), 197–200.

solid, unmistakable jolt has been landed. It would be mere idleness to give his *ars poetica* in more presumptuous terms. The process is simply this: There is the eye, and there is the thing upon which that eye alights; while the relationship existing between the two is a poem.

The difficulty here lies in conveying the virtues of such a method. For the method itself is as common as mud. The minute fixating of a mood, an horizon, a contrast; if one finds there any unusual commendation for Williams it is not in the excellence of his poetics, but in the excellence of his results. His first virtue, therefore, lies in the superiority of *his* minute fixations over those of his ten million competitors. He is a distinguished member of a miserable crew.

Honest people who really think highly enough of words to feel unhappy when they are vague will rejoice that Wiliiams' new volume, Sour Grapes, is more sober in this respect than the Improvisations. For the Improvisations were not finally satisfactory. Clear notes were there in abundance, but they were usually preceded and followed by the usual modern data for mental tests. (How beautiful the association of ideas would have been in art if used in one work, by one man, for one page, and for some end other than that of a beautiful association of ideas.) True, by the mere dissatisfaction of their context, such momentary beatitudes of expression received their full share of enthusiasm, but having twenty sentences of chaos to heighten one sentence of cosmos is too much like thanking God for headaches since they enable us to be happy without them.

Sour Grapes, however, skips a generation and takes after the volume, Al Que Quiere. And in these two works, it seems to me, Williams is at his best, since here he is not handicapping his remarkable powers of definition, of lucidity. You may wonder, perhaps, just why the poet is going off in some particular direction; but you are always aware just what this direction is. Here also his inveterate lustiness is up to par; for Williams knows Walt Whitman's smile down to the last wrinkle. If there are logs in the grate, he puts a match to them; if it is a warm Easter morning, he throws off his coat. And if, behind it all, there is evidence of a strong tendency towards transgression, towards, let us say, the mountains of Tibet or a negro harem in Madagascar, such things are there as an irritant rather than as a subject. The face value of the poems will always remain the definition of the poet's own gatepost. His peculiar gifts of expression, if nothing else, dictate this simplification. Williams evidently realizes that his emotions are one thing and his art another, and that those who wish to go beyond his minute fixations can find a great deal more implicated in them; but in the meantime, let the minute fixations suffice.

I should say, therefore, that Williams was engaged in discovering the shortest route between object and subject. And whether it is a flamingo befouling its own tail, or the tired ogling at little girls, or trees stark naked in a wind, one must always recognize the unusual propriety of his poetry, the sureness and directness with which he goes at such things. A fact with him finds its justification in the trimness of the wording.

If a man is walking, it is the first principle of philosophy to say that he is *not* walking, the first principle of science to say that he is placing one foot before the other and bringing the hinder one in turn to the fore, the first principle of art to say that the man is *more than* walking, he is *yearning*: then there are times when scientist, philosopher, and poet all discover of a sudden that by heavens! the man is walking and none other. Now, a good deal of this discovery is in Williams' poetry, and, if I understand the word correctly, is contained in his manifesto praising Contact in art. For I take Contact to mean: man without the syllogism, without the parode, without Spinoza's Ethics, man with nothing but the thing and the feeling of that thing. Sitting down in the warmth to write, for instance, Kant might finally figure it out that man simply must have standards of virtue in spite of the bleakness of the phenomenon-noumenon distinction, and that this virtue could be constructed on the foundations of a categorical imperative. But Williams, sitting down in the warmth to write, would never get over his delight that the wind outside was raging ineffectually; and, in his pronounced sense of comfort, he would write:

JANUARY

Again I reply to the triple winds
running chromatic fifths of derision
outside my window:

                        Play louder.
You will not succeed. I am
bound more to my sentences
the more you batter at me
to follow you.

                    And the wind,
as before, fingers perfectly
its derisive music.

Seen from this angle, Contact might be said to resolve into the counterpart of Culture, and Williams becomes thereby one of our most distinguished Neanderthal men. His poetry deals with the coercions of nature—and by nature I mean iron rails as well as iron ore—rather than with the laborious structure of ideas man has erected above nature. His hatred of the idea in art is consequently pronounced, and very rightly brings in its train a complete disinterest in form. (Note: Form in literature must always have its beginnings in idea. In fact, our word for idea comes from a Greek word whose first meaning is "form.") The Contact writer deals with his desires; the Culture writer must erect his desires into principles and deal with those principles rather than with the desires; the *Urphenomen*, in other words, becomes with the man of Culture of less importance than the delicate and subtle instruments with which he studies it.

Williams, however, must go back to the source. And the process undeniably has its beauties. What, for instance, could be more lost, more uncorrelated, a closer Contact, a greater triumph of anti-Culture, than this poem:

THE GREAT FIGURE

Among the rain
and lights
I saw the figure 5
in gold
on a red
firetruck
moving
with weight and urgency
tense
unheeded
to gong clangs
siren howls
and wheels rumbling
through the dark city.

In the American Grain

◆

American Sagas

LOLA RIDGE

The words of William Carlos Williams either rend and pull apart or set about erecting a new building. Strong, hard-beaked words, the one thing they cannot do is to leave things as they are, and they rarely carry to a pile already begun.

In this book they serve a fresh and beautiful interpretation of American history. Williams has found a new way of approach. His mind is of the fleet and narrow type that is built for speed. It makes men think of a horse in flight, a racer, with his ears back and here and there a fleck of foam . . . His objective is beauty: that which is not beauty is an obstacle, not to be walked around, to be attacked and if possible demolished. Yet his anger never swells into a chant as does his homage and his wonder; his disgusts are the intervals in his song. For, except for some chapters on Puritanism, in which there is so little to sing about, his book is an interrupted song. It opens with the saga of Red Eric and ends on Lincoln—a sensitive minor note, where so many readers will expect a trumpeting major, and be annoyed because it is not sounded. He speaks very softly of Lincoln, almost as though to himself; he might be remembering twilights in which they had sat together. He has hushed himself—who seldom hushes himself—and gone close to listen. He is the first to touch the brooding mother in that lonely man. Another for whom he has listened is Walter Raleigh, that shadow-

Reprinted from the New Republic 46 (24 March 1926): 148–49.

man, lost in a queen's lover. In histories he has seemed always remote to me; a posturing figure, covering a gutter with his coat, later, a sawdust head rolling off. Williams's staccato chant leaves him a song in the air, a song long over-laid with more importunate sounds, but not again to be forgotten.

Biased Carlos Williams is, accepting with passion or rejecting with intolerance. It is a proud mask, and fiercely meek, that head of Montezuma he raises above the ruins of Tenochtitlan. He throws only waste glances at the hardy bandit Cortez who serves his own lusts and Spain's as one god. To Montezuma, alone, no dried blood clings—unless some out-splashing from the blood-baths of the idols. Suave, smiling in despair, the Aztec is as untarnished as a golden image that has been dug up out of a dirty ruin. Williams has invested him, and the old jeweled civilization he rested on, with the strange glamor that surrounds beautiful things and people who die by violence before their time. You catch the intermittent glimmer of "gold and silver and precious stones," and moving shadows of birds over blue pools, over all the boding idols. . . . Tenochtitlan is a bloodied and desecrated tapestry over which the Spaniards swarm insatiate. They seized beauty and it died—still-born for those who destroyed it—only to be again and yet again resurrected by some such sensitively groping hand as has here achieved it.

There is in Williams a higher fealty than that demanded by mere factual truth. He has in him the truth that can only be proven by emotional recognition. Such a truth, beyond the scope of records, is that love-duel of de Soto with the New World. Thus She sings to her Black Jasamine: You are mine and I will strip you naked—jealous of everything that touches you. Down, down to me—in and under and down, unbeaten, the white kernel, the flame—the flame burning under water that I cannot quench.

The man has a boy's passion for the virginal America of de Soto and Daniel Boone. He, too, would have followed that savage mistress who starved and bled and isolated her weary lovers, or consumed them with her voracious tenderness. Like his favorite hero, Boone, he would have accepted whole-heartedly the hateful as well as the lovely aspects of his beloved. To the large ruthlessness of natural forces he submits without protestation, yet without cowering. But he vigorously rejects that amalgamated pressure of small souls that imposes itself as an organized will.

He has achieved here as searching an analysis of Puritanism as was possible to one not yet quite convalescent from its effects. But the residue of it that is in him has both colored his thought with an obscure violence, and prevented his near approach. You cannot touch intimately what you hate, except by a blow, and the blow feels only itself. But there is a light in Williams, and this light he has thrown upon the Puritans. It illuminates them for intense moments, burning over if not into them, and making their drabness vivid. With what precision he impales them on a phrase: "the first

American Democracy." And this for Poor Richard, smuggest of their proph-
ets: "the face on the penny stamp." Yet he joins foreigners, who have not
the knowledge that contact gives, in regarding New England women as
sexless. But they are no more sexless than any other women, merely encased
in congealed opinion that resists thaw like the long snows that persist upon
their hills.

His treatment of the Negroes, a people who have given so much to
America's spiritual and aesthetic life, is singularly inadequate. He is not
unsympathetic—far from it. But he approaches them as a spectator and
seems to watch, fascinated, a single gesture that, in all its variations, becomes
his beauty—to be segregated and kept pure for his perpetual enjoyment.
He is grateful for their joy, the "quality" they brought to America—and
of which they had so much that all their giving has not yet left them
bankrupt. But: "all the rest is to keep from having to say anything more
. . . it is their beauty."

In the American Grain is chaotic and unequal, but it is a great adventure. From time to time, especially in Jacataqua, the motion slackens. An
excited interest takes the place of intensity—something of the vivacity of
the expansive male in an after-dinner mood. I find in Williams signs of sex-
antagonism. There seems to be in him a streak of what is not so much
commonness as a desire, almost a hunger, to share its contacts. Not the
plush sofa variety, that he would execrate, but those of the gutters. Some
of his words have the rank immediacy of the gutters. But no one has a more
subtle sense of word-values. Sometimes, by re-examining and airing the
content of a word, he regains that first transparency through which we can
see afresh the delicate structure of the thought. Genius, for instance, has
never been better re-fitted than to "that stream-like purity of purpose"—
that filled Columbus on his first voyage.

In him the Indian lives. I say the Indian, advisedly, for the race looms
as one man, an over life-sized figure, ruthless, vivid, stark, moving swiftly.
It is the Indian who really dominates this book. To Williams he is as much
a part of the New World as are her prairies and great rivers; a being never
to be exterminated, a red power passing silent, subtle, into the white bodies,
in and under the white skins: "I do believe the average American to be an
Indian, but an Indian robbed of his world." Here again is that which I
recognize as truth, living and shifting under the static fact. It does not even
need the superstructure of a fact, because it is of that unknowable stuff that
life is made of, and that, in turn, vibrates to its touch.

This book leaves me with a sense of vast spaces, luxuriance arrested,
pressed back forces; a lonely, stark beauty, silent, grim, dying as the Indian
dies. A new world passing, unknown, having been touched only blindly,
as one jostles, without knowledge, a savage splendid queen riding by in
darkness.

American Heroes

D. H. LAWRENCE

Mr. Williams quotes Poe's distinction between "nationality in letters" and the *local* in literature. Nationality in letters is deplorable, whereas the *local* is essential. All creative art must rise out of a specific soil and flicker with a spirit of place.

The local, of course, in Mr. Williams's sense, is the very opposite of the parochial, the parish-pump stuff. The local in America is America itself. Not Salem, or Boston, or Philadelphia, or New York, but that of the American subsoil which spouts up in any of those places into the lives of men.

In these studies of "American" heroes, from Red Eric of Greenland, and Columbus and Cortes and Montezuma, on to Abraham Lincoln, Mr. Williams tries to reveal the experience of great men in the Americas since the advent of the whites. History in this book would be a sensuous record of the Americanization of the white men in America, as contrasted with ordinary history, which is a complacent record of the civilization and Europizing (if you can allow the word) of the American continent.

In this record of truly American heroes, then, the author is seeking out not the ideal achievement of great men of the New World but the men themselves, in all the dynamic explosiveness of their energy. This peculiar dynamic energy, this strange yearning and passion and uncanny explosive quality in men derived from Europe, is American, the American element. Seek out *this* American element—Oh Americans!—is the poet's charge.

All America is now going hundred per cent American. But the only hundred per cent American is the Red Indian, and he can only be canonized when he is finally dead. And not even the most American American can transmogrify into an Indian. Whence, then, the hundred per cent?

It is here that Mr. Williams's—and Poe's—distinction between the *national* and the *local* is useful. Most of the hundred per centism is national, and therefore not American at all. The new one hundred per cent literature is all *about* Americans, in the intensest American vernacular. And yet, in vision, in conception, in the very manner, it still remains ninety-nine per cent European. But for "Ulysses" and Marcel Proust and a few other beetling high-brows, where would the modernest hundred per centers of America have been? Alas, where they are now, save for cutting a few capers.

What then? William Carlos Williams tries to bring into his consciousness America itself, the still-unravished bride of silences. The great continent, its bitterness, its brackish quality, its vast glamor, its strange cruelty. Find this, Americans, and get it into your bones. The powerful, unyielding breath of the Americas, which Columbus sniffed, even in Europe, and which sent the Conquistadores mad. National America is a gruesome sort of fantasy. But the unravished *local* America still waits vast and virgin as ever, though in process of being murdered.

The author sees the genius of the continent as a woman with exquisite, super-subtle tenderness and recoiling cruelty. It is a myth-woman who will demand of men a sensitive awareness, a supreme sensuous delicacy, and at the same time an infinitely tempered resistance, a power of endurance and of resistance.

To evoke a vision of the essential America is to evoke Americans, bring them into conscious life. To bring a few American citizens into American consciousness—the consciousness at present being all bastardized European—is to form the nucleus of the new race. To have the nucleus of a new race is to have a future: and a true aristocracy. It is to have the germ of an aristocracy in sensitive tenderness and diamond-like resistance.

A man, in America, can only *begin* to be American. After five hundred years there are no *racial* white Americans. They are only national, woebegone, or strident. After five hundred years more there may be the developing nucleus of a true American race. If only men, some few, trust the American passion that is in them, and pledge themselves to it.

But the passion is not national. No man who doesn't feel the last anguish of tragedy—*and beyond that*—will ever know America, or begin, even at the beginning's beginning, to be American.

There are two ways of being American; and the chief, says Mr. Williams, is by recoiling into individual smallness and insentience, and gutting the great continent in frenzies of mean fear. It is the Puritan way. The other is by *touch*; touch America as she is; dare to touch her! And this is the heroic way.

And this, this sensitive touch upon the unseen America, is to be the really great adventure in the New World. Mr. Williams's book contains his adventures; and, therefore, for me, has a fascination. There are very new and profound glimpses into life: the strength of insulated smallness in the New Englanders, the fascination of "being nothing" in the Negroes, the *spell-bound* quality of men like Columbus, de Soto, Boone. It is a glimpse of what the vast America *wants men to be*, instead of another strident assertion of what men have made, do make, will make, can make, out of the murdered territories of the New World.

It would be easy enough to rise, in critical superiority, as a critic always feels he must, superior to his author, and find fault. The modernist style is sometimes irritating. Was Tenochtitlan really so wonderful? (See Adolf Bandelier's "The Golden Man.") Does not Mr. Williams mistake Poe's agony of *destructive penetration*, through all the horrible bastard-European alluvium of his 1840 America, for the positive America itself?

But if an author rouses my deeper sympathy he can have as many faults as he likes, I don't care. And if I disagree with him a bit, heaven save me from feeling superior just because I have a chance to snarl. I am only too thankful that Mr. Williams wrote his book.

Collected Poems

◆

Preface to *Collected Poems, 1921–1931*

WALLACE STEVENS

The slightly tobaccoy odor of autumn is perceptible in these pages. Williams is past fifty.

There are so many things to say about him. The first is that he is a romantic poet. This will horrify him. Yet the proof is everywhere. Take the first poem, "All the Fancy Things." What gives this its distinction is the image of the woman, once a girl in Puerto Rico in the old Spanish days, now solitary and growing old, not knowing what to do with herself, remembering. Of course, this is romantic in the accepted sense, and Williams is rarely romantic in the accepted sense.

The man has spent his life in rejecting the accepted sense of things. In that, most of all, his romantic temperament appears. But it is not enough merely to reject: what matters is the reason for rejection. The reason is that Williams has a romantic of his own. His strong spirit makes its own demands and delights to try its strength.

It will be observed that the lonely figure in "All the Fancy Things" and the person addressed in "Brilliant Sad Sun" have been slightly sentimentalized. In order to understand Williams at all, it is necessary to say at once that he has a sentimental side. Except for that, this book would not exist and its character would not be what it is. "The Cod Head" is a bit of pure

From *Opus Posthumous* by Wallace Stevens, ed. Samuel French Morse. Copyright 1957 by Elsie Stevens and Holly Stevens. Reprinted by permission of Alfred A. Knopf.

sentimentalization; so is "The Bull." Sentiment has such an abhorrent name that one hesitates. But if what vitalizes Williams has an abhorrent name, its obviously generative function in his case may help to change its reputation. What Williams gives, on the whole, is not sentiment but the reaction from sentiment, or, rather, a little sentiment, very little, together with acute reaction.

His passion for the anti-poetic is a blood-passion and not a passion of the inkpot. The anti-poetic is his spirit's cure. He needs it as a naked man needs shelter or as an animal needs salt. To a man with a sentimental side the anti-poetic is that truth, that reality to which all of us are forever fleeing.

The anti-poetic has many aspects. The aspect to which a poet is addicted is a test of his validity. Its merely rhetorical aspect is valueless. As an affectation it is a commonplace. As a scourge it has a little more meaning. But as a phase of a man's spirit, as a source of salvation, now, in the midst of a baffled generation, as one looks out of the window at Rutherford or Passaic, or as one walks the streets of New York, the anti-poetic acquires an extraordinary potency, especially if one's nature possesses that side so attractive to the Furies.

Something of the unreal is necessary to fecundate the real; something of the sentimental is necessary to fecundate the anti-poetic. Williams, by nature, is more of a realist than is commonly true in the case of a poet. One might, at this point, set oneself up as the Linnaeus of aesthetics, assigning a female role to the unused tent in "The Attic Which Is Desire," and a male role to the soda sign; and generally speaking one might run through these pages and point out how often the essential poetry is the result of the conjunction of the unreal and the real, the sentimental and the anti-poetic, the constant interaction of two opposites. This seems to define Williams and his poetry.

All poets are, to some extent, romantic poets. Thus, the poet who least supposes himself to be so is often altogether so. For instance, no one except a *surrealiste* himself would hesitate to characterize that whole school as romantic, dyed through and through with the most authentic purple. What, then, is a romantic poet now-a-days? He happens to be one who still dwells in an ivory tower, but who insists that life would be intolerable except for the fact that one has, from the top, such an exceptional view of the public dump and the advertising signs of Snider's Catsup, Ivory Soap and Chevrolet Cars; he is the hermit who dwells alone with the sun and moon, but insists on taking a rotten newspaper. While Williams shares a good deal of this with his contemporaries in the manner and for the reason indicated, the attempt to define him and his work is not to be taken as an attempt to define anyone or anything else.

So defined, Williams looks a bit like that grand old plaster cast, Lessing's Laocoön: the realist struggling to escape from the serpents of the unreal.

He is commonly identified by externals. He includes here specimens of abortive rhythms, words on several levels, ideas without logic, and similar minor matters, which, when all is said, are merely the diversions of the prophet between morning and evening song. It will be found that he has made some veritable additions to the corpus of poetry, which certainly is no more sacred to anyone than to him. His special use of the anti-poetic is an example of this. The ambiguity produced by bareness is another. The implied image, as in "Young Sycamore," the serpent that leaps up in one's imagination at his prompting, is an addition to imagism, a phase of realism which Williams has always found congenial. In respect to manner he is a virtuoso. He writes of flowers exquisitely. But these things may merely be mentioned. Williams himself, a kind of Diogenes of contemporary poetry, is a much more vital matter. The truth is that, if one had not chanced to regard him as Laocoön, one could have done very well by him as Diogenes.

Life Along the Passaic River

♦

X-Ray Realism

EDA LOU WALTON

Dr. Williams takes no detours around life. Using realism with the precision of a surgeon exposing the vital organs, he achieves art. His materials are those of his own life, the experience of a busy doctor engaged often in clinical and charity work. His vision is stated in his own words: "I defend the normality of every disease, every amputation. I challenge anyone who thinks to discomfit my intelligence by limiting the import of what I say to the expounding of a shallow morbidity, to prove that health alone is inevitable." His political position is implied in this bit of dialogue: " 'A clear miss,' he said. 'I think if we'd gone in there earlier, we'd have saved her.' 'For what?' said I. 'Vote the straight Communist ticket?' 'Would it make us any dumber?' said the ear man."

These sketches—many cannot be called short stories—teem with life, with the urgency, the fury with which life continues despite all that our general ignorance and our society do to kill it. Dr. Williams sees the heroism and the glory in corruptible flesh, among the diseased, the poor, the ignorant, and the immoral—the people, in short, who are "cuckoo as a funny strip. But at that it is not so funny." One of these stories is about a girl with a pimply face who is cured not only of her pimples but of ineffectual living by her will to find out causes; another is an account of a child's violent physical struggle to keep the doctor from examining her throat because she

Reprinted from the *Nation* 146 (19 March 1938) 334–45, by permission of the Nation company.

knows she has diphtheria. The doctor's anger at and admiration for the little fighting "animal" are both part of the comedy. One could point out that each of these sketches is, in a way, symbolic, but the reader discovers this for himself. The impact of these tales is due to the fact that everything expressed in them is pared down to the bone, to the essential structure. The shock of each story is the shock of observing bone suddenly and cleanly unfleshed. Without any sentimentality, and with the utmost dexterity, each little piece of the human pattern of living is made significant.

The comedy and tragedy, and always the human dignity, of birth and death—which a doctor observes daily—are Williams's subject matter. He stresses the psychology of the doctor-patient relationship, the exchange of feeling between healer and diseased. His scene is the Passaic River town, its tenements, its dirty streets, and its hospital clinic where the dramatic fight for the preservation of seemingly worthless lives takes place. Williams's art lies in his ability not only to paint his picture with unforgettable exactness but to expose what he himself *makes* of his picture. He has been compared to Hemingway because of his clipped prose. But in truth he is neither philosophically nor technically like the author of "The Sun Also Rises." He is not a sentimentalist, or a romanticist; he is not disillusioned. He faces life at its ugliest and reacts to it with a kind of gusto and faith. In his prose as in his poetry he is an imagist, a painter of pictures. He so uses commonplace, concrete words that they live again, expressive of new violence or tenderness, revealing a new awareness.

Williams's art is realism intensified with a skill as of X-ray in penetration and analysis—realism, in other words, vitalized by an imaginative way of viewing life which is unique, comprehensive, and very American. Despite the evidence in his writings of a clear political position arrived at through practical experience, Williams is never a propagandist. He lets his material speak for itself. Because he is a fine artist, he can make the picture, the action, the facts illuminate his theme; he need not comment.

Paterson I

◆

The Poet and His Public

RANDALL JARRELL

Paterson (Book I) seems to me the best thing William Carlos Williams has ever written; I read it seven or eight times, and ended up lost in delight. It seems a shame to write a little review of it, instead of going over it page by page, explaining and admiring. And one hates to quote much, since the beauty, delicacy, and intelligence of the best parts depend so much upon their organization in the whole; quoting from it is like humming a theme and expecting the hearer to guess from that its effect upon its third repetition in a movement. I have used this simile deliberately, because—over and above the organization of argument or exposition—the organization of *Paterson* is musical to an almost unprecedented degree: Mr. Williams introduces a theme that stands for an idea, repeats it over and over in varied forms, develops it side by side with two or three more themes that are being developed, recurs to it time and time again throughout the poem, and echoes it for ironic or grotesque effects in thoroughly incongruous contexts. Sometimes this is done with the greatest complication and delicacy; he wants to introduce a red-bird whose call will stand for the clear speech of nature, in the midst of all the confusion and ugliness in which men could not exist except for "imagined beauty where there is none": so he says in disgust, "Stale as a whale's breath: breath! / Breath!" and ten lines later (during which three themes have been

Reprinted from *Partisan Review* 13 (September–October 1946): 493–98, by permission of Partisan Review and Mary von Shradon Jarrell.

repeated and two of them joined at last in a "silent, uncommunicative," and satisfying resolution) he says that he has

> Only of late, late! begun to know, to
> know clearly (as through clear ice) whence
> I draw my breath or how to employ it
> clearly—if not well:
>
> Clearly!
> speaks the red-breast his behest. Clearly!
> clearly!

These double exclamations have so prepared for the bird's call that it strikes you, when you are reading the poem, like the blow which dissolves an enchantment. And really the preparation has been even more complicated: two pages before there was the line "divorce! divorce!" and half a page before the birds and weeds by the river were introduced by

> . . . white, in
> the shadows among the blue-flowered
> Pickerel-weed, in summer, summer! if it should
> ever come . . .

If you want to write a long poem which doesn't stick to one subject, but which unifies a dozen, you can learn a great deal from *Paterson*. But I do not know how important these details of structure will seem to an age which regards as a triumph of organization that throwing-out-of-blocks-upon-the-nursery-floor which concludes *The Waste Land*, and which explains its admiration by the humorless literalness of believing that a poet represents fragments by eliminating metre, connectives, and logic from the verses which describe the fragments.

The subject of *Paterson* is: How can you tell the truth about things?— that is, how can you find a language so close to the world that the world can be represented and understood in it?

> Paterson lies in the valley under the Passaic Falls
> its spent waters forming the outline of his back. He
> lies on his right side, head near the thunder
> of the water filling his dreams! Eternally asleep,
> his dreams walk about the city where he persists
> incognito. Butterflies settle on his stone ear.

How can he—this city that is man—find the language for what he dreams and sees and is, the language without which true knowledge is impossible? He starts with the particulars ("Say it, no ideas but in things") which stream to him like the river, "rolling up out of chaos, / a nine months' wonder"; with the interpenetration of everything with everything, "the drunk the sober; the illustrious / the gross; one":

> It is the ignorant sun
> rising in the slot of
> hollow suns risen, so that never in this
> world will a man live well in his body
> save dying—and not know himself
> dying . . .

The water falls and then rises in "floating mists, to be rained down and / regathered into a river that flows / and encircles"; the water, in its time, is "combed into straight lines / from that rafter of a rock's / lip," and attains clarity; but the people are like flowers that the bee misses, they fail and die and "Life is sweet, they say"—but their speech has failed them, "they do not know the words / or have not / the courage to use them," and they hear only "a false language pouring—a / language (misunderstood) pouring (misinterpreted) without / dignity, without minister, crashing upon a stone ear." And the language available to them, the language of scholarship and science and the universities, is

> a bud forever green
> tight-curled, upon the pavement, perfect
> in justice and substance but divorced, divorced
> from its fellows, fallen low—
>   Divorce is
> the sign of knowledge in our time,
> divorce! divorce!

Girls walk by the river at Easter and one, bearing a willow twig in her hand as Artemis bore the moon's crescent bow,

> holds it, the gathered spray,
> upright in the air, the pouring air,
> strokes the soft fur—

>   Ain't they beautiful!

(How could words show better than these last three the touching half-success, half-failure of their language?) And Sam Patch, the drunken frontier hero who jumped over the Falls with his pet bear, could *say* only: "Some things can be done as well as others"; and Mrs. Cumming, the minister's wife, shrieked unheard and fell unseen from the brink; and the two were only

> a body found next spring
> frozen in an ice-cake; or a body
> fished next day from the muddy swirl—
>
> both silent, uncommunicative.

The speech of sexual understanding, of natural love, is represented by three beautifully developed themes: a photograph of the nine wives of a Negro chief; a tree standing on the brink of the waterfall; and two lovers talking by the river:

> We sit and talk and the
> silence speaks of the giants
> who have died in the past and have
> returned to those scenes unsatisfied
> and who is not unsatisfied, the
> silent, Singac the rock-shoulder
> emerging from the rocks—and the giants
> live again in your silence and
> unacknowledged desire . . .

But now the air by the river "brings in the rumors of separate worlds," and the poem is dragged from its highest point in the natural world, from the early, fresh, and green years of the city, into the slums of Paterson, into the collapse of this natural language, into "a delirium of solutions," into the back streets of that

> great belly
> that no longer laughs but mourns
> with its expressionless black navel love's
> deceit.

Here is the whole failure of Paterson's ideas and speech, and he is forced to begin all over; Part II of the poem ends with the ominous "No ideas but / in the facts."

Part III opens with this beautiful and unexpected passage:

> How strange you are, you idiot!
> So you think because the rose
> is red that you shall have the mastery?
> The rose is green and will bloom,
> overtopping you, green, livid
> green when you shall no more speak, or
> taste, or even be. My whole life
> has hung too long upon a partial victory.

The underlying green of the facts always cancels out the red in which we had found our partial, temporary, aesthetic victory; and the poem now introduces the livid green of the obstinate and compensating lives, the lifeless perversions of the industrial city: here are the slums and the adjoining estate with its acre hothouse and weedlike orchids and French maid whose sole duty is to "groom / the pet Pomeranians—who sleep"; here is the university with its clerks

> spitted on fixed concepts like
> roasting hogs, sputtering, their drip sizzling
> in the fire
>
> Something else, something else the same.

Then (in one of the fine prose quotations—much altered by the poet, surely—with which the verse is interspersed) people drain the lake there, all day and all night long kill the eels and fish with sticks, carry them away in baskets; there is nothing left but the mud. The sleeping Paterson, "moveless," envies the men who could run off "toward the peripheries—to other centers, direct" for some "loveliness and / authority in the world," who could leap like Sam Patch and be found "the following spring, frozen in / an ice cake." But he goes on thinking to the very bitter end, reproduces all the ignorance and brutality of the city; and he understands its pathos and horror:

> And silk spins from the hot drums to a music
> of pathetic souvenirs, a comb and nail-file
> in an imitation leather case—to
> remind him, to remind him! and
> a photograph-holder with pictures of himself
> between the two children, all returned
> weeping, weeping—in the back room
> of the widow who married again, a vile tongue
> but laborious ways, driving a drunken
> husband . . .

Yet he contrasts his own real mystery, the mystery of people's actual lives, with the mystery that "the convent of the Little Sisters of / St. Ann pretends"; and he understands the people "wiping the nose on sleeves, come here / to dream"; he understands that

> Things, things unmentionable
> the sink with the waste farina in it and
> lumps of rancid meat, milk-bottle-tops: have
> here a still tranquillity and loveliness . . .

Then Paterson "shifts his change," and an earthquake and a "remarkable rumbling noise" frighten but do not damage the city—this is told in the prose of an old newspaper account; and, at the end of the poem, he stands in the flickering green of the cavern under the waterfall (the dark, skulled world of consciousness), hedged in by the pouring torrent whose thunder drowns out any language—

> the myth
> that holds up the rock,
> that holds up the water thrives there—
> in that cavern, that profound cleft

—and the readers of the poem are shown, in the last words of the poem, "standing, shrouded there, in that din, / Earth, the chatterer, father of all / speech. . . ."

It takes several readings to work out the poem's argument (it is a poem that *must* be read over and over), and it seemed to me that I could do most for its readers by roughly summarizing that argument. There are hundreds of things in the poem that deserve specific mention. The poem is weakest in the middle of Part III—I'd give page numbers if good old New Directions had remembered to put in any—but this is understandable and almost inevitable. Everything in the poem is interwoven with everything else, just as the strands of the Falls interlace: how wonderful and unlikely that this extraordinary mixture of the most delicate lyricism of perception and feeling with the hardest and homeliest actuality should ever have come into being! There has never been a poem more American (though the only influence one sees in it is that of the river scene from *Finnegans Wake*); if the next three books are as good as this one, which introduces "the elemental character of the place," the whole poem will be far and away the best long poem any American has written. I should like to write a whole article about it; I leave it unwillingly.

Paterson II

♦

Paterson II

ROBERT LOWELL

"Paterson," Book Two, is an interior monologue. A man spends Sunday in the park at Paterson, New Jersey. He thinks and looks about him; his mind contemplates, describes, comments, associates, stops, stutters, and shifts like a firefly, bound only by its milieu. The man is Williams, anyone living in Paterson, the American, the masculine principle—a sort of Everyman. His monologue is interrupted by chunks of prose: paragraphs from old newspapers, textbooks, and the letters of a lacerated and lacerating poetess. This material is merely selected by the author. That the poetry is able to digest it in the raw is a measure of power and daring—the daring of simplicity; for only a taut style with worlds of experience behind it could so resign, and give way to the anthologist. The didactic chapters in "Moby Dick" have a similar function, and are the rock that supports the struggles of Captain Ahab.

The park is Everywoman, any woman, the feminine principle, America. The water roaring down the falls from the park to Paterson is the principle of life. The rock is death, negation, the *nul*; carved and given form, it stands for the imagination, "like a red basalt grasshopper, boot-long with window-eyes." The symbols are not allegorical, but loose, intuitive, and Protean.

"Paterson," like Hart Crane's "Marriage of Faustus and Helen," is about marriage. "Rigor of beauty is the quest." Everything in the poem is masculine or feminine, everything strains toward marriage, but the marriages never come off, except in the imagination, and there, attenuated, fragmentary, and uncertain. "Divorce is the sign of knowledge in our time." The people "reflect no beauty but gross . . . unless it is beauty to be, anywhere, so flagrant in desire." "The ugly legs of the young girls, pistons without delicacy"; "not undignified"; "among the working classes *some* sort of break-down has occurred." The preacher in the second section, attended by the "iron smiles" of his three middle-aged disciples, by "benches on which a few children have been propped by the others against their running off," "bends at the knees and straightens himself up violently with the force of his emphasis—like Beethoven getting a crescendo out of an orchestra"—ineffective, pathetic, and a little phony. He has given up, or says he has given up, a fortune for the infinite riches of our Lord Jesus Christ. Interspersed through his sermon, as an ironic counter-theme, is Alexander Hamilton, whose fertile imagination devised the national debt and envisioned Paterson as a great manufacturing center. Nobody wins. "The church spires still spend their wits against the sky." "The rock-table is scratched by the picnick-ers' boot-nails, more than by the glacier." The great industrialists are "those guilty bastards . . . trying to undermine us." The legislators are "under the garbage, uninstructed, incapable of self-instruction." "An orchestral dulness overlays their world." "The language, tongue-tied . . . words without style!"

This is the harsh view. Against it is the humorous, the dogs, the children; lovely fragments of natural description; the author's sense of the human and sympathetic in his people.

Williams is noted as an imagist, a photographic eye; in Book One he has written "no ideas but in the facts." This is misleading. His symbolic man and woman are Hegel's *thesis* and *antithesis*. They struggle toward *synthesis*—marriage. But fulness, if it exists at all, only exists in simple things, trees and animals; so Williams, like other Platonists, is thrown back on the "idea." "And no whiteness (lost) is so white as the memory of whiteness." "The stone lives, the flesh dies." The idea, Beauty, must be realized by the poet where he lives, in Paterson. "Be reconciled, Poet, with your world, it is the only truth," though "love" for it "is no comforter, rather a nail in the skull."

"Paterson" is an attempt to write the American Poem. It depends on the American myth, a myth that is seldom absent from our literature—part of our power, and part of our hubris and deformity. At its grossest the myth is propaganda, puffing and grimacing: Size, Strength, Vitality, the Common Man, the New World, Vital Speech, the Machine; the hideous neo-Roman personae: Democracy, Freedom, Liberty, the Corn, the Land. How hollow, windy, and inert this would have seemed to an imaginative man of another culture! But the myth is a serious matter. It is assumed by Emerson, Whit-man, and Hart Crane; by Henry Adams and Henry James. For good or for evil, America *is* something immense, crass, and Roman. We must unavoidably place ourselves in our geography, history, civilization, institutions, and future.

The subjects of great poetry have usually been characters and the passions, a moral struggle that calls a man's whole person into play. One thinks of the wrath of Achilles, Macbeth and his conscience, Aeneas debating whether he will leave Dido, whether he will kill Turnus. But in the best long American poems—"Leaves of Grass," "The Cantoes," "The Waste Land," "Four Quartets," "The Bridge," and "Paterson"—no characters take on sufficient form to arrive at a crisis. The people melt into voices. In a recent essay Eliot has given his reasons why a writer should, perhaps, read Milton; Williams has answered with an essay that gives reasons why a writer should *not* read Milton—Eliot and Williams might learn something from "Paradise Lost" and "Samson Agonistes," how Milton populated his desert.

Until Books III and IV are published, it is safer to compare "Paterson" with poems that resemble it; not with "The Bridge," that wonderful monster, so unequal, so inexperienced—dazzling in its rhetoric at times in the way that Keats is dazzling; but with a book in which its admirers profess to find everything, "Leaves of Grass." Whitman is a considerable poet, and a considerable myth. I can never quite disentangle the one from the other. I would say that Whitman's language has less variety, sureness, and nerve than Williams's; that his imagination is relatively soft, formless, monotonous, and vague. Both poets are strong on compassion and enthusiasm, but these qualities in Whitman are *simpliste* and blurred.

"Paterson" is Whitman's America, grown pathetic and tragic, brutalized by inequality, disorganized by industrial chaos, and faced with annihilation. No poet has written of it with such a combination of brilliance, sympathy, and experience, with such alertness and energy. Because he has tried to understand rather than excoriate, and because in his maturity he has been occupied with the "raw" and the universal, his "Paterson" is not the tragedy of the outcast but the tragedy of our civilization. It is a book in which the best readers, as well as the simple reader, are likely to find *everything*.

ESSAYS

"It Is a Design"

LINDA WELSHIMER WAGNER

Important though metaphor is to the content of Williams' poems, it is even more significant as a principle of organization. All Williams' comments about the figure stress its ability to increase both the depth and the speed of the poem. He saw metaphor as an integral part of the poem's "anatomy," never an "addition" to it. As he wrote in "Preface to a Book of Poems," metaphor identified with "all the pretty glass balls, all the thrilling details of writing verse, must today be subjugated to . . . the structure of ideas."[1]

It is difficult to find a metaphor in Williams' poems which does not have structural importance. Most figures hold prominent positions in the poem, falling at the beginning, center, or end. Often the figure is isolated dramatically in the midst of literal expression, gaining much force from the contrast between kinds of speech.

Dr. Williams did not use metaphor for shock effect, however, as T. E. Hulme had once conceived of its value. Non-figurative lines relate to the metaphoric image, either by anticipating it or by elaborating it, so that the metaphor is the core of the entire poem. Frequently the isolated figure appears at the end, with detail building toward it, as in "A Negro Woman":

> carrying a bunch of marigolds
>> wrapped
>>> in an old newspaper:
> She carries them upright,
>> bareheaded, . . .
>>> as she walks
> looking into
>> the store window which she passes
>>> on her way.
> What is she
>> but an ambassador
>>> from another world
> a world of pretty marigolds . . .
>>> *(Pictures*, p. 123.)

Reprinted from *The Poems of William Carlos Williams: A Critical Study*, © 1964 by Linda Welshimer Wagner, Wesleyan University Press. By permission of University Press of New England.

Literal lines lead to the concluding metaphor as Williams describes the woman with fitting simplicity and dignity. She carries the flowers proudly, "upright"; while she walks, she looks about her—curious and attentive. The literal description indicates that she is well suited in her dignity to be "an ambassador" and, in her naturalness, to represent "a world of pretty marigolds."

Dr. Williams often used a complex of metaphors in which one was structurally dominant, with the others acting to expand the chief figure. As a rule, the dominant figure of several occurs early in the poem so that its relationship with the others is clear. "The Pink Locust," for example, begins with the simile, "I'm persistent as the pink locust," the comparison between the poet and the flower being the subject of the poem. Other figures—all related to the initial comparison—occur at intervals throughout.

From this basic structure grew several types of organization. The simplest is the elaboration of an initial metaphor, to be found in "To Waken an Old Lady":

> Old age is
> a flight of small
> cheeping birds
> skimming
> bare trees
> above a snow glaze.
> Gaining and failing
> they are buffeted
> by a dark wind—
> But what?
> On harsh weedstalks
> the flock has rested,
> the snow
> is covered with broken
> seedhusks
> and the wind tempered
> by a shrill
> piping of plenty.
> (*CEP*, p. 200.)

The effectiveness of this poem results from the purity of the single metaphor carried throughout, non-figurative lines in keeping with the figurative. Through the careful progression of detail, the last nine lines quietly reverse the direction of the opening, resolving the poem so that it *is* well suited for its purposes. Because of Williams' expert choice of adjectives, the shift after the interrupting question is gradual; *harsh* weedstalks continues the tone of early lines, as does *broken* seedhusks when read in the early context. That the flock has rested and has access to seeds, however, turns the poem toward the concluding "piping of plenty."

Vivid as this depiction is, it presents a relatively simple experience; such structure can be used with only limited subjects. Consequently, Williams expanded his use of metaphor as structure by juxtaposing images which employed singly each of the subjects fused in the metaphor. "A Widow's Lament in Springtime" utilizes this device, as does "Love Song."

> Sweep the house clean,
> hang fresh curtains
> in the windows
> put on a new dress
> and come with me!
> The elm is scattering
> its little loaves
> of sweet smells
> from a white sky!
>
> Who shall hear of us
> in the time to come?
> Let him say there was
> a burst of fragrance
> from black branches.
> (*CEP*, p. 137.)

Drawing from the subject areas of human relationships and nature, Williams gives the entire first strophe a domestic orientation. Especially striking details are the cleanliness of the sky and the elm's "loaves / of sweet smells"—a figure effective for its reversal as well as its coupling with the elm. (The expected order would be "sweet smells of loaves.")

Although no metaphor has specifically united the lovers with nature, the position of the four-line nature description immediately after the poet's invitation suggests the intended relationship. In the second strophe, by "answering" the poet's question with another nature description, Williams again uses juxtaposition, heightened here by a new intensity in the familiar image of smell. Now that the lovers are together, fragrance "bursts" rather than being scattered.

In Chapter III this technique was termed "transitional metaphor" because it creates much the same impact as does metaphor. The reader is forced to provide his own "meaning," his own transition for the sections as they appear, just as in metaphor he must complete or at least recognize the suggested relationship. In poems like "A Widow's Lament" and "Love Song" the position of images is nearly as important as their content. This principle of organization is central to many of Williams' poetic techniques, providing as it does the basis of structure for many poems throughout his career.

Montage, for example, is one variation of juxtaposition. Single elements are arranged to create a complex scene in accurate perspective. Each detail is listed separately, with no explanation for its position and no transition connecting it with other images:

> One
> black (of course, red)
> rose; a fat old woman backing
> through a screen door. Two,
> from the armpits
> down, contrasting in bed,
> breathless; a letter from
> a ship; leaves filling,
> making, a tree . . .
>> ("A Place (Any Place)
>> To Transcend All Places,"
>> *CLP*, p. 113.)

The effectiveness of what Williams called "a fascinating sort of composition" is derived from the presentation of details without comment: "nothing 'about' the subject, a bare placing of the matter before the attention, as an object, that which with wit a man might see for himself—swiftly and to the point."[2] By eliminating slowing transitions, the poet can achieve what Williams called "the white light" of perception, an almost instantaneous poetic "apprehension" (*SE*, p. 122):

> The shell flowers
> the wax grapes and peaches
> the fancy oak or mahogany tables
> the highbacked baronial chairs
>
> Or the girls' legs
> agile stanchions
> the breasts
> the pinheads . . .
>
> Then unexpectedly
> a small house with a soaring oak
> leafless above it
>
> Someone should summarize these things
> in the interest of local
> government or how
> a spotted dog goes up a gutter—. . .
>> ("11 / 10," *CEP*, pp. 309–310.)

Through this series of vignettes, Williams creates a definite conclusion as he "summarizes these things." The effectiveness of the local scene, however, is derived from the total cumulative structure rather than from individual figures. Each image helps to create the whole impression, but its meaning in the entire composite is often very different from that in isolation. Williams depended heavily on *montage* as an organizational principle during the nineteen-twenties and thirties, using it as the rationale for later more complicated structures.

That the effects of this technique were far-reaching is evident in his 1956 praise of René Char for his achievement of "cumulative interest": "once he gets the theme he follows it in example after example with telling effect until gradually it becomes clear by the sheer persistence of what he has to say. It is a perfectly legitimate device of the artist and increases the pleasure of the reader by piling up the emphasis with variations of detail until the total effect is overwhelming."[3] Perhaps the late principle of organization most dependent on the single phrase or detail is that of "words, rhythmically organized" which Williams defended in a television interview:

Q: . . . here's part of a poem you yourself have written: . . .

> 2 partridges
> 2 mallard ducks
> a Dungeness crab
> 24 hours out
> of the Pacific
> and 2 live-frozen
> trout
> from Denmark . . .

Now, that sounds just like a fashionable grocery list!

A: It is a fashionable grocery list.

Q: Well—is it poetry?

A: We poets have to talk in a language which is not English. It is the American idiom. Rhythmically it's organized as a sample of the American idiom. It has as much originality as jazz. If you say "2 partridges, 2 mallard ducks, a Dungeness crab"—if you treat that rhythmically, ignoring the practical sense it forms a jagged pattern. It is, to my mind, poetry . . .

Q: But shouldn't a word mean something when you see it?

A: In prose, an English word means what it says. In poetry, you're listening to two things . . . you're listening to the sense, the common sense of what it says. But it says more. That is the difficulty.

(*Pat*, p. 262)

Williams early recognized the need for the rhythmic arrangements of words and for structures that could contain complex subjects while at the same time moving fast enough to hold a reader's attention. Achieving a structure which satisfied these requirements, however, took many years of experimentation, experimentation which was put to the test of use only when Williams' subject matter became correspondingly complex. Structure was no problem until he began writing *Paterson* in the early forties.

To arrive at a satisfactory epic structure, Williams had to pass through his period of greatest transition. The tenets of Objectivism had dominated his poetry for fifteen years. The fact that Objectivism allowed as subject only the concrete "thing" (presented literally and in isolation from even the poet) gradually drove Williams into stalemate and then into change as he realized that he was ignoring more of the local than he had included. In the late thirties, Williams decided that what he needed was to modify his definition of both the poem and the role of the poet.

Still maintaining that the poem was to re-create the local, Williams now saw that it must present a complex view rather than a simple one. It must include many components of life: the poet and his perception, the subject and its surroundings, related objects in the fabric of life. In short, Williams felt that the poet must take the details of his observation and combine them into a meaningful whole. Man observes; the poet interprets the observation and relates it to life. And he cannot suppress or exclude his own reactions: they are an integral part of his local, probably the part he knows best. As Williams wrote in 1947, "The objective in writing is, to reveal. It is not to teach, not to advertise, not to sell, not even to communicate (for that needs two) but to reveal, which needs no other than the man himself . . ." (*SE*, p. 268).

Once Williams began writing the epic which would present life "whole," he found that many changes in technique were necessary. His new point of view forced him back to an even wider acceptance of figures of speech, now useful in presenting thought sequences and abstractions. The increased scope of the poem also necessitated more connective figures—symbolic metaphor as well as transitional. And, in structure, the self-determined forms of the previous limited poems could not carry the multiple segments of the new, particularly not of the epic.

Rather than evolve a definite formula for structure, however, Williams continued to rely on his faith in language and in experimentation: "In my mind, all along, I was disturbed as to how I would put the thing [*Paterson*] down on the page. Finally I let form take care of itself; the colloquial language, my own language, set the pace" (*IWWP*, p. 73). With Williams following the demands of language, line and stanza were largely self determined. And for structural format, he returned to the only expansive techniques he had—those of transitional metaphor and montage—and to a new concept of structure, that of *design*. As he wrote metaphorically in the opening of his 1948 *The Clouds*: "In the bare trees old husks make new designs /

Love moves the crows before the dawn / The cherry sun ushers in a new phase. . . ."

It is precisely the "old husks" of objective description and the "new phase" of more figurative subjectivity which form the "new designs" of these poems. Williams' reaction against the single image viewed in isolation is evident in his comment from "Tribute to the Painters":

> there came to me
> just now
> the knowledge of
> the tyranny of the image
> and how
> men
> in their designs
> have learned
> to shatter it. . .
> (*Pictures*, p. 137.)

Static representations of objects are no longer valid; only when fitted with other components in a design of total life does the image have a part.

Notes

1. "Preface to a Book of Poems," p. 3 (unpublished typescript, State Univ. of New York at Buffalo). Parenthetical references in this essay are to the following volumes: *Collected Earlier Poems* (Norfolk, Conn.: New Directions, 1951); *Collected Later Poems* (Norfolk, Conn.: New Directions, 1963); *I Wanted to Write a Poem*, ed. Edith Heal (Boston: Beacon Press, 1958); *Paterson* [I–IV] (Norfolk, Conn.: New Directions, 1963); *Pictures from Breughel and Other Poems* (Norfolk, Conn.: New Directions, 1962); *Selected Essays* (New York: Random House, 1954).

2. First complete draft (23 May 1944) of Williams's "Commentary" to his translation of Quevado's *The Dog and the Fever*, p. 19 (typescript, Yale University).

3. "Poet Who Cannot Pause," *New Republic* 135 (17 September 1956): 18.

William Carlos Williams

J. Hillis Miller

Words as things incarnating their meanings become a set of fluid energies whose life exists only in the present.[1] Such words, isolated and cleaned, can be put down on the page like splashes of paint on a canvas and allowed to explode into the multitude of meanings which emerge from their juxtaposition. One version of "The Locust Tree in Flower" is an extreme example of this use of words. Here each word has a line to itself, and is surrounded on all sides by the blank page. Logic and grammar almost disappear, but not quite, and prepositions, adjectives, nouns, verbs, and adverbs are put side by side to establish a simultaneous pattern of linguistic forces. This effect is enhanced by the fact that the poem begins with two prepositions, which must be held side by side in the mind as alternatives. Then follow a series of somewhat contradictory adjectives without the article which would be expected before a singular noun. Are these all meant to modify "branch," or will a later noun attract some of them to itself? The words hang freely in the air. Moreover, the verb presupposes a plural subject, so the reader must balance between the possibility that the word "has" may have been left out and the assumption that "come" is to be taken as an imperative. This grammatical uncertainty forces him to hold all the words before his attention at once as he tries various ways to make a sentence of them. He is like a seal juggling thirteen brightly colored balls, and this is exactly what the poet wants. The poem is as much all there at once as the locust tree itself in its tension of branches, leaves, and flowers. The poem is not a picture of the tree, but is itself something substantial echoing in its structure of verbal forces the birth of white blossoms from stiff boughs. In "The Locust Tree in Flower," to borrow Williams' praise for Miss Moore, the "purely stated idea," the idea embodied in words which are things, "has an edge exactly like a fruit or a tree or a serpent" (SE, 130):

                    Among
                    of
                    green

                    stiff
                    old
                    bright

                    broken
                    branch
                    come

                    white
                    sweet
                    May

                    again
                    (CEP, 93)

Words, nevertheless, are different from splashes of paint or musical sounds. However consubstantial their meaning and their physical presence, they still refer to things other than themselves. The word "parsley" is the name of a small green crinkly plant. Williams cannot escape the referential meaning of words, and curiously enough he has none of that tormenting fear of reference which haunts modern art, no desire to abolish the naming power of words in order to create a poem which will be entirely free of objects, like an abstract painting. In his poetry words are one thing, trees and flowers are another, but both are possessed within the same inner space. As a result he replaces the romantic or symbolist aesthetic of transformation with an art which is calm description, naming one by one the visible and tangible qualities of an object. Texts of this sort abound in his work:

                In brilliant gas light
                I turn the kitchen spigot
                and watch the water plash
                into the clean white sink.

                On the grooved drain-board
                to one side is
                a glass filled with parsley—
                crisped green.
                                (CEP, 145)

    Such a passage is the exact opposite of a poetry of indirection or of transposition, Mallarmé's hints at the fan which he never names or Stevens' tangents of a pineapple. Williams can look straight at the object because it offers no threat. There is nothing alien or distant about it. It proposes no invitation to the poet's violence. The objectivity of his descriptions affirms his security. The parsley does not need the poem. The poem does not need the parsley. The parsley and the poem about the parsley are separate things, each existing within the universal realm made of the poet's coextension with the world. Poetry of this kind is a way of letting things be. A good poet, consequently, "doesn't *select* his material. What is there to select? It *is*" (Intro, xi).

To let the parsley be in the poem does not mean transposing the parsley into the poem. It means using the referential meaning of words to name the parsley in its self-sustaining independence. The parsley is a stubborn and irreducible fact, nonverbal in nature, and the poem in the simplicity of its description recognizes it as such. Just as the parsley is separate from the poem about it, so it is separate from the things around it. It stands alone in its glass, side by side with the grooved drainboard, the clean white sink, the water, the spigot, the gaslight. Each thing has its own intrinsic particularity, its own precise edges cutting it off from other things, just as each word in "The Locust Tree in Flower" stands by itself, surrounded by the white page. There is no blurring, no flowing of a ubiquitous force which melts distinctions and makes things alike. In the "Prologue to *Kora in Hell*" the poet affirms that the value of his poem about the chicory flower (see CEP, 122) is the way it praises the resolute isolation of the plant. Free of the poem, it is also free of the things around it: "A poet witnessing the chicory flower and realizing its virtues of form and color so constructs his praise of it as to borrow no particle from right or left. He gives his poem over to the flower and its plant themselves" (SE, 17). In Williams' world there are no resonances or similarities between things, no basis for metaphor. There is in fact little figurative language in his poetry. He is deeply suspicious of it. Its place is sometimes taken by a version of imagist technique, the juxtaposition of dissonant things so that a meaning may emerge from their contrast:

> Like a cylindrical tank fresh silvered
> unpended on the sidewalk to advertise
> some plumber's shop, a profusion
> of pink roses bending ragged in the rain—
> (CLP, 24)

Most often even this doubling of particulars is not permitted. Williams has an extraordinary ability to pick a single thing out of the multitude existing and focus on it with intense concentration, as if it were the only object in the world, incomparable, unique. He has the power of "seeing the thing itself without forethought or afterthought but with great intensity of perception" which he praises in his mother (SE, 5). His attitude toward things, like Ezra Pound's, is nominalist. Each object is itself and nothing more should be said about it: "Although it is a quality of the imagination that it seeks to place together those things which have a common relationship, yet the coining of similes is a pastime of very low order, depending as it does upon a nearly vegetable coincidence. Much more keen is that power which discovers in things those inimitable particles of dissimilarity to all other things which are the peculiar perfections of the thing in question" (SE, 16).

Nor are there vertical resonances. Since there is no "behind" or "beyond" in Williams' world, no depth or transcendence, there can be no symbolic meaning in things, no reference to a secret heaven of ideal values. "No symbolism is acceptable" (SE, 213); "Those who permit their senses to be despoiled of the things under their noses by stories of all manner of things removed and unattainable are of frail imagination" (SE, 15). A primrose is just a primrose, and there are no deep thoughts in flowers, trees, or tables. The table "describes / nothing: four legs, by which / it becomes a table" (CLP, 91). The wheelbarrow, in a famous poem, does not stand for anything or mean anything. It is an object in space dissociated from the objects around it, without reference beyond itself. It is what it is. The aim of the poem is to make it stand there for the reader in its separateness, as the words of the poem stand on the page.

If the poem affirms the independence of the object and lets the object be, what good is the poem in itself? The parsley already is, and there seems little use for a poem which merely says that it is. Williams' response to this problem is the basis of his theory of imagination. The poet must make use of the referential meaning of words to relate them to physical objects as a springboard from which they may leap into a realm of imagination carrying with them the things named in a new form. Williams rejects those modern poets who "use unoriented sounds in place of conventional words" (SA, 92). Words should not be wholly independent of things, but they should not be completely attached to things either. That would be the kind of description in which "words adhere to certain objects, and have the effect on the sense of oysters, or barnacles" (SA, 90). Poetry is an effect of the imagination, and "words occur in liberation by virtue of its processes" (SA, 90). How can this freedom be attained? It is not a matter of "a removal from reality" (SA, 90). There must be no return to the idea of the imagination as a power which can take the reader beyond the world. The imagination is one of the conditions or regions of the inner-outer space which is all there is. In poetry words must still have their old meanings, and, therefore, "the writer of imagination would attain closest to the conditions of music not when his words are disassociated from natural objects and specified meanings but when they are liberated from the usual quality of that meaning by transposition into another medium, the imagination" (SA, 92).

This liberation takes place by a paradoxical movement both toward and away from the object, a movement of which the poem about parsley is an example. By illuminating the object exactly, the poem affirms the object's independence and thereby frees the words to execute their dance of imagination above the body of the world. The words carry with them some of the substance of the world and are vitalized by their possession of that substance. The thing "needs no personal support but exists free from human action" (SA, 91), and the poem is real too, but only because it is both related to and free from the thing it names. "The word is not liberated," says Williams, "therefore able to communicate release from the fixities which destroy it until it is accurately tuned to the fact which giving it reality, by its own reality establishes its own freedom from the necessity of a word, thus freeing it and dynamizing it at the same time" (SA, 93). This crucial passage explains what the poet means earlier when he says that "the same things exist, but in a different condition when energized by the imagination" (SA, 75). An image of sublimation is fundamental to his concept of the action of imagination. Poetry lifts things up. Its aim is "to repair, to rescue, to complete" (SL, 147). John of Gaunt's speech in *Richard II*, for example, is not an escape from reality, nor is it a mere description of his state. It is "a dance over the body of his condition accurately accompanying it" (SA, 91). This idea of a free play of words above reality but not separate from it appears again in an image of poetry as like a bird in flight: "As birds' wings beat the solid air without which none could fly so words freed by the imagination affirm reality by their flight" (SA, 91). In another passage, "the poet, challenging the event, recreates it as of whence it sprang from among men and women, and makes a new world of it" (Intro, xii).

This tense interaction between words and things is the basis of Williams' repeated affirmation that a poem is "a field of action" (SE, 280). Only if the words are both free of things and related to them can it be said that "poetry does not tamper with the world but moves it" (SA, 91). This avoids both the Scylla of defining art as a mirror of reality and the Charybdis of accepting an art of romantic evasion, a music of pure sounds cut off from life. The poem and the thing are both real, both equally real: "A rose *is* a rose / and the poem equals it / if it be well made" (PB, 141). Again and again the poet repeats his rejection of any representational theory of art. Poetry is "not a matter of 'representation' " (SA, 45), "nor is it description nor an evocation of objects or situations" (SA, 91). A poem "creates a new object, a play, a dance which is not a mirror up to nature" (SA, 91), "not 'like' anything but transfused with the same forces which transfuse the earth—at least one small part of them" (SA, 50). The prose parts of the original edition of *Spring and All*, never reprinted by the poet, are his fullest expressions of a subtle theory of poetry which rejects both the mirror and the lamp, both the classical theory of art as imitation, and the romantic theory of art as transformation. In their place is proposed a new objectivist art in which a poem is "Not prophecy! NOT prophecy! / but the thing itself!" (P, 242). This new art is becoming increasingly dominant in both America and Europe, and, as this happens, Williams' place as a poet helping to bring about a radical change in literature is more apparent.

If the same energies flow through a poem as flow through the earth, then a poem is "natural" because it is a growth, a process. The poet must try to write "the poem that lifts the dish / of fruit . . . like / a table" (CLP, 91), or compose fiction "so that when [he speaks] of a chair it will stand upon four legs in a room. And of course it will stand upon a four-legged sentence on a page at the same time" (SL, 312). These passages emphasize the activity of the poem. The poem "lifts" the dish of fruit, or "stands up" on the page. Elsewhere the way the essence of poetry is its power to do something is even more explicit. Only if the poem shifts from the adjective which copies a dead nature to the verb which is alive with natural forces can the words be an extension of the processes of the earth, "not 'realism' but reality itself" (SA, 45): "To copy nature is a spineless activity; it gives us a sense of our mere existence but hardly more than that. But to imitate nature involves the verb: we then ourselves become nature, and so invent an object which is an extension of the process" (SL, 297). "It is not to place adjectives, it is to learn to employ the verbs in imitation of nature—so that the pieces move naturally—and watch, often breathlessly, what they *do*" (SE, 302). "Only the made poem, the verb calls it / into being" (PB, 110). The verbal energy of the poem makes it part of nature and asserts the poet's approximate coextension with the universe. Williams ridicules the idea that this means some impossible Roman feast in which man ingurgitates the earth: "the powers of a man are so pitifully small, with the ocean to swallow— that at the end of the feast nothing would be left but suicide" (SA, 28). Through the action of imagination the poet frees himself from this absurd thirst or hunger. When he has rooted himself in objective reality his poems become "as actual, as sappy as the leaf of the tree which never moves from one spot" (SA, 22). His coextension with the universe need be only approximate, for the sap in his poems flows everywhere. This sharing in universal energies produces the sense of "enlargement," of "expansion," which men feel "before great or good work" (SA, 29).

The need to have the poem rooted in the ground of reality is the reason for Williams' insistence that art must start with the local and particular, and raise those to the universal. The poet is "taught by the largeness of his imagination to feel every form which he sees moving within himself" (SA, 27). His problem is "to be both local (all art is local) and at the same time to surmount that restriction by climbing to the universal in all art" (SL, 286). By concentrating on the individual in its uniqueness the poet may reach the universal. The particular *is* the universal. The same forces stream through it as stream through all existence, and therefore the poet "seems to make the world come toward him to brush against the spines of his shrub. So that in looking at some apparently small object one feels the swirl of great events" (SE, 294). It is for this reason that so much depends upon the red wheelbarrow. The wheelbarrow, red and glazed with rain water, occupying silently its small spot in time and space, contains everything. In the same way a single word may concentrate the poet and his world in a breath, as the poet somewhat whimsically proposes in *The Great American Novel*: "I shall make myself into a word. One big word. One big union. . . . I begin small and make myself into a big splurging word: I take life and make it into one big blurb." Whatever the specific content of the here and now may be, it can still be said that "all things enter into the singleness of the moment and the moment partakes of the diversity of all things" (SE, 97). The poems about chicory and parsley, like the chicory and parsley themselves, concentrate in themselves the universe, and the basic method of art is that recommended at the beginning of *Paterson*: "To make a start, / out of particulars / and make them general . . ." (P, II).

A poem written on the basis of this theory of art may be defined as "the mind turned inside out" (KH, 72), or, alternatively, as things turned inside out, taken into a different condition, energized by the imagination. It will also be the reader turned inside out. When a man reads a poem he should enter not so much into the words as into the depths of himself by means of the words, just as a play

> should be the
> audience itself, come out of itself
> and standing in its own eyes, leaning
> within the opening of its own ears,

"seeing itself / in the action" (ML, 33). Poet, things, and reader are absorbed into the poem and lifted there into a new dimension of intimacy, a place where the unity of mind and world, often obscured or lost, is validated, realized, and possessed. The poem alone "focuses the world" (SE, 242). What is it like inside such a poem?

The major difficulty in reading Williams' poetry is to become accustomed to the ways in which he uses words not as names but as things. This is especially evident in his rejection of visual imagery. Like Charles Olson, he dismisses all "pictorial effects" (ML, 9), all that " 'evocation' of the 'image' which served us for a time" (SA, 20). Eyesight is the most abstract and detached of the senses. It opposes man to a world which he sees from a distance. A poem made of word-pictures compounds these divisions. The reader contemplates language which generates mental pictures of an absent reality. Poem, reader, and world are kept in separate compartments. The aesthetic theory which defines poetry as images for the mind's eye is a natural product of a literate, subjectivistic culture, a culture which would develop photography and the printed book. A poetry of this sort would be a return to the abstraction Williams abhors.

His practice confirms his theoretical choice. His poems are often nonsense if the reader tries to make a coherent mental picture of the sequence of phrases. "To All Gentleness" (CLP, 24–29), for example, moves bewilderingly from the silvered tank to the pink roses bending ragged in the rain, to a girl practicing archery, to a sailor knocked into the sea by the shattering prop of a plane, and so on. *Paterson* is often a sequence of images which seem disconnected if the reader thinks of them visually:

>   like a bull
>   or a Minotaur
>   or Beethoven
>   in the scherzo
>   from the Fifth Symphony
>   stomped
>   his heavy feet
>   I saw love
>   mounted naked on a horse
>   on a swan
>   (P, 260)

The sense of bewilderment disappears if the reader understands that the words are not primarily visual at all. They are meant to energize the mind in certain ways, and express in their sonority some quality of matter, thickness and weight, or airy delicacy, or any one of the other innumerable textures which our senses may know through words. The poet assumes "that we smell, hear and see with words and words alone, and that with a new language we smell, hear and see afresh" (SE, 266). Words marry the reader to the solidity of things and to their movement. All words are both verbs and nouns for Williams, both action and matter, and his poetry is the product of an imagination which puts the mind within the life of objects. To express this identification in language the poet must break up the fixities of words and make them flow together like figures in a dance or ice melted into a stream. "Then it begins," he says, "that happy time when the image becomes broken or begins to break up, becomes a little fluid—or is affected, floats brokenly in the fluid. The rigidities yield—like ice in March, the magic month" (SE, 307). How can this melting be brought about? It seems plausible enough in theory or as a metaphor, but words are after all fixed sounds, and even the volume occupied by the falling Passaic seems bound by the universal laws of space. Any one place in it is excluded from all other places. The poet must transcend the limitations of logical, visual, or geometrical space in order to bring into existence the new poetry of multiple elements in fluid intimacy.

To think of space as always characterized by rigid exclusions and limitations is to universalize illegitimately one mode of space. There are other spaces all men and women inhabit, regions less capable of being deformed by the preconceptions of the logical mind, and these are dominant in Williams' poetry.

Consciousness is not a separate thing filling a hollow place in a man's skull. My whole body is conscious, to the tips of my fingers and toes. The mind is incarnate in "warm self-flesh" (CEP, 182), and the body is also a means of possessing the world. This is achieved partly through the senses, which are so many different ways of assimilating things. Perhaps even more important is the way the body in action "open[s] up the world" (CEP, 453), and takes it in. The position of my arms and legs, the force of gravity on my flesh, my gestures, gross and subtle movements of my muscles—these make of my body a kinesthetic pantomime internalizing the world. Williams' poems are a dance of words rising from this pantomime. They express that state of bodily knowledge the poet praises in *Kora in Hell*: "A thing known passes out of the mind into the muscles" (KH, 71).

When a thing has passed into the muscles, then language can express the thing by matching the movement of those muscles. Here is another reason for Williams' praise of the verb. His language is often a way of knowing the world through the posture and quality of bodily life which a certain state of the world induces. He thinks with his muscles and bones rather than with ideas: "I have heavy bones, I am afraid—there's little here for me—gravity must drag me down—over the horizon—I'm too slippery— and it doesn't matter—but so it seems" (SL, 64). The reader must accustom himself to words which express the flowering of chicory, the growing of a tree, the flowing of water as if it were happening in the interior of his own body. There is often a soft, muted, thick, blurred quality in Williams' language, something quiet, delicate, almost feminine, and this is the "gentleness that harbors all violence" (CLP, 29), the violence of a power to enter into a natural process and experience it inwardly. In one poem a series of "external" actions expresses the gradual relaxation of a child's body as it falls asleep. The verbs carry the weight of the thickening of consciousness as it is absorbed by the sleeping body: "Gentlefooted crowds are treading out your lullaby. / Their arms nudge, they brush shoulders, / hitch this way then that, mass and surge at the crossings—" (CEP, 192).

In the admirable poem about the "contention" of the yachts (CEP, 106, 107), the water through which the boats sail is felt as "an entanglement of watery bodies": "Arms with hands grasping seek to clutch at the prows. / Bodies thrown recklessly in the way are cut aside." A wild cherry, in another poem, is "continually pressing back / peach orchards," and this image is equated with "the feel of good legs / and a broad pelvis" (CEP, 140). Another tree is "tense with suppressed excitement" (CEP, 141). Still another is "bent" "from straining / against the bitter horizontals of / a north wind" (CEP, 142). Chicory is bid by the poet to "lift" its flowers, to "strain under them" (CEP, 122), and in spring all plants "grip down and begin to awaken" (CEP, 242). All these images urge the reader to respond to the words with subliminal movements of his muscles mimicking the energy of trees, yachts, plants, or water. "Young Sycamore" is a beautiful poem of this sort. The movement of the poem follows the shape of the tree not as a visual outline but as an "undulant / thrust" from "round and firm trunk" all the way to the "two / eccentric knotted / twigs" at the top (CEP, 332). In the same way a charming poem catches in its rhythm and in the placing of end stops the tension of a cat's feet as it climbs over the top of a jam closet:

> first the right
> forefoot
>
> carefully
> then the hind
> stepped down
> (CEP, 340)

Sometimes the space of a poem is a multiplicity of things felt together as a tension of muscle against muscle. The transformation of words into vectors of power is accomplished by an emphasis on their weight as expressions of movements within the body. In "Spring Strains" the pun in the title prepares for the energizing of sky, sun, buds, and "rigid jointed" trees in a wrestle of opposing forces which the poem incarnates in its own movement:

> . . . the blinding and red-edged sun-blur—
> creeping energy, concentrated
> counterforce—welds sky, buds, trees,
> rivets them in one puckering hold!
> Sticks through! Pulls the whole
> counter-pulling mass upward, to the right
> locks even the opaque, not yet defined
> ground in a terrific drag that is
> loosening the very tap-roots!
> (CEP, 159)

In such poems the space the words create is the volume of the body. This body-world has the same kind of intimacy that events inside a man's body have for him. A pain is located in one place, but also permeates the whole body until a man may become one pervasive pain. In the same way

Williams' kinesthetic poems transcend the limitations of abstract visual space and bring into existence a realm in which all places are everywhere.

Note

1. Parenthetical references in this essay are to the following works: *Collected Earlier Poems* (New York: New Directions, 1951); *Collected Later Poems* (New York: New Directions, 1963); Williams's Introduction to Byron Vazakas, *Transfigured Night* (New York: Macmillan, 1946); *Kora in Hell* (San Francisco: City Lights, 1957); *Many Loves and Other Plays* (New York: New Directions, 1961); *Pictures from Breughel and Other Poems* (New York: New Directions, 1962); *Spring and All* (Dijon: Contact, 1923); *Selected Essays* (New York: Random House, 1954); *Selected Letters* (New York: MacDowell, Obolensky, 1959).

Spring and All: A New Lyric Form

JAMES E. BRESLIN

In its original version, published by an obscure expatriate press in France in 1923, *Spring and All* was a serial poem consisting of twenty-seven untitled but numbered poems, introduced and accompanied throughout by a sometimes fierce, sometimes flamboyant prose polemic. The *Spring and All* poems, striking for their toughness and spontaneity, their abrupt and radical shifts of tone and direction, generate all the intensity and persistence of a pitched battle; and they get their extraordinary power from their proximity to chaos—from their capacity to bring together violently antagonistic forces and to leave them, suspended and unresolved, in a moment of agonizing tension. Individual poems, as we move through them, seem to fly off in several directions simultaneously and, by doing so, become the first in Williams's career to illustrate what he later called "the poem as a field of action." No argument, no narrative—no linear mode of organization— imposes a single direction on the full, rounded moment of experience. Instead of relations that are stated and therefore fixed, we get relations that are left open and therefore fluid and multiple. Instead of a designated *path* we can follow through the poem, we get the poem as a *field*—as a field of *action*. *Spring and All*, for its startling originality and tensed force, must be ranked as one of the major documents of modern literature. . . .

Yet the power of the *Spring and All* poems frequently comes from the way they create an intense, ego-shattering concentration upon physical objects. Williams has here created a literary style that is uniquely his, but one from which he has entirely disappeared as a conscious personality. The voice of these poems, coming from far below the level of conscious will or reason, gives poetic speech to bodily consciousness. We enter a world where seemingly banal objects, carefully perceived, can generate ecstatic emotion—as in "The Red Wheel-barrow."

so much depends

upon

Reprinted from *William Carlos Williams: An American Artist*. Copyright © 1970 by James E. Breslin. By permission of The University of Chicago Press.

a red wheel
barrow

glazed with rain
water

beside the white
chickens

How can a poem about things as hopelessly ordinary as a wheelbarrow and white chickens be anything but flat? Again, Williams is deliberately seeking flatness—through banal objects and an impersonal manner. The personal element—the instructing, argumentative "I" of *Al Que Quiere!*—has disappeared; we get instead an impersonal assertion: "so much depends. . . ." With the disappearance of the poet comes a close focus upon the object: short, jagged lines and long vowels slow down our movement through the poem, breaking off each part of the scene for exact observation. Any symbolic reading of the scene, a possible imposition by the observer, is carefully resisted; its hard, literal, objective reality is insisted upon.

But Williams risks banality in order to push through to startling discoveries. The scene is not entirely bare: the wheelbarrow is red and it has just been rained on, giving it a fresh, "glazed" appearance. A spare, clinical manner, it is clear, asserts by relief the primary color and novelty that are there. We are brought down, into a new world. Similarly, the effect of the impersonal subject "so much" is not to empty the poem of feeling but to fill it with the ecstatic emotion which these particulars inspire. By its slow movement the poem not only forces us to concentrate on the physical scene, but also renders the intensity of the emotion; intensity means a stretching out. Originally, there is the feeling of a laborious thrust downward, away from all conscious activity and toward a heightened receptivity; but the final effect is the sense of a slow lifting, with the discovery of a distinct beauty in the commonplace. The poem *is* impersonal; its impersonality, however, is not that of the indifferent God paring his fingernails, but one that comes from the way the poet has yielded himself intimately to the scene. The particulars in the poem, broken apart to be seen clearly, are drawn together by the ecstatic feeling generated by the poet's discovery. This kind of crisp, intense lyric, in which self is dissolved into scene, is one way Williams had of constantly renewing himself. . . .

In *Spring and All* we find a new power of affirmation and acceptance. Whitman had opened Williams to the myth of plenitude; Eliot had confronted him with the myth of sterility. Together, they prompted Williams to identify his own informing myth—the discovery of plenty lodged, as it must be in the contemporary landscape, amid barrenness. Characteristic of the poems in this volume, "The Eyeglasses" begins with descriptions of the

flowers that grow near the edges of garbage heaps and of the delicate beauty
of the farmer's daughter issuing from the crude strength of her father:

> The universality of things
> draws me toward the candy
> with melon flowers that open
>
> about the edge of refuse
> proclaiming without accent
> the quality of the farmer's
>
> shoulders and his daughter's
> accidental skin, so sweet
> with clover and the small
>
> yellow cinquefoil in the
> parched places.

The constant subject of the *Spring and All* poems is the emergence of
life out of death, ecstasy out of despair, poetry unexpectedly blossoming in
a parched industrial landscape. Once again the presiding mythic figure is
Persephone, whose savage force is hidden but still alive in our world. Her
power is evident in the roots that "grip down and begin to awaken" in the
first poem and in the wildflower ("Arab / Indian / dark woman") of the last.
Persephone is explicitly named in "At the Faucet of June"; she appears as a
gypsy woman in "Quietness" and "The Avenue of Poplars," the farmer's
daughter in "The Eyeglasses," Kiki in "Young Love" and Elsie in "To Elsie."
Persephone is always embattled, surrounded by "white" "crowds" as she is
in "The Wildflower"; but she is fierce as well as beautiful, "rich / in savagery,"
and she persists along with the mechanical and industrial realities of modern
life.

Like so many works of the 'twenties, *Spring and All* is often apocalyptic
in tone; the prose commentary, which opens the book, moves toward a vision
of cataclysmic destruction. Yet Williams, who believed that "destruction
and creation / are simultaneous" (*Collected Earlier Poems*, p. 266), celebrates
the "end." The root sense of apocalypse is "uncover" and what excites him
is that the upheaval will uncover Persephone, the buried creative principle.
In fact, what Williams imagines is the release of the imagination from the
"rock" (*Spring and All*, p. 14), the very place where Eliot was attempting
to secure it. At the moment of release, the rigid forms of the old order are
shattered and we are forced to enter a new world. Everything exists from
the beginning. "It is spring," Williams asserts after the catastrophe, "THE
WORLD IS NEW" (*SA*, pp. 10–11). The major impetus behind *Spring and
All* is the reaffirmation of a creative power which is often thwarted, repressed,
surrounded by blankness, but which ardent pursuit can still uncover.

All of the books of poetry Williams had written since "The Wanderer" had begun with a spring poem. But in 1923, as the poet of birth in a seemingly sterile environment—as the poet of spring *and all*—Williams invented a new spring for poetry. The poem that follows the cataclysm, genuinely new, does not take us into the traditional spring song world of bounding lambs, gamboling children, gentle breezes and universal fecundity. We are moved down, from a literary to an actual landscape. And instead of jocund song, Williams gives us a rough, harsh music, broken rhythms that jolt us into an awakened perception of the scene.

> By the road to the contagious hospital
> under the surge of the blue
> mottled clouds driven from the
> northeast—a cold wind. Beyond, the
> waste of broad, muddy fields
> brown with dried weeds, standing and fallen
>
> patches of standing water
> the scattering of tall trees
>
> All along the road the reddish
> purplish, forked, upstanding, twiggy
> stuff of bushes and small trees
> with dead, brown leaves under them
> leafless vines—
>
> Lifeless in appearance, sluggish
> dazed spring approaches—
>
> They enter the new world naked,
> cold, uncertain of all
> save that they enter. All about them
> the cold, familiar wind—
>
> Now the grass, tomorrow
> the stiff curl of wildcarrot leaf
> One by one objects are defined—
> It quickens: clarity, outline of leaf
>
> But now the stark dignity of
> entrance—Still, the profound change
> has come upon them: rooted, they
> grip down and begin to awaken

This poem does not simply describe the physical qualities in a landscape; its center is an *act* of perception, "the stark dignity of / entrance," the slow penetration of a desolate landscape by an awakening observer. We follow the thrust of his imagination downward, through obstacles, to a new union with the physical environment. The progression in the poem is literally downward: the observer goes from "the blue / mottled clouds," across a distant view of "broad, muddy fields," to the quickening plant life right before him—and then penetrates even further downward, into the dark earth, as he imagines the roots taking hold again. The panoramic view, with its prospect of "muddy fields," dried weeds, "patches of standing water," offers nothing with which the imagination might joyously connect itself. At first an apparently blank and "lifeless" nature invites the observer to passivity and despair; but Williams pushes through vacancy to uncover dormant life.

Implicitly, "By the road" argues that Eliot's despair derives from his cosmopolitanism, his detachment from a locality. What the tenacious observer here finally perceives is no "waste" land but a "new world" and he makes his discovery by narrowing and focusing Whitman's panoramic vision upon the near and the ordinary. In the torpor of ordinary consciousness, what we find by the road to the contagious hospital is a desolate landscape. But the awakened consciousness, focused sharply and including everything in the scene, discovers novelty and life, the first "sluggish / dazed" stirrings of spring. Hence poet and landscape are gradually identified—as he too grips down and begins to awaken.

In Eliot's early poetry, spoken by "voices dying with a dying fall," the characteristic movement is the fall of anti-climax; for instance, Prufrock's romantic "visions" of communion are continually undercut by his fear of self-exposure. In Williams's verse, movement is typically through a slow, downward thrust toward an ecstatic lift. The poems move us down into the physical world, back to our origins, to release creative power. In "By the road," even after he has discovered the burgeoning life in the amorphous "stuff" around him, Williams slips forward into a dream of April definition: "tomorrow / the stiff curl of wildcarrot leaf." The abrupt shift back to the "now" in the last stanza partly accounts for its great force. At the beginning, a plain diction, use of short, disconnected phrases, loose, flat rhythms create a sense of stasis; but the poem tightens at the end with the pounding stresses, heavy pauses, and epigrammatic force of its final stanza. We get a final, compact moment of illumination.

As Williams asserts in one of the commentaries in Kora, "*Between two contending forces there may at all times arrive that moment when the stress is equal on both sides so that with a great pushing a great stability results giving a picture of perfect rest.*" Each of the poems in Spring and All gives us such a moment when contending forces, pushing and pulling in opposite directions simultaneously, achieve a dynamic equilibrium. "By the road" grows out of the elemental contest between winter and spring, death and life; so does "The Black Winds." "The Eyeglasses" brings together gross strength and delicate beauty; "Shoot It Jimmy!" plays off classical and jazz language: "Our orchestra / is the cat's nuts"; "Rigamarole" shows "the *veritable* night" (my emphasis) which now contains "wires" as well as "stars." At the end of that poem Williams says that "moonlight // is the perfect / human touch": its scene includes both light *and* darkness. "At the Faucet of June" creates a modern June morning in which we hear the sound of the motor car as well as the more delicate music of nature. . . .

"The rose is obsolete," Williams muses at the beginning of one of these poems, but an act of imagination can make even this traditional symbol new. He proceeds from a consideration of the way to renew the impact of the figure to a joyous affirmation of its rediscovered power. "The Rose" appears at a point in the prose commentary of *Spring and All* when Williams is praising the Cubist painter Juan Gris for dealing with "things with which [the onlooker] is familiar, simple things—at the same time to detach them from ordinary experience to the imagination" (*SA*, p. 34). Williams is thus experimenting here with a kind of literary Cubism. He takes the familiar rose out of amorphous, ordinary contexts by making his subject inorganic, by considering a rose cut onto "metal or porcelain"; he hardens his soft subject in this way and by the mathematical language the Cubists employed: "so that to engage roses / becomes a geometry." Finally, he places the rose in a world of infinite, empty space. There, he contemplates it playfully, turning his argument on the ambiguity of the word "end." "The rose carried weight of love," he says, "but love is at an end—of roses." Just as he constantly asserts that life must be caught as it emerges out of death, so here he argues that at the end of the rose, its death and its edge, a new beginning can be found.

To see the rose anew, we must concentrate on the locus of its singularity, its edges. Raised from a flat surface, carefully worked onto china, these edges are perceived more distinctly.

> Sharper, neater, more cutting
> figured in majolica—
> the broken plate
> glazed with a rose

Only when the flower has been worked painstakingly, lovingly, onto a hard, inorganic substance will its fragile life be preserved—a paradox which gives his meditation a subtle wit; the language keeps shifting, crisply, between organic and inorganic, soft and hard, words:

> Crisp, worked to defeat
> laboredness—fragile
> plucked, moist, half-raised
> cold, precise, touching

In its abstracted realm, the realm of the imagination, the rose touches—nothing. There is a surrounding blankness which at once threatens and defines the flower, just as the white crowd and the dark sea activate the poet's individuality. In Williams, a finely wrought distinction always asserts itself at the edge of emptiness.

When he speaks of the need for objects and words to have hard edges, as he does in both poems and essays, Williams is using a phrase that can be found in the writings of a whole gamut of moderns—from Hemingway to Wittgenstein. The importance of edges for Williams is that they are the locus of maximum tension and thus of maximum life. In "The Rose" a careful, hard-edged perception of the object generates an infinite line of force.

> From the petal's edge a line starts
> that being of steel
> infinitely fine, infinitely
> rigid penetrates
> the Milky Way
> without contact—lifting
> from it—neither hanging
> nor pushing—
>
> The fragility of the flower
> unbruised
> penetrates space

The image is bold, playful, entirely characteristic: a delicate strength, a fine steel line—emerging out of the dead porcelain—triumphantly asserts its distinction through infinite space.

In the *Spring and All* sequence Williams keeps returning us to that moment, abstracted from temporal sequence, when life begins to begin. He adjusts us to a level of consciousness where historical time, and thus literary associations, do not yet exist. He pushes spring back from April to March, he deals with those weeds and wildflowers shunned as too coarse by his poetic predecessors. In short, he strips objects bare of all acquired associations and it is this neutralization of things that makes it possible for him to accept *any* thing as suitable for poetry. But Williams is not, as he is often regarded, a poet who moves simply from the object as symbol to the object as literal fact; this *is* the tendency of *Al Que Quiere!*, but *Spring and All* develops out of the pull between these two ways of apprehending things. A reader who gets to the first stanza of the last poem, "The Wildflower"—"Black eyed susan / rich orange / round the purple core"—should remember the "reddish / purplish, forked, upstanding, twiggy / stuff of bushes" from the first poem, the "horned purple" of the nineteenth and the anemones in "At the Faucet of June." The "white daisy" and the "white" "crowds" of the next two stanzas of "The Wildflower" take the reader back through the numerous references to "nothing," "without being," empty spaces, blank fields in the poems. The black-eyed susan clearly manifests that rich primitive force found in almost all of the poems—a notion reenforced by reading "core" as a pun for "Kore," as it is earlier in "to solve the core / of whirling flywheels." As always, this force tensely defines itself against a surrounding blankness. At the same time the tight sensual music (r's, long vowels) and the precisely observed detail show the poet's intense devotion to the actual flower. The point is that the serial poem genre enables Williams to create a special kind of poetic field. Williams liked to point out that poems are made of words and the spaces between them; a serial poem is then made of poems and the spaces between them. There is no articulated surface of connections that a narrative or explicit argument would provide; instead, there is a buried coherence—of recurrent words, images—which the reader himself must uncover. Literal details, in context, suddenly reverberate into mythic significance. The breaking of narrative surface, the spacing within and between poems, establish a field that is thick in texture, multidimensional. Nature and society move, according to Williams, in recurrent cycles. Movement in the serial poem, too, is circular rather than linear; the reader is constantly forced to go back before he can go on, the poem thereby becoming an *experience* of recurrence. Williams's bare, neutral objects do acquire associations, but these are developed entirely from the inside, within the poem itself. Individual poems, by their juxtaposition in a series, create a poetic field, a context; but the spaces between them enable the poet to preserve each poem's pull toward the instant. The all—the universal, the mythical—is discovered *in* the moment, not imposed upon it. Again, everything exists from the beginning. . . .

Relations are fluid. The objects in the poem are like parts of a mobile in the further sense that they are in motion. Syntactic units pull back and forth—seeming at first to go with what has come before, then shifting into relationship with what follows; both versions must be suspended in the reader's mind. In the introduction to his *Bending the Bow*, Robert Duncan (like Charles Olson and Robert Creeley, importantly influenced by Williams's handling of the line) approvingly quotes from Heraclitus: "They do not apprehend how being at variance it agrees with itself. There is a connection working in both directions." A particularly intense use of this making a phrase connect back and forth simultaneously occurs in Williams's "The Avenue of Poplars"; these are the first eight stanzas:

> The leaves embrace
> in the trees
>
> it is a wordless
> world

> without personality
> I do not
>
> seek a path
> I am still with
>
> Gypsy lips pressed
> to my own—
>
> It is the kiss
> of leaves
>
> without being
> poison ivy
>
> or nettle, the kiss
> of oak leaves—

Most readers, confronted with these lines and asked to produce an oral interpretation, will look through them several times in an effort to make certain decisions—e.g., What words get emphasis? Which parts go with what other parts? Does "without being" mean "without existence" (as it does in the previous poem, "Rigamarole") and go therefore with "leaves"? Or is "being" a verb form, in which case it goes with what follows: "without being / poison ivy"? Such an approach seeks "a path" through the poem—which is precisely the opposite of Williams's intent. We must yield to the poem; we must approach and read it "without personality." To read the poem in a voice that is more flat than dramatically expressive—giving equal weight to each of the words and observing the slight pauses marked by lines and stanzas—is to discover a new world, one that is open, fluid, and shifting. To give up the need for a path through the poem is to discover the poem as a field of action.

The poem is a kind of Gordian knot; paraphrasing is cutting, in the mode of J. P. M., but does yield a sense of the poem's tight multiplicity—a quality not usually associated with Williams's work. It begins simply enough: "The leaves embrace / in the trees." Yet the second line cuts loose from the first as we move into the second stanza: in the trees it is a "wordless / world." A wordless world is a world "without personality." That phrase, however, moves in another direction, to go with "I do not." Without personality I do not act, as we have already seen in "To Have Done Nothing." The next stanza converts "do" to an auxiliary verb; (without personality) I do not "seek a path"—and then, I do not seek a path "I am still with." But "I am still with" begins as well as ends a sentence: I am still with "Gypsy lips pressed / to my own," a sentence which has two possible meanings, given the ambiguity of "still." It can mean, I am quiet when Gypsy lips are pressed to mine (a wordless world), or, I am yet kissing Gypsy lips. Even this analysis is not exhaustive, but it is enough to show that in Williams's work, a word retains more of its energy, its possible connections, than any linear method of development would allow. In fact, the edge of his line is like the edge of the rose which "cuts without cutting"—releases rather than inhibits energy—"meets nothing"—the second of silence at the end of the line— then "renews itself" in the following line. Ends dissolve into beginnings. Each poem, then, becomes a series of lines, each of which, spaced off from all the others, pulls toward isolation, independence, at the same time that it is pulled back by syntax, by recurrences, toward all the other lines. At the edge of chaos, containing the pressure of its pushing and pulling, the poem trembles with force.

"The Red Wheelbarrow"

Hugh Kenner

Not what the poet *says*, insisted Williams; what he *makes*; and if ever we seem to catch him *saying* ("So much depends upon . . ."), well, he has cunningly not said *what* depends. He has levered that red wheelbarrow into a special zone of attention by sheer torque of insistence.

> so much depends
> upon
>
> a red wheel
> barrow . . .

Attention first encounters the word "upon," sitting all alone as though to remind us that "depends upon," come to think of it, is a rather queer phrase. Instead of tracing, as usage normally does, the contour of a forgotten Latin root, "depends upon" ignores the etymology of "depend" (*de* + *pendere* = to hang from). In the substantial world "upon" goes nicely with "wheelbarrow": *so much*, as it were, *piled upon*. In the idiomatic world, inexplicably, "upon" goes with "depends." In the poem, since we're paying unaccustomed attention, these two worlds are sutured, and "depends" lends its physical force, an incumbency as though felt by the muscles, to what must be a psychic depending.

    (Here, to keep ourselves straight, let's borrow Eli Siegel's statement of the scope of this poem: "Williams is saying that if a curved useful thing, a wheelbarrow, can be red; and if the red can be glazed with rain water— that is, make a one with something different from red, something not of color; and if the oneness of a red wheelbarrow and rain can be attended by living things in white—the white chickens—the diversities of the world, seen boldly, can satisfy human life and a particular mind.")

    En route to which, after "upon," there's what looks like a stanza break. What are these stanzas? Small change symmetrically counted, always three words and then one word; the one word, moreover, always of two syllables,

Reprinted from *A Homemade World: The American Modernist Writers*. Copyright © 1975 by Hugh Kenner. By permission of Hugh Kenner.

but the three-word line having four syllables the first time and the last, but only three syllables on its two middle occurrences. These are stanzas you can't quite *hear*, especially as one very simple sentence runs through all four of them. They are stanzas to see, and the sight of them, as so often in Williams, inflects the speaking voice, the listening ear, with obligations difficult to specify. "Upon," "barrow," "water," "chickens," these words we punctuate with as it were a contraction of the shoulders, by way of doing the stanzas' presence some justice. And as we give "barrow" and "water" the emphasis their isolation requests, two other words, "wheel" and "rain," isolate likewise:

> a red wheel
> barrow
>
> glazed with rain
> water . . .

"Wheelbarrow" and "rainwater," dissociated into their molecules, seem nearly kennings: not adjective plus noun but yoked nouns, as though new-linked. And "red" goes with "white," in a simple bright scheme, and "chickens" with "barrow" for an ideogram of the barnyard, comporting with the simplicities of rain; and the rain glazes a painted surface but (we are left to imagine) does not glaze the chickens, merely soaks them if they are chickens enough to stand in it. (And yet they need it, and may not be wise enough to know how much depends, for them, on the rain.) So much depends on all that pastoral order: food, and the opportunity to touch actualities (while trundling a wheelbarrow), and the Sabine diastole to counter the urban systole.

Are these reflections penumbral to the poem? Probably. Probably even external to it. This poem tends to ignore what it doesn't state. But let them serve to remind us that a farmer would know every one of the words in this little poem, but would be incapable of framing the poem, or even uttering its sentence. We need to be at a picturesque distance from such elements to think of how much depends (for us) on them.

"Mobile-like arrangement," said Wallace Stevens. Yes. The lines, the words, dangle in equidependency, attracting the attention, isolating it, so that the sentence in which they are arrayed comes to seem like a suspension system. This was one thing Williams meant by "making," not "saying." Yet you do say, you do go through the motions of saying. But art lifts the saying out of the zone of things said. For try an experiment. Try to imagine an occasion for this sentence to be said: "So much depends upon a red wheelbarrow glazed with rainwater beside the white chickens." Try it over, in any voice you like: it is impossible. . . .

Not only is what the sentence says banal, if you heard someone say it you'd wince. But hammered on the typewriter into a *thing made*, and this without displacing a single word except typographically, the sixteen words exist in a different zone altogether, a zone remote from the world of sayers and sayings.

That zone is what Williams in the 1920's started calling "the Imagination." It is the place where mental clarities occur, for you no more experience clarities in your head than you experience vision in your eye. Where is the seen world? It is behind the eye, in a space you have learned to create. And where, likewise, is the clarified world (where "so much depends")? Ah, in the Imagination.

Which, Williams meant, is where poems are, in a space you must likewise learn to create. "There is a 'special' place which poems, as all works of art, must occupy, but it is quite definitely the same as that where bricks or colored threads are handled": are handled, of course, by the intending mind that can reach through the fingers. The poem that doesn't succeed in existing there is "the usual 'poem,' the commonplace opaque board covered with vain curlicues."

"Lines Converging and Crossing"

Marjorie Perloff

How can the poet infuse his compositions with the "power TO ESCAPE ILLUSION" (SAA, 112)?[1] A power to be found, so the poet of *Spring and All* believes, in certain Cubist paintings, most notably those of Juan Gris.[2] Williams, who was to remark in later life: "I would rather have been a painter than to bother with these god-damn words" (IWWP, 29), puzzled over this question for years. In the Marianne Moore essay, he observes: "Unlike the painters the poet has not resorted to distortions or the abstract in form. Miss Moore accomplishes a like result by rapidity of movement. A poem such as 'Marriage' is an anthology of transit. It is a pleasure that can be held firm only by moving rapidly from one thing to the next. It gives the impression of a passage through" (IMAG, 311).

Spring and All, published three years after *Kora*, is just such an "anthology of transit": "from all angles lines converging and crossing establish points" (IMAG, 309). One chapter or poem opens up into the next; sentences are left hanging, as in

> The farmer and the fisherman who read their own
> lives there have a practical corrective for—
>
> (SAA, 100)

> It is very typical of almost all that is done by the writers
> who fill the pages every month of such a paper as
> (SAA, 100)

The poems themselves now display a kind of cutting new to Williams. Perhaps the first difference to note between the lyrics collected in *Sour Grapes* (1921) and those of *Spring and All* is that the ubiquitous exclamation point of the former book is now replaced by the dash. Within the space of twenty-seven poems, there is only a single instance of the exclamation point: "I was your nightgown / I watched!" (SAA, 115). An exclamation point implies, of course, a momentary finality, a stop however ecstatic, whereas the dash stresses fluidity, a rapid shift from one thing to another. In *Sour Grapes*, the poetic surface is not yet broken; words are organized into complete sentences:

> The sky has given over
> its bitterness.
> Out of the dark change
> all day long
> rain falls and falls
> as if it would never end.
> ("Spring Storm," CEP,
> 202)

Or

> They call me and I go.
> It is a frozen road
> past midnight, a dust
> of snow caught
> in the rigid wheeltracks.
> The door opens.
> I smile, enter and
> shake off the cold.
> ("Complaint," CEP, 199)

In these poems, Williams has already discovered his characteristic imagery. As James Breslin notes: "he strips objects bare of all acquired associations"; "details do not combine into symbolic clusters but instead create a literal specificity."[3] But between the writing of these sharply etched Imagist poems and the lyrics of *Spring and All*, a marked change has occurred. To call Williams' early poems "Cubist," as does Bram Dijkstra, is, I think, to overstress the pictorial component of Cubist art. Dijkstra maintains, for example, that "Spring Strains" (1916) "is an elaborate attempt at painting a Cubist picture in words": "It represents a visual plane, a visual field of action, within which objects are analyzed in a strictly pictorial fashion. They are isolated, intensified through compression, then broken into parts:

> two blue-grey birds chasing
> a third struggle in circles, angles
> swift convergings to a point that bursts
> instantly!

Williams shatters the forms in his picture just as a Cubist painter fragments his forms, and in doing so he achieves the 'constructive dispersal of these fragments over the canvas' of his poem which Kandinsky mentions in discussing the work of Picasso."[4] But in fact the structure of the passage cited is still essentially linear; form is not shattered and fragmented. "Spring Strains" is a highly pictorial poem, a sequence of clear visual images. In *Spring and All*, such images are not just "isolated" and "intensified through compression"; they are decomposed:

> The red paper box
> hinged with cloth
>
> is lined
> inside and out
> with imitation
> leather
>
> It is the sun
> the table
> with dinner
> on it for
> these are the same—
>
> Its twoinch trays
> have engineers
> that convey glue
> to airplanes
>
> or for old ladies
> that darn socks
> paper clips
> and red elastics—
>
> What is the end
> to insects
> that suck gummed
> labels?
>
> for this is eternity
> through its
> dial we discover
> transparent tissue
> on a spool
>
> But the stars
> are round
> cardboard
> with a tin edge
>
> and a ring
> to fasten them

to a trunk
for the vacation—
            (SAA, 123–124)

This is not as radical an experiment as Gertrude Stein's "box" poems in *Tender Buttons*,[5] but its Cubist style recalls the fragmentation and superposition of planes, the tension between compositional game and representational reference that characterizes Stein's work. Juan Gris, Williams' "favorite painter" at this time, uses geometric analogies to confound the absolute identities of objects and their spatial positions, but he does not submit his objects to the large-scale decomposition we find in, say, Picasso's *Ma Jolie*.

Consider *Still Life Before an Open Window: Place Ravignan*, painted in 1915. Here we can identify the objects on the table—carafe, bowl of fruit, goblet, newspaper—and the window view—shuttered windows across the street, trees, balcony rails—quite easily. We can also make out the label "MEDOC" and the block letters of "LE JOURNAL." But Gris' "real" objects are seen as through a distorting lens; they are rigidly subordinated to the geometric structure of the painting: a complex set of interlocking triangles and rectangular planes whose spatial positions are ambiguous. Here structure calls attention to itself: carafe, tree trunks, window frames, an apple—all become relational parts of Gris' charged surface.

Just so, Williams' poem is not a "description" of a red paper box in the sense that "Spring Strains" presents the image of "two blue-grey birds" struggling in circles, against the backdrop of a "tissue-thin monotone of blue-grey buds." Like the mysterious boxes of Joseph Cornell, Williams' "box" immediately becomes a kind of open sesame, waiting to be entered:

The red paper box
hinged with cloth

is lined
inside and out
with imitation
leather

Each of the four-line stanzas that follows has the shape of a box, being roughly a small square centered on the wide empty space of the page.[6] The squareness of the stanza is further enhanced by the pervasive presence of consonance at line ends:

or for old ladies
that darn socks
paper clips
and red elastics

On the other hand, syntactic units within a given stanza are regularly broken up by line breaks and internal alliteration as in

> through its
> dial we discover
> transparent tissue
> on a spool

Here the lineation urges us to take "dial we discover" as a separate semantic unit even though its meaning is totally dependent on the lines in which it is embedded.

The poem's particulars, moreover, refuse to cohere. The red *paper* box turns out to be "hinged with cloth." If it is lined "inside and out" (an odd description for lining usually refers to what is inside) not outside, with "imitation / leather," how can it be made of paper? If its "two-inch trays" have "engineers / that convey glue / to airplanes," it may have large hinges; if, on the other hand, it holds "paper clips / and red elastics" for "old ladies / that darn socks," it must be one of those delicate little boxes with tiny compartments and drawers. "What is the end," the poet asks, "to insects / that suck gummed labels"? But how do insects get at these drawers? And what is the "dial" by means of which "we discover / transparent tissue / on a spool"? Perhaps the combination lock of a jewelry box. But then, would a box that contains airplane glue have a lock? Finally, and most confusing, are the "stars" made of "round / cardboard / with a tin edge" inside the box or do they decorate its surface? How and why would one fasten "them" as opposed to "it" (the box) "to a trunk / for the vacation"?

By the time we reach the end of the poem with its deceptive "boxy" stanzas, we realize that the "box" is purely the poet's construction. We cannot visualize it. "If illusion," writes E. H. Gombrich, "is due to the interaction of clues and the absence of contradictory evidence, the only way to fight its transforming influence is to make the clues contradict each other and to prevent a coherent image of reality from destroying the pattern in the plane."[7] Like a Cubist painting, Williams' poem introduces contradictory clues that resist all attempts to apply the test of consistency. Thus the red paper box turns out to be made of cloth or leather; its "dial" may lead us to "eternity," but then again it may just be a ring attaching cardboard stars to a steamer trunk. For that matter, the box is also "the sun" and "the table / with dinner on it," not because there is a metaphoric analogy between these items but by sheer creative fiat. As Williams asserts in the prose section preceding this lyric, "The objects of his world were real to him because he could use them and use them with understanding to make his inventions" (SAA, 122).[8] "The red paper box" begins with an image of a concrete object only to break that image into fragments, making of these fragments a new verbal construct. The form of the poem is one of calculated indeterminacy. One is reminded of the Gris painting in which the house front and trees ostensibly outside the painter's window are rendered as a brightly lit violet-blue plane that seems to be inside the room.

Poem after poem in *Spring and All* is characterized by such Cubist mobility and indeterminacy. No. V is a composition on wind:

> Black winds from the north
> enter black hearts. Barred from
> seclusion in lilies they strike
>
> to destroy—
>
> Beastly humanity
> where the wind breaks it—
> (SAA, 102)

It is a conventional enough opening: the wind as Shelleyan destroyer and preserver. Williams plays with this notion only to push it aside and replace it with one equally hackneyed—the wind that bloweth where it listeth:

> salt winds—
>
> Sold to them men knock blindly together
> splitting their heads open
>
> That is why boxing matches and
> Chinese poems are the same—That is why
> Hartley praises Miss Wirt.
> (SAA, 103)

Vacant shuttles weave the wind. But Williams is not Eliot and he wants to be matter-of-fact, scientific. "There is nothing in the twist / of the wind but—dashes of cold rain."

If the poem ended here—and many Williams poems do end on such a "hard-boiled" note—it would be merely clever. But the poet of *Spring and All* refuses to take this easy way out. He wants to experience wind as fully as possible. In the erotically charged universe of *Spring and All*, the wind cannot remain a symbol, viewed from the outside:

> Black wind, I have poured my heart out
> to you until I am sick of it—

> Now I run my hand over you feeling
> the play of your body—the quiver
> of its strength
>
> (SAA, 103)

It is a striking transformation, the poem enacting the rejection of symbolism which has been the subject of the prose section that precedes it, a section that ends with the sentence: "The word must be put down for itself, not as a symbol of nature but a part, cognizant of the whole—aware—civilized" (SAA, 102). All the talk of black winds entering black hearts, of beastly humanity broken by the wind, of day as the time of flower and rocks, and night as the time of hate, gives way to a sense of *living*. How can the black wind be anything but an object of love, a female presence, waiting to be touched so that the "quiver / of its strength" can manifest itself?

"Black winds" also functions within the larger serial structure of *Spring and All*. The orchestration of symbolic images which characterizes a poem like *The Waste Land* gives way, in *Spring and All*, to what David Lodge has called a "field of contiguities."[9] Williams' images—wind, flower, farmer, white, purple—are perfectly transparent; all are nature images, reflecting the sexual energy of the universe, the life force. They are images without depth, but in the shallow space in which they coexist, they create enormously varied configurations. Thus we first meet the word "wind" in the opening pages of *Spring and All*: "Houses crumble to ruin, cities disappear giving place to mounds of soil blown thither by the winds . . ." (SAA, 91). Here the wind is part of the holocaust, but when it next appears, it announces the coming of spring:

> By the road to the contagious hospital
> under the surge of the blue
> mottled clouds driven from the
> northeast—a cold wind.
>
> (SAA, 95)

And again, some fifteen lines further into the poem, we meet "the cold, familiar wind." In poem III about the farmer, "A cold wind ruffles the water / among the browned weeds" (99). In IV, we have, by contrast, "dove-tame winds— / stars of tinsel" (99). And so on.

Each time we meet the word *wind*, two things happen. First, we experience the pleasure of recognition, coming, as we do, upon a familiar image we had almost forgotten we knew. Secondly, we distinguish this particular manifestation of the word from all others. As Williams had said in the Prologue to *Kora*, "the coining of similes is a pastime of a very low order. . . . Much more keen is that power which discovers in things those inimitable particles of dissimilarity to all other things which are the peculiar perfections of the thing in question" (IMAG, 18).

Notes

1. The following abbreviations are used in this essay: CEP: *Collected Earlier Poems* (Norfolk, Conn.: New Directions, 1951). IMAG: Shorter prose pieces in *Imaginations* (New York: New Directions, 1970). IWWP: *I Wanted To Write a Poem* (Boston: Beacon Press, 1958). SAA: *Spring and All,* in *Imaginations* (New York: New Directions, 1970).

2. See esp. SAA, 107, 110, 112, 117, and cf. *A Novelette* (1932), whose fourth section is called "Juan Gris" (IMAG, 283–86).

3. *William Carlos Williams: An American Artist* (New York: Oxford UP, 1970), pp. 78, 52.

4. *Hieroglyphics of a New Speech* (Princeton: Princeton UP, 1969), pp. 64–65.

5. There are two poems called "A Box" in *Tender Buttons.* Here is the first:

Out of kindness comes redness and out of rudeness comes rapid same question, out of an eye comes research, out of selection comes painful cattle. So then the order is that a white way of being round is something suggesting a pin and it is disappointing, it is not, it is so rudimentary to be analysed and see a fine substance strangely, it is so earnest to have a green point not to red but to point again.

—"Objects," *Selected Writings of Gertrude Stein,* ed. Carl Van Vechten (New York: Vintage, 1962), p. 463. See also pp. 465–466 for the second "A Box."

6. Strictly speaking, stanzas 2 and 6 (following the opening couplet) have five rather than four lines, but the analogy to the box still holds.

7. *Art and Illusion, A Study in the Psychology of Pictorial Representation* (New York: Pantheon Books, 1960), p. 282. In *Skyscraper Primitives*, Dickran Tashjian argues that the lyrics in *Spring and All* are comparable to Duchamp's Readymades: thus the red wheelbarrow is a "readymade transposed into language through accurate, concise description and subtle phrasing. The wheelbarrow on the page gains its reality as an addition to nature because it already exists as a reality in human experience" (p. 108). I would argue that, on the contrary, Williams' "wheel / barrow" exists nowhere but in the words on the page.

8. Here Williams is referring to Shakespeare, but he is, of course, also talking about himself as artist.

9. *The Modes of Modern Writing: Metaphor, Metonymy, and the Typology of Literature* (London: Edward Arnold), p. 107.

"The Desert Music"

Paul Mariani

Considering the seriousness of [his stroke in 1951], Williams's recovery was amazingly rapid. It was as if Williams—having suffered whatever he had to suffer—wanted to get back to business as usual as quickly as he could. But he also realized that he could just as easily have been dead now, and so he began to look at this poststroke period as a time of grace, as the space between lightning stroke and thunder clap. He would use it for his art. At the beginning of '51, the Alpha Chapter of Phi Beta Kappa at Harvard had invited him to be their poet of the year and deliver a "fifteen-minute poem" for the group's commencement exercises on June 18. Until the time of the stroke he'd done nothing about actually composing his poem, other than that he knew that his bridge—the one at El Paso—would somehow figure in it. But now, in the hospital, unable to write, he had time to think about his life and about his poem.

By early May he had sent the third part of the *Autobiography* to his typist, Mrs. Pettengill, and had written his foreword, telling McDowell that he hoped he would not object to his saying there that the *Autobiography* would *not* talk about the women he had been to bed with "or anything about them," and he was warning his readers not to look for that side of his life in his book. Such encounters and intimacies, he argued, had really not had anything to do with him as a writer. Besides, the *Autobiography* was a public document, unlike *Paterson*, where he had talked—confessed—about the problem of intimacy. Then he and Floss were dropped off at the summer home of a colleague of Williams', Dr. Sullivan, up in Schuylerville, New York, outside of Saratoga, for a two weeks' rest. For the moment Williams was free of his Random House commitments and so free to tackle his poem for Harvard. And since he was unable to drive and now found himself isolated in a still-wintry Saratoga, where spring was a cold, raw, and drizzly affair, Williams spent most of his time mildly depressed, just sleeping and thinking or reading Rouse's translation of the *Iliad* and trying to shape his poem. At first, try as he might, nothing happened. But finally, "after a good deal of labor," he managed to midwife the thing into life, "forcing" himself, as he told one person, "to put the words down." He was back home on Monday, May 21, and by Friday he had "finished the first, faulty but complete draft: 17 pages." By the end of the month he had a clean and corrected copy ready for his stenographer. It had taken him five weeks of close work to produce one fifteen-minute poem, and though he still had mixed feelings about what he'd written, Harvard had ordered a poem "sight unseen," and now, like it or not, "they were going to get it."

What Harvard was getting was "The Desert Music," and Williams had written it quite simply to prove to himself that—in spite of very strong intimations of his own mortality—he was still a poet. It was a highly self-conscious piece of work, this poem: words in search of a form consonant with Williams' dramatic sense of his own radical deformation. He'd created a desert music for a desert time, the poet afoot in a wasteland of his own with a poem moving out of embryonic formlessness toward the assertion that Williams could still write a poem. So the shadowy presence of his old friend McAlmon, wandering toward his own desert oblivion, stood behind the poem, a figure embodying Williams' own fears that he too might be swallowed up, his ability to create cut off permanently, without warning, before he'd had the chance to say what it was he'd felt compelled to say.

To create: the verb-centeredness of that act. And to *imitate* reality, not merely copy it. It was a pervading concern of Williams', particularly in the months when he'd worked on the *Autobiography* at top speed, when he found himself day after day writing at that level: not reenacting his life, not driving toward its intimate center as he had in *Paterson*, but simply copying the surface of his life over. One could keep busy that way, as the memory selected out thousands of discrete events without revealing the essential figure of the man himself. He had engaged only part of himself in the act of writing his life, so that now "The Desert Music" became a necessary and welcome counterresponse to the finger exercises of the *Autobiography*. In "The Desert Music" he would try once again to touch the self. The poem would need another dimension, then, other than what prose had been able to give him if he was to imitate the descent into hell once more. A descent with its necessary sense of disintegration, its formlessness moving once again toward its opposite, form, like a fetus moving toward the form of the child.

Writing to Ken Burke in late January, Williams had told him how only recently he had come to understand the *real* "significance of Aristotle's use of the word 'imitation.' " It was the central word for the creating artist; in fact it had become for Williams a "new" word, fraught with new significance for him: "The imagination has to imitate nature, not to copy it—as the famous speech in *Hamlet* has led us to believe. There is a world of difference there. The whole dynamic of the art approach is involved, to imitate invokes the verb, to copy invokes nothing but imbecility. It is the very essence of the difference between realism and cubism with everything in favor of the latter." The *Autobiography* was, after all, only a mode of realism: page on page of narrative, most of it "true," and much of it somehow missing the revelation he was after. But in "The Desert Music" he used a cubist strategy, with the poem's dislocated, shattered forms bringing his images into high relief. Thus the poem's sharp edges and dissociated voices, its crazy quilt of forms ranging from sprawled prose to tight quatrains to heighten the "realistic" narrative of the poem grinding against those self-consciously sharp patterns revealing the man's deepest anxieties.

Like *Paterson*, "The Desert Music" provided a narrative thread and a journey. This time it was a journey between worlds, and the poem began literally in a no-man's land: the international boundary between two countries—the U.S. (English-speaking, masculine, assertive, manipulative) and Mexico (Spanish-speaking, feminine, passive, generative, exploited). It was a mirror of the split, then, in Williams himself between his dead father and his recently dead mother, and recollections of Williams' journey to Potosí forty years before—"You see, we do not all live like *los negros*, gringo"—stirred in Williams, his entry into Juárez at nightfall triggering the split—and regression—into that side of his psyche which he identified with his female half.

He went even further, personifying the debased female—his artist double—in the figure of a stripteaser from the States, whom he'd watched in one of the local Mexican spots, gyrating one more time to her honky-tonk music. Here once more was the eternal feminine: his old muse, battered and badly used, but still dancing, still giving the poet courage. What struck Williams was how closely this brassy, tired music fit the woman's performance. So here, then, just here was the deeper music he'd searched for and which he now reenacted in his turn, fitting her music to his poem:

> There is a fascination
> seeing her shake
> the beaded sequins from
> a string about her hips
>
> She gyrates but it's
> not what you think,
> one does not laugh
> to watch her belly.

In *The Bridge*—the poem Williams had had to confront in order to write *Paterson* 1—Hart Crane had reduced his own Indian / American muse at one point to the level of a burlesque queen. Now, twenty years later, in a complex crossing with this dead poet, Williams responded to Crane's high romantic figure with his own low romantic, using a countermusic and a rhythm he clearly saw as being more in tune with the truth of such matters. Williams' bridge across the Rio Grande would answer Crane's vision of hell in *The Bridge*, as his stripped, jerky quatrains countered Crane's own Eliotic quatrains with their complex, artificial Elizabethan music. "Her eyes," Crane had written,

> Her eyes exist in swivellings of her teats,
> Pearls whip her hips, a drench of whirling strands.
> Her silly snake rings begin to mount, surmount
> Each other—turquoise fakes on tinselled hands.

Williams' music was by far the flatter, like his dancer, "heavy on her feet," yawning her way through her accustomed moves, cold eyes watching, aware that she was "part of another tune." As Williams watched her he could see that she too knew her customers, knew her audience, and could hold the "same / opinion" of them that they held of her. "What," the poem asks,

> What in the form of an old whore in
> a cheap Mexican joint in Juárez, her bare
> can waggling crazily can be
> so refreshing to me, raise to my ear
> so sweet a tune, built of such slime?

The answer comes as he crosses back over the bridge, after having come in contact with the people of that place by literally touching them, as his hero in *In the American Grain* had touched the Abnaki Indians in Maine. Once more, then, he must confront the deathlike figure asleep on the bridge, who is not after all dead but instead promises "a birth of awful promise." For now Williams sees that that shapeless mass has become "a child in the womb prepared to imitate life." The force of that infinitive—*to imitate*—should not escape our attention, for it was with the verb that Williams had promised to enact the poem. The shapeless figure is, of course, an extension of Williams' own crippled condition, both physically and artistically, except that he could be protected against the fact of his own encroaching annihilation by a "music" that acted like a "mucus." That punning echo suggests that the act of writing the poem could itself act like a film, an amniotic fluid, to protect the crippled poet, ironically, from returning to preconsciousness. Poetry, then, could be "a benumbing ink," staining and coloring the mind, and giving Williams a way of coping with the terrible reality of what had happened to him. So "The Desert Music" is in a sense an action painting, like Jackson Pollock's paintings concerned with the process of their own enactment. It is a poem built out of the need to locate the moment of life-sustaining inspiration: the recall of a distant music remembered on the other side of the bridge when he was still in his prestroke, prelapsarian condition.

Out of his fears about creative impotence following the shock of his first stroke, out of the need to assert that, in spite of his accident, he was still a poet, Williams managed to create his fifteen-minute poem for that Harvard audience. But facing them, facing those who were synonymous for him with the academy and more especially with the camp of Eliot (one of Harvard's most famous sons), Williams had a crippling anxiety as well to deal with. Especially now that he'd been hit in mind and eye and tongue. What would it be like to be up there on that platform in Cambridge performing his poem before the curious or indifferent or openly hostile shadows surrounding him? Williams: that old trouper from the States, made more comic than ever by his stroke. The day after his reading he'd told Zukofsky that the atmosphere at Harvard had been just what he'd expected: "semi-ecclesiastic, a hall hallowed by tradition," and that his own poem had been "low" church in comparison to such high church surroundings.

What was all this "nauseating prattle" about platonic love in the face of a sordid reality everywhere about him? Williams the revolutionary would give his audience a new kind of music, performing his own rebellious strip in church, singing about—of all things—a whore in a cheap Mexican joint in his own rendition of the American West. And if the academicians there shook their heads or gritted their teeth or dismissed this American naif: no matter. The feeling was mutual. Williams still believed the universities were "rank / with" the old music of Eliot and Eliot's disciples, the New Critics. Like his stripper, he was "part of another tune," knew his customers and knew their worth, and—though he might be "heavy" on his feet—he would keep on dancing.

Self-lacerating, self-contemptuous, determined to survive, Williams would dance for them, maintaining in their very faces that, in spite of indifference, in spite of neglect, in spite of his brain's self-betrayal, he was still a poet: "I am a poet! I / am. I am. I am a poet, I reaffirmed, ashamed." "The Desert Music" had been written to allow Williams to make that statement. And yet, with that poem and that reaffirmation made, it would cost him another year before he could bring himself to compose another poem. In the meantime he had demonstrated to himself that he still could write a poem, still "keep his pecker up." It was not without its own pathos, his effort. *I / am*: that line break reinforcing the sense of the poet in the act of doing that which constituted Williams' deepest sense of self. *I / am*: creation and affirmation at the poem's close simultaneously realized. *I am.*

The Descent Beckons

MARILYN KALLET

It is tempting to read the secrets of an initiatory ritual into "Asphodel"—
even if the more esoteric parallels are only unconsciously alive there—to see
in the "greeny" but "wooden" flower the ancient vegetation goddesses Rhea,
Kore, Demeter, Persephone. It is tempting to see Persephone, the hidden
one, the spiritual mystery of rebirth, in the cave drawings Williams reminds
us of, and to see her veiled in the marriage ceremony. But such secrets, if
they are in the poem, lie deeply embedded in its more obvious and deliberate
mythic pattern.

Williams drives deep in his poetry as a result of his yearning to see.
Inevitably, his curiosity leads him to examine the depths of a situation, even
an explosive, emotionally dangerous situation.

> There is beauty in the bellow of the BLAST . . . —To me beauty is
> purity. To me it is discovery . . .
>   And for this you are willing to smash—
>   Yes, everything. —To go down into hell. —Well let's look.
>   (I, 171)[1]

We may assume that Williams did not deliberately seek out suffering but
had it in his nature to follow his feelings and to look at them honestly. As
he says to Flossie in "Asphodel," often he "found himself" in difficulty.

> I cannot say
>   that I have gone to hell
>   for your love
>   but often
>   found myself there
>   in your pursuit.
>   (PB, 156)

As the lines move downward on the page, speaking of Williams' journies
to hell, they signal to us that this poem will make an inner journey. By

repetition, Williams etches a memory, a picture of depths. The poem has several ways of achieving its journey to emotional depths. "Asphodel" is reflexive, referring to Williams' life and literary life in a way that adds resonances to his images. The image of "Asphodel," found in *Kora*, reminds us of the poet's early struggle and early work, of the connection between "asphodel" and the underworld in myth and art, of the continuity of dreams and the unconscious. Williams tells us in "Asphodel" about how he pressed flowers into his book as a boy, "The asphodel, / forebodingly, / among them." He brings us "reawakened, / a memory of those flowers" (*PB*, 155), a memory of his boyhood, and of the *Autobiography*, where he speaks of gathering asphodel while at school in Switzerland. "Any poem that has worth expresses the whole life of the poet," Williams says in *Paterson* (261). But some poems are more densely packed with life than others; perhaps more than any of his other poems "Asphodel" sings to us of what Williams has lived and written.

This personal mythology, recall of meaningful images and "spots of time," adds depth to the poem, as do the folkloric and mythic elements. The contest between light and darkness in "Asphodel" is an agon found in fairy tales and folklore. Persecution is old, Williams reminds us, with his references to the witchcraft trials. The bomb threatens us with darkness, while the poets, explorers and great men of culture move through the lines of "Asphodel" with their "palms going / always to the light." The outcome is by no means certain, though in the "Coda" Williams asserts that "The light / for all time shall outspeed / the thunder crack."

We can also interpret the "Coda" in the light of an older drama. The Hierophant at Eleusis, home of Persephone's mysteries, beat an "echeion," an "instrument with the voice of thunder." The thunder signaled the opening of the underworld, heralded a vision of death. The torchlights that followed thunder were a sign of revelation and rebirth in the midst of this meeting with death. Williams reverses the order of the archaic ceremony, "light takes precedence," as the poem celebrates a mystery of awakening and re-union. . . .

In "Asphodel" Williams is still on the quest for wholeness dramatized in "The Wanderer"; he continues to search for Euridice. But in old age the images for absence or presence of the female beloved take on a lifetime of meaning; her presence becomes a matter of life or death.

"Asphodel," with its scope and depth, is primarily a love lyric. Euridice, not mentioned now, but still sought after in the imagination and in the flesh, is Flossie. In order to rescue her, Williams must himself be rescued; he needs his wife's forgiveness. Her compassion will help to restore him.

> What power has love but forgiveness?
> In other words
>   by its intervention

>   what has been done
>   can be undone.
>   What good is it otherwise?
>   (PB, 169)

Williams is poetically articulate with his new measure and emotionally articulate, able to make his plea. If Flossie can forgive him, not only will his "mind be cured" but the image of Persephone will be lifted from hell. The luminous marriage will be a sign of restitution.

C. Kerényi says of the Eleusinian mysteries that the first function of the ritual was to "perfect the world . . . in order that men might die more confidently after having lived better." "But," Kerényi continues, "the second condition was that men should also *know* about the happy marriage of the ravished Maiden—the prototype of all marriages. This knowledge was communicated to them by the beatific vision of Kore at Eleusis—vision of the innermost 'divine maiden' of men and women."[2]

In "Asphodel" Euridice is the living, human self whom the poet tries to redeem from death through art. In the triadic lines the imagination defies death, insisting that love will stay on through "abiding" song. The heart of the Eleusinian mysteries seems to have been a dramatization and a promise of rebirth. Lyric poetry is not religious mystery, and yet Williams tells us that his poem concerns "every man / who wants to die at peace in his bed / besides" (PB, 162). Williams wrote "Asphodel" to keep his imagination alive and thereby to keep himself alive. The poem enriches our experience, giving us new memories, even if it will not make us live forever.

Persephone, the dark, elusive one, is also memory. "Asphodel" is about memory's power to renew experience, even as the poem is a quest for memory. Williams had had a severe stroke in 1952, resulting in partial memory loss. Literally for the poet, "Memory is a kind / of accomplishment" (PB, 73), a return to life.

Early in the poem Williams speaks from the point of view of a ghost, a revenant. We remember how close he had come to death as a result of his recent illnesses. The living may "little prize" asphodel,

>   but the dead see,
>   asking among themselves:
>   What do I remember
>   that was shaped
>   as this thing is shaped?
>   (PB, 153)

Like the shaman, Williams hears the voices of spirits; he lets their questions inform him. "In the great night (his) heart will go out" to gather images of healing and renewal.[3] Williams brings himself back alive, giving emotion and at least a "wash of crimson," the tint of roses, to shapes that started out ghostly pale.[4]

The three-line stanzas of "Asphodel" move the images, accommodating the descent myth well. Each line is taut with both the descent, the return to memory, and the yearning for ascent, for the rescue from time. Though the poem has a narrative movement from the quest for love and speech to a resolution in the wedding song, the triadic lines incorporate descent and ascent in such a way that there is no separation of the two gestures or needs. The lines may descend on the page, but the music rises above them, an odor, Williams sings, "as from our wedding." Williams developed a poetry of "continual flowering" at the end of his life. "Each line or phrase" of the late poems "gathers the elements into inextricable union. Rising and sinking are not sequential but simultaneous."[5] The tension between descent and ascent is a "poised flower," which opens for Williams at the end of "Asphodel," in a release from time. For

> . . . love and the imagination
>   are of a piece,
>   swift as the light
> to avoid destruction.
>   So we come to watch time's flight
>   as we might watch
> summer lightning
>   or fireflies, secure,
>   by grace of the imagination,
> safe in its care.
>
> (*PB*, 179–80)

Williams' spirit rises from the ashes of his life's struggles to celebrate the light. He reduces time, the enemy, to size, and renders it not merely harmless but illuminating. As the poet rescues his world through love expressed in his art, he seems to observe the mysterious process of defeating ordinary time, as if its flight were occurring before him. An old man, and one who has long reflected on the imagination's powers, Williams is a spectator as well as a participant in his drama. The result of the poet's work is a sense of release, of imaginative freedom gained through the poetic line. The mythic pattern of descent can be translated into psychological terms. "According to depth psychologists, the two patterns of thinking [concerning Orpheus and Kora] are related and involved with the double. In 'Archetypes of the Collective Unconscious,' Carl Jung clears up some of the relationship by associating the Orphean descent with the archetype of the 'wise old man' or 'meaning.' "[6]

According to Jung, " 'the Wise Old Man appears in dreams in the guise of a magician, doctor, priest, teacher, professor, grandfather, or any other person possessing authority.' "[7] He appears the way Williams presents himself in "Asphodel," as the aging poet who comes to rescue the self in jeopardy. Jung sees the Wise Old Man as one who appears in dreams at a time of crisis to bring wholeness to a fragmented spirit. Williams performs this role for himself and his wife; he plays Demeter or Orpheus in the form of the Wise Old Man, a rescuer in his own voice. This time Williams draws upon the descent myth deliberately, to find and preserve imaginative treasures that might otherwise be lost forever. The old man descends, returns to his boyhood memories, returns to the present with a new sense of wholeness that defies time's blows. He gives this sense of wholeness as a gift in song to his wife.

The lines of "Asphodel" move like the chorus of an ancient drama, weaving back and forth in the dance of words. The truth of the measure goes back to the body's truth. As Williams says in *Kora*, "A thing known passes out of the mind into the muscles, the will is quit of it, save only when set into vibration by the forces of darkness opposed to it."

Jung has this to say about the creative, restorative quality of the descent undertaken with purpose; he hails those who "go down the sunset way with open eyes."

> Things go very differently when the sacrifice is a voluntary one. Then it is no longer an overthrow, a "transvaluation of values," the destruction of all that we held sacred, but transformation and conservation. Everything young grows old, all beauty fades, all heat cools, all brightness dims, and every truth becomes stale and trite. For all these things have taken on shape, and all shapes are worn thin by the working of time; they age, sicken, crumble to dust—unless they change. But change they can, for the invisible spark that generated them is potent enough for infinite generation. No one should deny the danger of the descent, but it *can* be risked. No one *need* risk it, but it is certain that someone will. And let those who go down the sunset way do so with open eyes, for it is a sacrifice which daunts even the gods. Yet every descent is followed by an ascent; the vanishing shapes are shaped anew, and a truth is valid in the end only if it suffers change and bears new witness in new images, in new tongues. . . .[8]

Within Jung's words we can also hear Williams' songs of descent; the poet trusts that there will be a corresponding ascent in his music if he can complete his journey.

The sources for "Asphodel" are the oldest sources of art, archaic; there are ancient and contemporary sources for the poem as well. In Book II the poet begins by "approaching death"; "place and condition," Williams' mainstays, begin to lose their particularity. He awakens as if from a bad dream. In order to prevent the shapes of things from growing dim, Williams advises us and himself:

> If we are to understand our time,
>   we must find the key to it,
>   not in the eighteenth
> and nineteenth centuries,
>   but in earlier, wilder
>   and darker epochs . .
> So to know, what I have to know
>   about my own death,
>   if it be real,
> I have to take it apart.
>
>   (*PB*, 162–63)

To face death the poet must "dream back" to "darker epochs," to a time when myths of origin flourished. He must examine his suffering, "take it apart," as the tribal shaman had to experience a sense of dismemberment to render myth as a source of wholeness and new beginnings to his tribe.

Williams' journey takes the form of a dreaming back to early memories, to his childhood, and back deep into human memory, to see the shapes drawn on the walls "of prehistoric / caves in the Pyrenees" (*PB*, 174). The movement of dreaming back and of descent are one; both represent an inner voyage to the depths of the self, in a quest for origins. The poet takes us down the steps of the triadic line with him into the subway, where he exchanges glances with a man who reminds him of his father. And the subway with its modern power jolts open the image of archaic caves, places that reveal the emergence of human consciousness and the origins of art.

Williams refers to the fact that Paleolithic shamanic artists "left their marks, / by torchlight," for the regions in which they painted were deep in the earth (*PB*, 174). Their art "was done deep down in the darkest and most dangerous parts of the caves, although the men lived only in the openings of the caves."[9] Most people live at the surface ("Look at / what passes for the new") but the poet goes deeper to provide for us; the passage down is tortuous. By going deep into the earth and creating animals in paint, the early draftsmen must have gained power over the animals, as Williams seeks to find words that will capture his most profound emotional stirrings and make the emotions vibrant in the dance of the poem. This hunt requires all of the poet's artistry.

Within the Paleolithic caves of Cantabria archeologists have found extraordinary figurines of the Great Mother as well as images of bison, of the hunt. At this point in his poem, having faced death and moved beyond it to the theme of love's forgiveness, the poet finds himself in depths that resonate with masculine and feminine powers, powers of creativity, fertility. Williams acknowledges the two principles.

> Their women
>   had big buttocks.
>   But what

> draftsmen they were!
>> By my father's beard,
>>> what draftsmen.
>>> (PB, 174)

The cave paintings, like early Chinese drawings and paintings, were not an expression of facile simplicity, but of craft and design. From 40,000 B.C. to the present day "there have been great numbers of primitive peoples living throughout the world, yet none has had a representational art to approach that of [the Paleolithic cave-painters]."[10] How could Williams not have felt a kinship with images "from the hands of men who knew the great animals well—knew the feel of their fur, the tremendous drive of their muscles, and the danger one faced when he hunted them"?[11] Williams had always respected artists who knew their materials and recognized things with a "glandular perception of their uniqueness." At the end of Book III his poem touches the first traces of humanness, with a source that revels in the particularities of art. The newspapers may carry the terrible news of the burning of "priceless Goyas" by Perón's goons, but the paintings on the cave walls, the memory of the origins of art, remain intact and living for the poet.[12]

On his dangerous journey Williams carries "torchlight" in the image of the flower. Having missed contact with him, the man on the subway is "a flower / whose savor had been lost." The cave drawings have not lost their savor, they are "lilacs" left by the archaic draftsmen (PB, 174). As in tribal poetry, where through repetition and association of imagery one image brings together the cosmos and is used to explore it in all its sacred ramifications, Williams uses the flower image both as a center and as a place of change.

Out of the flower, or memory of his father and of the "great fathers" resting within the mountain beds, Williams creates a world: "in a subway train / I build a picture / of all men" (PB, 174). Williams reminds us that the poem brings its life to the present. Yet like the earth diver in tribal mythology, the poet goes deep for materials with which to begin again. The poem's journey, like the earth-diver myth, reinforces the singer's identity, that of the "mythopoeic male." Through his contact with origins, the poet revitalizes an image of himself as a creator, as a man who gives birth.[13]

The descent myth that recurs in Williams' poems is universal and need not refer to specific tribal mythologies. Yet Williams does open the book *Pictures from Brueghel* with a quotation about tribal practices: " ' . . . the form of a man's rattle may be in accordance with instructions received in the dream by which he obtained his power' " (Frances Densmore, *The Study of Indian Music*). Williams was an accomplished dreamer.

Frazer's *Golden Bough*, with its descriptions of ancient myths and rituals, comes to mind when one reads "Asphodel, That Greeny Flower." As indi-

cated in chapter 3, Williams takes the image of the flower with him throughout his poetry as a protection against chaos, reminiscent of the way that
Aeneas carried the golden bough through Hades as a protection against
death. Frazer's account of why Virgil chose the mistletoe or golden bough
for Aeneas, accurate or not, is lyrical and suggestive for our comments on
Williams' use of flower imagery. Frazer says of the mistletoe that "its fiery
nature marks it out, on homeopathic principles, as the best possible cure or
prevention of injury by fire. . . ." Frazer continues, "If the mistletoe, as a
yellow withered bough in the sad autumn woods, was conceived to contain
the seed of fire, what better companion could a forlorn wanderer in the
nether shades take with him than a bough that would be a lamp to his feet
as well as a rod and a staff to his hands? Armed with it he might boldly
confront the dreadful spectres that would cross his path on his adventurous
journey."[14] For Williams, the "yellow flower" or "sacred flower" (PB, 89)
of any color to match the poet's mood is his emblem for art's power to bring
the poet safely through the hell of his experience. The triadic line, the
measure, is the solid "rod and staff" that Williams uses to hold off time
and his own terror. Unlike Paterson, which "refuses to claim a center,"[15]
"Asphodel" has a formal center that permits the poet to take a dangerous
journey, and to dance.

Notes

1. Parenthetical references in this essay are to the following volumes: I: Imaginations
(New York: New Directions, 1971). PB: Pictures from Brueghel (New York: New Directions,
1962).

2. C. Kerényi, Eleusis (New York, 1977), 174.

3. This line comes from a "dream song" belonging to Owl Woman, a Papago healing
woman. She said the chant was taught to her by the dead, to help her in her fight for the
life of a sick man. One version of the song is found in William Brandon (ed.), The Magic
World: American Indian Songs and Poems (New York, 1971), 42.

4. A handwritten note in the worksheets, found on the back of a typed page marked
Paterson, Book V: The River of Heaven, refers to "the weak wash of crimson color" as the means
"by which the rose is celebrated." YALC.

5. J. Hillis Miller, Poets of Reality: Six Twentieth Century Writers (Cambridge, Mass.,
1966), 355.

6. Jerome Mazzaro, William Carlos Williams: The Later Poems (Ithaca, 1973), 15.

7. C. G. Jung, Psyche and Symbol (Garden City, 1952), 70–71. Quoted by Mazzaro,
William Carlos Williams: The Later Poems, 16.

8. C. G. Jung, The Collected Works of C. G. Jung, trans. R. F. C. Hull, Bollingen
Series XX, Vol. 5: Symbols of Transformation (Princeton, 1956), 357.

9. Robert J. Braidwood, Prehistoric Man (Chicago, 1967), 72.

10. Jacquetta Hawkes, Prehistory (New York, 1963), 286.

11. Braidwood, Prehistoric Man, 72. For a provocative personal and poetic exploration
of the drawings in prehistoric caves (and for an argument against seeing these figures as mere
depictions of the hunt), see Clayton Eshleman's Hades in Manganese (Santa Barbara, 1981).

12.   New York *Times*, April 16, 1953, Sec. 1, p. 4. This event took place two days before Williams' release from the mental hospital.

13.   Alan Dundes, "Earth-Diver: Creation of the Mythopoeic Male," *American Anthropologist*, LXIV (October, 1962), 1032–48.

14.   Sir James George Frazer, *The Golden Bough* (1922; rpr. New York, 1972), 819.

15.   Joseph N. Riddel, *The Inverted Bell: Modernism and the Counterpoetics of William Carlos Williams* (Baton Rouge, 1974), 186.

Machines Made of Words

CECILIA TISCHI

It has been by paying naked attention first to the thing itself that American plumbing, American shoes, American bridges, indexing systems, locomotives, printing presses, city buildings, farm implements and a thousand other things have become notable in the world. Yet we are timid in believing that in the arts discovery and invention will take the same course. And there is no reason why they should unless our writers have the inventive intelligence of our engineers.
—William Carlos Williams, "Yours, O Youth," 1921

To make two bald statements: There's nothing sentimental about a machine, and: A poem is a small (or large) machine made of words. When I say there's nothing sentimental about a poem I mean that there can be no part, as in any other machine, that is redundant.
—William Carlos Williams, *The Wedge*, 1944

William Carlos Williams spoke literally when he called the poem a machine made of words. And he spoke sincerely when summoning American writers to show the inventive intelligence of the nation's engineers. In the age of ubiquitous structural and machine technology Williams understood that writers in search of new forms could benefit from the conception of art as a structure with a framework and various fixed and moving parts intended to transmit energy. He understood that the poem was a design or arrangement of prefabricated component parts. Like Frank Lloyd Wright, Williams knew this principle was crucial for the contemporary artist. In fiction Ernest Hemingway and John Dos Passos demonstrated their understanding that component parts were central to the conception of the sentence and the narrative.

On the subject of design components in imaginative literature, however, Williams became the most articulate spokesman. As we shall see, the medical education that prepared him for a poetics of kinetic efficiency also taught him to perceive the world in ways congenial with the values of engineering technology. Williams was able to call the poem "an organization of materials

From *Shifting Gears: Technology, Literature, Culture in Modernist America* by Cecilia Tischi, © 1987 the University of North Carolina Press. Reprinted by permission of Cecilia Tischi and the University of North Carolina Press.

. . . as an automobile or a kitchen stove is an organization of materials" because of his medical background (*Interviews* 73). In the era of the art-technology crisis Dr. Williams welcomed the opportunities afforded by technology. In large part he was freed from a decayed romanticism by his machines made of words.

Williams welcomed new technologies of all sorts in his poems and fiction. In *The Great American Novel* (1923) he proudly detailed his "great dexterity" in garaging his car and enjoyed making "a little Ford" his heroine (*Imaginations* 169–90). As we know, this poet of the age of "trees, animals, engines" freely intersperses technological figures with those of flora and fauna. Readers encounter images of "the weed-grown / chassis / of a wrecked car," "whirling flywheels," bridge "trestles," "machine shrieks," and "trip-hammers," along with the flowers and trees for which Williams's poems are well known (*Collected Earlier Poems* 96, 251, 194–95, 192, 262). His was a holistic world in which the natural mixed freely with objects of human manufacture.

And of course American culture brought Williams the same consciousness of engineers as was available to much of middle-class America. Popularized in movies and novels, and evidenced everywhere in the structures and machines that covered the landscape and the pages of magazines, engineers found their way into Williams's writings. He mused that invention or creation was a basic mark of intelligence "selecting and rejecting its materials—as it would be in an engineer that turns to the time for his opportunity" (*Embodiment of Knowledge* 22). He regretted communication barriers in a specialists' age ("Is there no conversation . . . between farmers and engineers?"). He fretted that "the knowledge of an engineer" would be likely to lure the man, then entrap him, in science where he would be "limited, segregated" (*EK* 46, 62–63). In the poem "The Red Paper Box" in *Spring and All* Williams writes in sportive tones that "twoinch trays / have engineers / that convey glue / to airplanes" (*I* 124). And when Williams disparages his brother Ed's position in a dialogue on art, saying "nobody gives a whoop in hell for such a viewpoint," Ed retorts, "Nobody but an engineer with a bridge to build," a line Williams recorded word for word (*Selected Essays* 182).

But the engineer, like machine and structural technology, was much more than a casual reference in Williams's work. For one thing, the poet was no stranger to the machine-age anxieties that Willa Cather, Sherwood Anderson, and for that matter Henry James felt in the face of engineering achievement. Williams understood that the arts and technology made competing claims for the imagination, and he acknowledged the rivalry between the technological and the literary mind, revealing his anxiety in "The Flower" in which he says, it

> makes me ill to see them run up
> a new bridge like that in a few months

> and I can't find time even to get
> a book written. They have the power,
>
> that's all, she replied. That's what you all
> want. If you can't get it, acknowledge
>
> at least what it is. And they're not
> going to give it to you. Quite right.
>
> For years I've been tormented by
> that miracle, the buildings all lit up—
>
> unable to say anything much to the point
> though it is the major sight
>
> of this region. But foolish to rhapsodize over
> strings of lights, the blaze of a power
>
> in which I have not the least part.
>   (*CEP* 238–39)

Seen across the New Jersey meadowlands, Manhattan's bridges, its skyscrapers, and its electrification all enter into the poet's complaint that twentieth-century power is objectified in engineering technology, while the slow-paced writer is left behind, tormented and sick at heart.

Williams is both anxious and frustrated. Yet unlike Cather and Anderson, he does not assert the superiority of the writer by condemning engineers, machines, and structures in a cluster of subversive, denigrating images. Instead, "The Flower" plays a game intended to demonstrate the supreme flexibility of the poet's imagination when it, too, builds bridges, for the shape of the arched bridge span suggests a flower petal to Williams, who is free to fling his flower-petal arch over time as well as space:

> One petal goes eight blocks
>
> past two churches and a brick school beyond
> the edge of the park where under trees
>
> leafless now, women having nothing else to do
> sit in summer—to a small house
>
> in which I happen to have been born.

Another petal, we learn, "reaches to San Diego," and a third

> into the past, to Puerto Rico
> when my mother was a child bathing in a small

> river and splashing water up on
> the yucca leaves to see them roll back pearls.
> (*CEP* 237, 238)

Even as he complains that the power of technology eludes him, Williams is showing the imaginative versatility which he presumes to be unavailable to the designer of fixed forms like bridges. The poet, Williams suggests, surpasses the engineer in his ability to imagine. The poet can bridge an entire continent at will. He can span decades, reaching back from the Atlantic seaboard of the present to the Spanish Caribbean of his mother's childhood. The poet can even see the yucca leaves as arched spans flowing with the traffic of water pearls.

There is, Williams suggests, no end to the imaginative possibilities available to the poet, who can be positively stimulated by the engineer's designs. He even mused that the writer must "have a *basis*, a local stanchion, by which to bridge over the gap between present learning and the classical" (*In the American Grain* 231). Williams thus differed from Cather and Anderson—and from Henry James, who shuddered at the bridges and skyscrapers and electrical devices that he felt threatened the repose of the imagination. In *The American Scene* James tried to dismiss the skyscrapers by reducing them to such mere domestic stuff as a snaggle-toothed comb or a jammed pin cushion. But Williams, unlike James, resolves to coexist with them, in fact to incorporate them. The poems of *Spring and All* are a record of that incorporation. Williams's candy box "skyscrapers / filled with nut-chocolates" and his "skyscraper soup" of a composite urban-medical-artistic life encompass the dominating technology (*CEP* 244, 253). The images show Williams laying claim to it. It is domesticized to be welcomed as a familiar and not to be dismissed.

Not uncritically, to be sure. Williams sees New York's tall buildings as "Agonized Spires" and describes Manhattan as a high-rise electrified coral colony of "sweaty kitchens" and "swarming backstreets." Its bridge stanchions are "long / sunburnt fingers" piercing deep down into the ventricular heart of the organism (*CEP* 262–63). But the prose gloss on the poems of *Spring and All* indicates Williams's incorporation of all material objects, including the technological. "The objects of the [poet's] world," says Williams, ostensibly of Shakespeare but essentially of himself, "were real to him because he could use them and use them with understanding to make his inventions" (*I* 122). The bridges, skyscrapers, and electrical circuitry that James experienced as a threat to imaginative literature thus become, in Williams, an opportunity for poetic design.

The dynamo, then, can enter Williams's work as a familiar object, not as a larger-than-life religio-social symbol for the age. In "Paterson" he speaks of "the grace and detail of / a dynamo," and in *The Great American Novel* (1923), his self-styled "travesty on . . . conventional American writing,"

Williams responds to Henry Adams by making the dynamo just one voice among many in contemporary speech. "I'm new, says the great dynamo. I am progress. I make a word. Listen! UMMMMMMMMMMMMM—"

It is not clear whether Williams welcomes or spurns the new monosyllabic hum-word. But he certainly incorporates the dynamo as a comic object. He demystifies it, first in an operatic spoof set in the sickroom: "Ow, ow! Oh help me somebody! said [the woman in distress]. UMMMMMM sang the dynamo in the next street, UMMMM." Williams next domesticates the dynamo, again for incorporation. Williams begins with the awesome, theatrical set of a great misty amphitheater of a power station. It is back-lighted from the interior, its doors flung wide open to the night. "In [stately] rows sat the great black machines saying vrummmmmmmmmmmmmm." For what purpose?—to light the cellar stairs, to warm the patient's heating pad, to cook supper by and iron her husband's pajamas (*I* 162–63). The dynamo, no quasi-religious symbol for the technological age, figures in Williams as a character in a boffo opera vignette, as a possible source of one new monosyllabic word, and as a backstage functionary in domestic life. It is incorporated as a comic object, just like the Ford car and Mack truck whose romance is also detailed in the novel.

In fact, it is Williams's comic vision, which is to say a vision of social inclusiveness, that enables him to embrace technology and inclines him to use utilitarian, engineering terms when defining culture and the writer's place in it. To be sure, like Ezra Pound he understood the shortcomings of the technical mind at its least imaginative. He regretted the disappearance of the apprentice system of the crafts and condemned the intellectual narrowness of technical education, which he thought made boys lambs to the slaughter ("This is not civilization but stupidity") (*EK* 23; *I* 140). In "The American Background" he deplores the meretricious American money culture, railing against "the unmitigated stupidity, the drab tediousness of the democracy, the overwhelming number of the offensively ignorant" (*SE* 119).

But Williams defines authentic culture and the poet's place in it in optimistic—and utilitarian—terms. "Let the hopeful artist manufacture . . . something . . . which will be an organization of materials on a better basis than it had been before." He continues, "It is the job of the workman-artist to manufacture a better world than he sees." Culture "isn't a thing: it's an act," he says in a characteristically kinetic phrase. "If it stands still, it is dead" (*In* 77–78).

Williams elaborates on his utilitarian conception of cultural progress. The poet's manufacture of a better world begins with a grasp of culture, itself "the realization of the qualities of a place in relation to the life which occupies it, embracing everything involved" including vegetation, minerals, geology, geography, "and the condition of knowledge beyond its borders." Culture, then, is "the act of lifting these things into an ordered and utilized whole." The poet, like the scientist or philosopher, plays his part in it, since the "material manifestations" of the human mind are "of equal value whether in clay, iron, or words" (*EK* 130). Asserting the values of organization and utility, Williams sustains his utilitarian argument with a phrase unsurprising to those aware of the art-technology crisis. He takes Willa Cather's title and inverts its meaning: "The slow, foot-weary ascent goes on . . . this painstaking construction from the ground up, this Alexander's Bridge" (*SE* 159). Borrowing Cather's title for the novel that condemns the engineer's flawed psyche, Williams argues instead that culture is an act of knowledgeable engineering. But his Alexander's bridge is a multi-part construction. . . .

Like Dos Passos, Williams often finds his design components in American popular culture. The poem "Rapid Transit" is a good example of the design formed largely of components manufactured, so to speak, in the word factories of the advertising agencies. Williams, the designer, selects and brings them into arrangement to make the poem:

> Somebody dies every four minutes
> in New York State—
>
> To hell with you and your poetry—
> You will rot and be blown
> through the next solar system
> with the rest of the gases—
>
> What the hell do you know about it?
>
> AXIOMS
>
> Don't get killed
> Careful Crossing Campaign
> Cross Crossings Cautiously
>
> THE HORSES   black
>   &
> PRANCED   white
>
> Outings in New York City
>
> Ho for the open country
>
> Don't stay shut up in hot rooms
> Go to one of the Great Parks
> Pelham Bay for example
>
> It's on Long Island Sound
> with bathing, boating
> tennis, baseball, golf, etc.

Acres and acres of green grass
wonderful shade trees, rippling brooks

Take the Pelham Bay Park Branch
of the Lexington Ave. (East Side)
Line and you are there in a few
minutes

Interborough Rapid Transit Co.
(*I* 146–47)

"Rapid Transit" is a poem of the kinetic Williams. It gives a contemporary twist to the "sic transit" motto (*sic transit gloria mundi*—thus passes
away the glory of the world). Twentieth-century life is both perilous and
fast-paced. Somebody dies in New York every four minutes, so "Don't get
killed." Instead, live in the moment. The glory of the world is here and
now. As poets see it, the much-vaunted future comes down to decay and
solar wind; their opportunity is to make poems immediately. The experience
of the poem is the experience of contemporary urban life, fast and disjunctive.
Its components include advertising copy, slogans, maxims. All are prefabricated elsewhere and renewed by reformulation in poetic design. Williams
remarked that such "common objects" about him have combined with the
"seriousness" of his life to make up "an actuality of which I am assembling
the parts" (*I* 294). In a state of "clarity" the poet, as designer, chooses
those parts that make the most efficient arrangement. Williams said that in
considering a poem, he did not care whether it was finished or not: "if it's
put down with a good relation to the parts, it becomes a poem. And the
meaning of the poem can be grasped by attention to the design" (*In* 53).

Efficient design is ever Williams's objective. From Pound he had learned
"the original lesson: Never use two words where one will do" (*In* 81). Given
his commitment to poems as arrangements of materials, as efficient machines,
we would expect Williams's personal history, *In the American Grain* (1925),
to treat Benjamin Franklin sympathetically. Yet the Colonial exponent of
American technology and efficiency becomes one of Williams's most con-
temptible figures, timid, fearful, guarded against passion, defended against
experience. "He sensed the power [of lightning] and knew only enough to
want to run an engine with it" (*AG* 155). No admirable designer, Franklin
figures as a despicable "Poor Richard."

It is Edgar Allan Poe, instead, who emerges as the exemplary American
designer, the writer with an algebraic mind whose sentences play with clauses
"as with objects." It is Poe who "feels and turns [words] about as if he fitted
them to his design with *some* sense of their individual quality." It is Poe,
not Franklin, whose efficiency has power ("he wanted a lean style, rapid as
a hunter and with an aim as sure"). Williams admired Poe, as readers have
noticed, for having achieved the universalizing local that was so important

to the New Jersey-based Williams as he prepared *Paterson.* But Poe is equally admirable for his successful "inventions" and for a construction method that "let[s] the real business of composition *show.*" Williams especially valued this trait as a doctor trained to let the composition of the human body show and as a citizen of the twentieth century, when the composition of structures and machines was apparent to streetside onlookers as well as to readers of magazines (*AG* 221–22, 227, 230). (In this connection it is worth recalling that the critic of American culture, Van Wyck Brooks, compared Poe with Edison, saying that "the greatest of inventors cannot be called a scientist . . . but a mechanic" and that "Poe is a mechanic of the same sort" [60–61].)

Admiring Poe's feeling for the word-object, Williams reveals his own pleasure in the word, itself a single structural or machine component that gives tactile pleasure just as Frank Lloyd Wright's boyhood blocks did. Williams credits another writer trained in medicine, Gertrude Stein, with using "words as objects out of which you manufacture a little mechanism you call a poem" (*In* 69). (It would, in fact, be interesting to consider Stein's work in this light.) Williams characterized the sentimental poetry around him, poetry of the kind he himself once wrote, as viscous and opaque ("gummy. . . . covered with vain curlicues") (*SE* 111; *I* 320). He couched his praise for Marianne Moore in terms of precision parts pleasing to the eye and to the touch. Cleansed in an acid bath, each word is dried and placed on a clean surface and inspected for nicks or other imperfections. Only those words with perfect edges qualify for assembly into the design (*I* 319–20). The word is "an objective unit in the design—but alive" (*SE* 111). Within the poem the word, the essential unit of design, keeps its identity just as the body part, the machine part, or the structural member does.

Hearing Williams affirm the vitality of poet and poem in the terms "dynamic" and "clarity," we anticipate his remark on component word-objects, vibrant with energy, "shin[ing] in the structural body" of the machines made of words. In *The Great American Novel* the dynamo and the new word hum with powerful currents. Even entropy can be described in these kinetic terms: "words are the reverse motion. . . . Words roll, spin, flare up, rumble, trickle, foam—Slowly they lose momentum. Slowly they cease to stir. At last they break up into their letters" (*I* 160, 162).

Williams's scorn, moreover, for the simile is essentially a rejection of the static adjective, that decorator's tool. The imperative of the writer, on the contrary, "is to learn to employ the verbs in imitation of nature— so that the pieces move naturally." Then, says Williams, "watch, often breathlessly, what they *do.*" For authentic writing is "a transit from the adjective . . . to verb." Writing, says Williams, "is an action, a moving process—the verb dominates" (*SE* 302–3, 306).

Williams's emphasis on the primacy of the verb may seem peculiar, considering his preference for word-objects ordinarily classed as nouns and adjectives. The "red wheel / barrow" and "white / chickens" come immediately to mind, as do other figures from Williams's best-known work—the plums, the young housewife, the figure five. There is not a verb among them—unless, of course, one dispenses with the entire system of classification of parts of speech in order to embrace instead a radically different linguistic theory. The theory argues that words in English, like Chinese ideographs, "carry in them *a verbal idea of action*" no matter what their conventional linguistic designation. This, apparently, was what Williams did, for Ernest Fenollosa's theory of language, published as of 1918 through the tireless effort of his literary executor, Pound, came at a propitious time for Williams. Whether he read Fenollosa's "The Chinese Written Character as a Medium for Poetry" in its four installments in the *Little Review* beginning September 1919, or in Pound's *Instigations* (1920), or heard Pound, in correspondence, sketch the argument, Williams must have found Fenollosa's theory to be as permissively liberating as Dewey's remarks on the universalizing local were fortifying when he began to conceive *Paterson*.

Fenollosa offered the poet a theory of language commensurate with the modern moment of speed and machine technology. For Fenollosa's was the perfect linguistic theory for the gear-and-girder world. Echoing Emerson, he said that "the verb must be the primary fact of nature, since motion and change are all we can recognize in her" (rpt. in E. Pound, *Instigations* 374–75). His exposition of the Chinese and Japanese ideograph demonstrated an entirely verbal basis for parts of speech in English. He argues that the color green, for instance, is not adjectival but verbal because "green is only a certain rapidity of vibration." Prepositions "are naturally verbs," and conjunctions, "since they mediate actions, are actions themselves." (Fenollosa, of course, was not alone in exploring this verbal basis of language. In *Principles of Psychology*, William James, discussing the stream of thought, also speculated that conjunctions, prepositions, and adverbial phrases signify experience [1:245–46].)

Within Fenollosa's theory, Williams's "red wheel / barrow" and "white / chickens" become fully active and interactive, as do his other so-called prepositions, adverbs, articles. This idea of the poem constructed as a formal integration of verbal components clearly fit Williams's definition of the poem as "a small (or large) machine made of words." The machine figure asserts energy-producing movement and implicitly warns the poet to rid the poem of inessential verbiage. "The Red Wheelbarrow" demonstrates Fenollosa's language theory and the compatible concept of the efficient machine in which "there can be no part . . . that is redundant":

> so much depends
> upon
>
> a red wheel
> barrow

> glazed with rain
> water
>
> beside the white
> chickens.
>
> (*CEP* 277)

Here, "pruned to a perfect economy," is the machine made of words, all of its parts perfectly, formally intergeared (as Williams put it, "undulant") and thus able to achieve its "exact meaning" (*SE* 256). "The Red Wheelbarrow," the kinetic machine, shows the standard of verbal efficiency of operation even as it encodes the rapid-transit, efficient moment.

Williams and the Female Principle

KERRY DRISCOLL

Despite his deep affinity for women and sensitivity to their plight, Williams was unable, except in a few rare instances, to surmount an inherently patriarchal bias involving notions of male primacy and dominance, and hence could not make the psychic transition from sympathy to truly empathic identification. Trapped by what he labeled "a counter stress, / born of the sexual shock" (*PB*, 78),[1] the poet viewed women from a compassionate, but external—and therefore "confused"—stance. The exteriority of his position is reflected in a tendency to depict them in two antithetical, but equally idealized ways. The first . . . proclaims the bewildering multiplicity and variation of feminine traits—"they were all different." The second, as the following passage from *January: A Novelette* reveals, reduces all women to a single, symbolic archetype, a Botticellian vision of beauty: "And what is a beautiful woman? She is one. Over and over again, she is one . . . So she—building of all excellence is, in her single body, beautiful; enforcing the mind by imperfections to a height. Born again, Venus from the confused sea. Summing all the virtues. Single. Excellence. Female" (*I*, 282).

These conflicting modes of representation are reconciled in Williams' later work, where female characters, though individuated, are treated primarily as avatars of this archetype. The convergence of the two styles can be clearly seen in the poet's nostalgic recollection in *Paterson* 4 of girls to whom he'd been attracted in his youth. His litany of praise to "Margaret," "Lucille," "Alma," and "Nancy," each of whom is delineated by a few specific details (which, quite tellingly, consist mostly of body parts—"big breasts and daring eyes," "gold hair," "steady hand," and a "mouth [that] never wished for relief"), concludes in this manner:

> All these
> and more—shining, struggling flies
> caught in the meshes of Her hair
>
> (*P*, 192)

These lines typify the technique of "drawing back" that Williams mentioned in the excerpt from *I Wanted to Write a Poem* quoted earlier. Through a sudden, distancing shift in authorial perspective, the four women lose not only their individual identities, but their humanity itself. They become helpless "flies," entrapped in and serving as adornments for the "invisible net" covering the hair of a primordial earth goddess who is associated throughout the poem with Garrett Mountain. The distinguishing personal features of Margaret, Lucille, Alma, and Nancy are thus subsumed into a single attribute of a mythic entity who incarnates the universal "female principle."

This same mythicizing tendency can also be observed in two of Williams' most celebrated later poems, "Of Asphodel, That Greeny Flower" and "For Eleanor and Bill Monahan." In "Asphodel," which is addressed to his wife Flossie, he states:

> All women are not Helen,
> I know that,
> but have Helen in their hearts.
> My sweet,
> you have it also, therefore
> I love you
> and could not love you otherwise.
> (*PB*, 159)

Though Williams stops short of literally equating all women with Helen of Troy in this passage, he nevertheless predicates his love for Flossie upon a subjective mythic association, namely, that "all women . . . have Helen in their hearts." Moreover, he insists on the necessity of this imaginative projection in order for love to exist and survive: "I could not love you otherwise." For the poet, the figure of Helen represents a male fantasy of female beauty, desirability, and possession; she epitomizes the concept of woman as object and prize. In asserting that all women somehow partake of Helen, he obliquely alludes to the possibility of their seduction, thereby unconsciously revealing more about himself (e. g., as a modern-day Paris) and his perceptions of women than about Flossie, his intended subject.

Fantasy also plays a significant role in "For Eleanor and Bill Monahan," although in this case, the poet's subject is not a female intimate but rather a religious deity, the Virgin Mary. Throughout the lyric, Williams humanizes the Mother of God by imaginatively describing her as a palpable, sexually attractive woman, "young / and fit to be loved" (*PB*, 85). This strategy, which anticipates his characterization of the virgin and the whore in book 5 of *Paterson* as dual facets of a single female identity, initially seems presumptuous, even irreverent; however, as the poem's concluding lines indicate, the piece is in fact a prayer, a plea for mercy and forgiveness, addressed to a being whom Williams clearly worships. Rather, the radicality of his interpretation lies in locating the source of Mary's divinity not in her remote, inviolable aura of virginity, as the Christian church has traditionally done, but in an attitude of tenderness, vulnerability, humility, and love which he considers quintessentially feminine:

> Mother of God
> > I have seen you stoop
> > > to a merest flower
> and raise it
> > and press it to your cheek.
> > > I could have called out
> joyfully
> > but you were too far off.
> > > You are a woman and
> it was
> > a woman's gesture.
>
> > > > (PB, 84)

The implications of this description are far-reaching: by emphasizing the womanly qualities of the Virgin Mary's character, Williams suggests that the archetypal feminine is in itself divine. All women, in addition to having "Helen in their hearts," resemble the Mother of God in the gentleness of their gestures and largesse of their spirits. The poet, in this instance, moves beyond the bounds of mythicizing into pure deification, declaring: "The female principle of the world / is my appeal / in the extremity to which I have come" (PB, 86). Interestingly, this exaltation of the feminine creates a corresponding diminution of his own status within the lyric. Williams portrays himself as a devotee and supplicant who willingly "submits" to the "holy rule" (PB, 83) of the redemptive female force embodied in Mary. The generosity of women and their capacity for forgiveness become for him synonymous with emotional salvation; hence, they are to be treated as objects of veneration. The archly romanticized nature of his depiction, though intended to be flattering, proves ultimately counterproductive in that it deepens the "riddle of a man and a woman" rather than taking steps to resolve it. In this respect, the glaring inequity of the relationship he proposes between himself and the "female principle" reaffirms the exteriority of his perceptual stance—that women are indeed the "other."

The attitudes Williams expressed about women in his writing range over a wide emotional spectrum, from candid acknowledgment of their potent erotic appeal to the mythic idealization so evident in the later poems. After lecturing to a predominantly female audience at Vassar, for example, he told a friend: "I [always] find it rather difficult to take the girls seriously enough except on the one topic"; similarly, in I Wanted to Write a Poem, he recalled a reading at Wellesley, commenting to Edith Heal, "The girls

. . . were so adorable. I could have raped them all!" (*IW*, 95). Although many of his statements, like the following passage from *Paterson*,

> Say I am the locus
>   where two women meet
> One from the backwoods
>   a touch of the savage
>   and of T. B.
>   (a scar on the thigh)
> The other—wanting,
>   from an old culture
> —and offer the same dish
>   different ways
>
>   (*P*, 110)

are both distasteful and flagrantly sexist from a contemporary feminist standpoint, the openness with which Williams attempted to record his varied responses to women, even when they were objectionable or taboo in nature, must also be taken into consideration. He describes, for example, his lust for little girls in a number of poems such as "The Ogre," where, upon viewing a "sweet child . . . with well-shaped legs," he contemplates thoughts which would "burn [her] to an ash" (*CEP*, 154). Whereas another writer might have suppressed such feelings, or at least chosen not to publicly commemorate them in print, Williams understood that passion was an integral component of his identity, and defied the prevailing puritanical morality of his time to repeatedly assert it. In the foreword to his *Autobiography*, he states unequivocally: "I am extremely sexual in my desires: I carry them everywhere and at all times. I think that from that [*sic*] arises the drive which empowers us all" (*A*, i). The intensity of this innate drive was, in his estimation, augmented by the isolated circumstances of his childhood: "I never had a sister, no aunts and no female cousins, at least within striking distance. So that aside from Mother and Grandma I never knew a female intimately for my entire young life. That was very important. It generated in me enough curiosity to burn up fifty growing boys" (*A*, 4–5).

Despite the poet's endeavor in this statement to minimize the importance of his mother, Elena Hoheb, and paternal grandmother, Emily Dickenson Wellcome, in formulating his early impressions of women, these two individuals undoubtedly comprised his primary female role models. Significantly, their relationship to one another was far from harmonious; another childhood memory recounted in *Autobiography* concerns the fierce rivalry that developed between the two women over the possession of little Willie himself. Immediately following the birth of his younger brother, Edgar, Williams had been begrudgingly surrendered to the care of his grandmother, who lived at home with the family; as a result, Emily came to think of him as "her boy": "Grandma took me over or tried to. But once Mother lost her temper and laid the old gal out good with a smack across the puss that my mother joyfully remembered until her death" (A, 5).

The legendary slap with which Elena ended her mother-in-law's attempt to usurp her eldest son had extensive repercussions for the poet's personal development. Through this act of symbolic reclamation, she asserted the primacy of the maternal relationship above all others, and established a hierarchy of familial bonds and devotion which was never again overtly challenged. Moreover, the incident's sexual configuration (a triangle, involving two females and a male) influenced and, to some extent, determined the pattern of Williams' mature interactions with women by revealing to him, at an early and impressionable age, that females "desired" him and would quarrel among themselves over the right to his possession. One of the most famous passages in *Paterson* illustrates how fundamental this notion of male singularity as the magnetic center of a multiplicity of females was to the poet's self-image:

> A man like a city and a woman like a flower
> —who are in love. Two women. Three women.
> Innumerable women, each like a flower.
> > But
> only one man—like a city.
>
> > > (P, 7)

Even in old age, Williams remained confident of his ability to charm women, telling Robert Lowell with characteristic aplomb: "I am sixty-seven, and / more attractive to girls than when I was seventeen."[2]

Within the large cast of female figures who populate Williams' writing, there stands a triumvirate of characters notable for both the careful detail with which they are delineated and the frequency of their appearance. Beyond the generic appeal that all women had possessed for the poet, these three— his mother, grandmother, and wife—are distinguished by the intimacy and long duration of their relationships with him, as well as by the powerful influences they exerted on his imagination. The poet's fictive representations of these three individuals offers a logical starting place for critically examining the evolution of his attitudes towards women and theories about "what made them tick" (IW, 64) for the simple reason that they were the ones whom he himself knew best and had the most extensive opportunities to observe.

To a certain extent, Williams consciously mythologized these three women in his work; each is elevated and ennobled in the process of transmutation from life into art. His grandmother, for example, who appears as the haggard old muse in his important early poem "The Wanderer," is by Williams' own admission, "raised to heroic proportions . . . [and] endowed with magic qualities" (IW, 26). She flies through the air with the poet, initiating him, through a series of visionary experiences, into the sordid realities of the modern world, and finally baptizes him in the filthy waters of her "old friend" (*CEP*, 11), the Passaic River. In a less fantastic, but still idealized manner, he describes her in the eulogy, "Dedication for a Plot of Ground," as a tough, adventurous individual who voyaged from the old world to the new and fought tirelessly to defend herself "against thieves / storms, sun, fire," as well as "against the weakness of her own hands" (*CEP*, 171). The great admiration Williams felt for his grandmother's passion, independence, and determination did not, however, allow him to transcend the exteriority of his male perceptions and penetrate to the hidden, inner core of her being. Emily Dickenson Wellcome remained, to the end, a mystery to him.

Similarly, Williams' treatment of Flossie in both his poetry and prose is also externalized. His trilogy of novels about her childhood and family background, *White Mule, In the Money*, and *The Build-up*, is narrated, significantly, from a limited third-person point of view. Little attempt is made to enter into and explore the development of the young girl's consciousness; instead, the narrative chronicles a progression of purely external events. Even in the heart-wrenching love poems of the 1950s, Flossie is a veiled, passive presence. Williams variously describes and interprets her, evokes tender moments in their long life together, and pleads for her forgiveness, but her responses to these overtures are unfortunately not recorded; as a result, she is elusive and inaccessible to the reader, a subjective "dream of love" (*ML*, 105) created within the poet's imagination.

The one instance in which Williams successfully overcame his perception of female "otherness" was the portrayal of his mother, Raquel Helen Rose Hoheb Williams. Aside from the poet's ubiquitous representations of himself, she is arguably the most fully realized of all his "characters," appearing regularly throughout his work from the very earliest pieces of the last. He upheld her, for example, as a symbol of the imagination in the prologue to *Kora in Hell*, related bits of her biography in *The Descent of Winter* and *January*, made her the subject of numerous poems ("Eve," "All the Fancy Things," "Two Pendants: for the Ears," "The Horse Show," "An Eternity," "The Painting," to mention only the most prominent), and devoted a book-length memoir, *Yes, Mrs. Williams*, to her stories and aphorisms.

The source of Williams' abiding fascination with Elena, which served as a crucial factor in his surmounting of the perceptual barriers typically imposed by gender difference, was his intuitive recognition of the extensive physical, spiritual, and psychic similarities that existed between them. Because the poet believed that he and his mother were, in many respects, fundamentally alike, he came to regard her as a living text in which he could read and discover the secrets of his own identity. The concept of female "otherness" thus yielded in the case of Elena to a perception not only of resemblance, but symbolic convergence. Within the fictive universe of Williams' writing, the figures of mother and son complement one another, conjoining male and female elements to form a single, unified whole; as Doc Thurber explains to his wife Myra in the play *A Dream of Love*, the process is one of reciprocal imaginative completion: "Just as a woman must produce out of her female belly to complete herself—a son—so a man must produce a woman, in full beauty out of the shell of his imagination and possess her, to complete himself also . . ." (*ML*, 200).

This analogy between the literal act of giving birth and artistic creation has particular relevance for the poet's depiction of Elena, in which the roles of "parent" and "offspring" are thoroughly conflated. The mother is engendered, "in full beauty," out of the womb of her son's imagination, in much the same way that she earlier gave life to him. As "Eve," the title of his 1936 poem about her, suggests, Elena represented the first, archetypal female for Williams, the Ur-mother from whom all other women are descended. In this respect, his characterization of her parallels Freud's theory of the three symbolic forms assumed by the figure of the mother as a man's life proceeds: "the mother herself, the beloved who is chosen after her pattern, and finally the Mother Earth who receives him again."[3] For Williams, Elena not only supplied the "pattern" for the beloved, but fulfilled that role herself in his imagination; as a young man studying medicine in Leipzig, he had written a letter to her, enclosing a poem that he described as "a pure love song and all the truer because of the impossibility of passion."[4] Through the intensity of this "impossible," multifaceted passion, Elena became the foundation upon which her son's later concept of a generic "female principle" was erected; following her example and instruction, he learned how to live, how to love, and ultimately, how to die. "What do I look for in a woman?" he asked in *Autobiography*. "Death, I suppose, since it's all I see anyhow in those various perfections. I want them all in lesser or greater degree" (*A*, 222).

But who exactly was this obscure woman to whom Williams ascribed such monumental significance? The answers are diverse: an immigrant to the U. S., born and raised on the island of Puerto Rico; a frustrated artist and musician; a misfit; a spiritual medium who fell into periodic trances; an isolated suburban housewife who bore two sons. Petite in stature and ethereal in temperament, Elena was also very much a lady, fond of fine dresses and polite society, extremely vain about her slender waist and size 4½ feet. The fragility of her appearance, however, concealed a tough, resilient inner fiber and potential for emotional volatility that manifested itself from time to time in violent, impetuous actions, like slapping Grandma Wellcome in the face or "whaling [the] hell" out of Williams and his brother with a piece of cord wood (*A*, 11–12). Yet, in terms of her son's poetry, Elena was most compellingly a voice—indeed, the primal voice of human contact, that of the mother. As nurturer and guardian, singer of lullabies and teller of bedtime tales, it was she who largely introduced Williams into the mysteries of language, and the powerful impression created in his mind by the exotic rhythms of her ungrammatical immigrant speech later became the wellspring of his interest in the American idiom.

Elena's centrality in the poet's life and imagination is illustrated by the following passage from *I Wanted to Write a Poem:*

> I was conscious of my mother's influence all through this time of writing, her ordeal as a woman and as a foreigner in this country. I've always held her as a mythical figure, remote from me, detached, looking down on an area in which I happened to live, a fantastic world where she was moving as a more or less pathetic figure. Remote, not only because of her Puerto Rican background, but also because of her bewilderment at life in a small town in New Jersey after her years in Paris where she had been an art student. Her interest in art became my interest in art. I was personifying her, her detachment from the world of Rutherford. She seemed an heroic figure, a poetic ideal. I didn't especially admire her; I was attached to her. I had not yet established any sort of independent spirit. (*IW*, 16)

Although these remarks pertain specifically to Williams' first two books, *Poems* (1909) and *The Tempers* (1913), they also attest to the enduring nature of his preoccupation with Elena. "I've *always* held her as a mythical figure," he states, suggesting that her appeal did not suddenly diminish at the end of his apprentice period, but continued throughout his career. Moreover, in attempting to describe the extent of his mother's early influence, Williams makes several revealing comments, the most significant of which is, "I was personifying her, her detachment from the world of Rutherford." Initially, he seems to be sketching a rather conventional portrait of spiritual legacy ("Her interest in art became my interest in art"), yet the weight of the mother's inheritance is so strong that it unsettles the poet's sense of personal identity and autonomy. From a semantic standpoint, his use of the verb "personify" is incorrect, since only inanimate objects can be personified, not people. But in this context, the verb accentuates the extent of Elena's imaginative hold on Williams: in his poetry, he is incarnating and acting out her interests, her ideals, her plight. This strange configuration is reinforced by two statements which occur at the end of the passage: "I was *attached* to her. *I had not yet established any sort of independent spirit*" (emphasis mine).

The exaggerated nature of these assertions implies that Williams' statement is more than an idle reminiscence; even at this late stage in his life, almost a decade after Elena's death in 1949, his identification with her remained active and unresolved. Furthermore, the subtle blurring of identities in the passage is not an aberration produced by the casual, oral quality of *I Wanted to Write a Poem*, but a motif that characterizes all the poet's descriptions of his mother. For this reason, I believe that Williams' textualization represents more than an extended illustration of the way life is mysteriously metamorphosed into art; rather, it exposes the essence, the "radiant gist" (*P*, 186) of his identity. Williams' mother was his muse, the spiritual source from which his creative genius sprang. As such, his numerous portrayals of her, especially the memoir, *Yes, Mrs. Williams*, have a dual resonance, simultaneously revealing essential facets of his own personality. In analyzing the memoir's genesis and slow evolution over the course of the poet's career, this study explores not only the complex configuration of the mother-son relationship, but Williams' progressive understanding of himself, particularly in terms of the androgynous, "female" aspects of his character.

The intimate and assiduous detail in which Williams delineated Elena was the result not only of psychic affinity but physical proximity. Because he spent his entire life within a few miles of the house where he was born, the poet was able to maintain extraordinarily close contact with Elena right up until the time of her death. When, for example, he left home in 1912 to marry Flossie, the newlyweds rented rooms which adjoined his parents' residence, and took meals with them. And in 1924, Elena, who was growing increasingly infirm, moved in with her eldest son at 9 Ridge Road, and lived there most of her last twenty-five years. Through the daily regularity of their contact, Williams became steeped in his mother's personal mythos— the figure of the defeated romantic "clinging desperately to the small threads of a reality which she thought to have left in Paris" (*YMW*, 33). He could not, however, easily reconcile Elena's sentimental self-image with his firsthand knowledge of her toughness and ability to survive adversity, and so resolved to break through this mythic facade and excavate her "true life, undefeated if embittered, hard as nails, little loving, easily mistaken for animal selfishness" (*YMW*, 33). Much of Williams' writing about his mother can thus be viewed as a hermeneutic exercise—an attempt to come to terms with conflicting interpretations of her identity and character which, by extension, offered insight into his own. The 1927 poem, "Brilliant Sad Sun," offers a concise example of the way in which he approached and articulated this dilemma:

Lee's
Lunch

Spaghetti   Oysters
a Specialty   Clams

and raw Winter's done
to a turn—Restaurant: Spring!
Ah, Madam, what good are your thoughts

romantic but true
beside this gaiety of the sun
and that huge appetite?

Look!
from a glass pitcher she serves
clear water to the white chickens.

What are your memories
beside that purity?
The empty pitcher dangling

from her grip
her coarse voice croaks
Bon jor'

And Patti, on her first concert tour
sang at your house in Mayagüez
and your brother was there

What beauty
beside your sadness—and
what sorrow

(*CEP*, 324)

This impressionistic poem concerns the disparity between past and present, memory and direct experience. The unusual arrangement of the first four lines mimics an advertisement, perhaps the signboard of an unpretentious local eatery. Although the dramatic situation of the poem is unclear, the sense of vividness and immediacy created by the opening stanzas suggests that mother and son may in fact be dining at Lee's Lunch or simply out for a drive in the spring weather. In any event, the text's focus and progression depend largely on Williams' pun on the word "restaurant," which derives from the French verb, "restaurer," meaning to restore, refresh, or reestablish. He moves deftly from the subject of food to the changing of the seasons by using the term simultaneously as a noun and verb, "raw Winter's done / to a turn—Restaurant: Spring!" This double entendre metaphorizes the concept of "restaurant" by linking it with a natural process of renewal; moreover, the highly kinetic quality of the phrase, "turn—Restaurant: Spring!" parallels the quick leap in the poet's train of thought.

The questions Williams poses to Elena are also intended to produce a "restaurant," drawing her out of a futile absorption with the past into an appreciation of the sensuousness and diversity of her present environs. He openly challenges the validity and worth of his mother's attitudes

. . . what good are your thoughts

romantic but true
beside this gaiety of the sun
and that huge appetite? . . .

> What are your memories
> beside that purity?

but does so in a polite, respectful manner. Indeed, he even calls her "Madam," as a waiter would a female customer. In lieu of Elena's direct response to these questions, Williams presents a pair of enigmatic images which form a veiled parable about the dangers of her condition. The first scene he enjoins her to observe, "Look! / from a glass pitcher she serves / clear water to the white chickens," is a pastoral paradigm of grace, plenitude, and order. And yet its pristine clarity, accentuated by the modifiers "glass," "clear," and "white," is ultimately deceptive, since the image is idealized and atemporal, as its degraded counterpart reveals:

> The empty pitcher dangling
>
> from her grip
> her coarse voice croaks
> Bon jor'

This anonymous female figure represents two antipodal aspects of memory— its benign ability, on the one hand, to crystallize, refine, and preserve individual experience, and its treacherous vacuity and insubstantiality on the other. As Williams states in the poem's conclusion, it is precisely this combination of beauty and sadness that makes the snare of memory so difficult to escape. He understands Elena's attraction to the distant, irretrievable past of her youth in Puerto Rico, but also recognizes its concomitant hazards. The sorrow he alludes to in the last line is thus not his mother's, but rather his own, arising from the failure of his "restaurant" to effect any change in her outlook on the present.

Like "restaurant," the poem's title, "Brilliant Sad Sun," is a double entendre that plays on the concept of turning. This celestial image refers most obviously to Elena, who occupies the center of the text and, in her old age, resembles the diminished splendor of the setting sun. Yet there is another possibility as well, that of "brilliant sad *son*." The sun's "gaiety," which Williams evokes in line 9 as a symbol of the beauty and vitality of the physical environment, epitomizes all that he seeks to restore to his mother. In this respect, the poet himself becomes the sun, the primary source of light in Elena's memory-bedimmed world. The title's ambiguity thus reflects the richness, complexity, and dynamic reciprocity of influence which characterizes the poet's depictions of himself and Elena throughout his work. Together, mother and son comprise an imaginative universe, "the he and the she of it" (*IW*, 65), spinning in perpetual orbit about one another, seeking coalescence.

Notes

1.   Parenthetical references are as follows: *A: Autobiography* (New Directions, 1951). *CEP: Collected Earlier Poems* (New Directions, 1951). *I: Imaginations* (New Directions, 1970). *IW: I Wanted to Write a Poem* (Beacon Press, 1958). *ML: Many Loves and Other Plays* (New Directions, 1961). *P: Paterson* (New Directions, 1963). *PB: Pictures from Brueghel and Other Poems* (New Directions, 1962). *YMW: Yes, Mrs. Williams* (New Directions, 1959).

2.   Lowell, "William Carlos Williams," *History* (Farrar, Straus & Giroux, 1973), p. 142.

3.   Freud, "The Theme of the Three Caskets," *On Creativity and the Unconscious* (New York: Harper, 1958), p. 75.

4.   Paul Mariani, *William Carlos Williams: A New World Naked* (New York: McGraw-Hill, 1981), p. 84.

"Young Sycamore"
and the Influence of Science

LISA M. STEINMAN

"Young Sycamore" (1927) is a brief poem of one sentence that opens:

> I must tell you
> this young tree
> whose round and firm trunk
> between the wet
>
> pavement and the gutter
> (where water
> is trickling) rises
> bodily
> (CEP 332)[1]

The poem follows the tree's rise to a fork, and then to smaller branches with cocoons in them,

> till nothing is left of it
> but two
>
> eccentric knotted
> twigs
> bending forward
> hornlike at the top
> (CEP 332)

The poem is based on an aesthetic shared with paintings and photographs by members of the Stieglitz circle; indeed, Bram Dijkstra argues that Williams is literally describing Alfred Stieglitz's photograph, *Spring Showers*.[2]

"Young Sycamore" and other Williams poems like it seem to resist explication, to be purely descriptive, although, as J. Hillis Miller points out, Williams takes a firm stance against "the falseness of attempting to 'copy' nature" (*I* 107), desiring "not 'realism' but reality itself" (*I* 117). Miller's argument is that the poem does not represent a tree, but rather as a poem it "is an object which has the same kind of life as the tree."[3] If, as he argues, "Young Sycamore" is not symbolic but an object in its own right, it nonetheless presents an analogy between the growth of a tree and the growth of a poem. The motion described is paradigmatic, familiar to any reader of *Kora in Hell, Spring and All,* or *In the American Grain.*[4] The tree's "bodily" rise ending in the near still life of the two twigs is a motion very like Williams's description of imaginative creation.[5] In "How to Write" from 1936, Williams says that poems begin with "the very muscles and bones of the body itself speaking, [although] once the writing is on the paper it becomes an object. . . . an object for the liveliest attention that the full mind can give it" (*SSA* 98). The poem takes its place as another artifact, an object in the world, but also refers to a series of parallel motions: Nature produces the tree, in a fashion very close to the way we have seen the production of inventions described; Williams produces his poem; and the reader is invited to join in the creative process, not by looking through the language to that which it describes, but by paying attention to the poem itself, and, if the paradigm of the poet and nature holds, producing some object of his own.[6]

Even without knowing Williams's theories about poetry, by turning mind and attention to the poem-as-object, the reader is referred to Williams's process of creation in language. Although the poem describes an act of detailed perception, and thus at first recalls Williams's statement that artists teach us to see,[7] a closer examination of "Young Sycamore" shows that it places equal emphasis on speaking and language. The urgency of the first line focuses attention on the poet's voice, while the careful syntax of the main clause and the enjambment suggest that Williams is not showing us a tree or even clearly telling us about one; he is creating a tree of language: "I must tell you / this young tree."

At the same time, it is no accident that the verbs, like the tree, thin out towards the end of the poem, nor that the one simile occurs in the last line, as the flow of language ends. Williams said he disliked similes: "The coining of similes is a pastime of very low order" (*I* 18). It has been a commonplace of Williams scholarship to use such statements as evidence of Williams's desire to present poems as objects or as being objective descriptions of discrete, nonsymbolic objects in the world.[8] As Henry Sayre argues, however, Williams's similes and metaphors are not lapses by someone who wished to but could not avoid "subjective observation and interpretation"; they serve rather to make the poems work as "the site of the interplay between the mind and reality."[9] The overt figure at the end of "Young Sycamore" deliberately calls attention both to the poet's act of interpretation and to his linguistic creation. It shifts our attention from trees to poems at the same time that it recasts the poem as an emblem or, at least, as a series of figures. Not only is the tree's growth like the poet's creative process, but the waxing and waning of the tree is also echoed more succinctly in the cocoons' simultaneous image of death and potential life, and in the contradictory motions finally abstracted in the stark image of the two knotted twigs.[10]

The central concern of the poem is the process of growth or creation with its inevitable culmination in an object. But objects can yield new realities, new life, like the cocoons or like the emblem of the eccentric twigs. The twigs are eccentric because they are off center, leaning forward,[11] but also because the literal center of the poem images the process of creation yielding both multiplicity and destruction as the trunk's "one undulant / thrust" begins to divide between the third and fourth stanzas, and the poem widens its focus to include the cocoons, which, as a gardener like Williams would have known, spell destruction for trees. The final image is eccentric as well because the twigs remain stubbornly particular, even as they tempt us to align their double nature with the other dualities to which the poem calls our attention—the process behind the product; the cocoons' destruction in creation; the poem as object and figure, physical and intellectual. As Williams says, "nothing is left of it / but two." Delaying the noun by a stanza break and a line of adjectives, Williams makes "two" seem for a moment the object itself. The final duality is formal or structural.

One might say that all of the oppositions suggested in the poem are given their purest expression—not resolved, but expressed—in the image, which is the fruition of the poem, but which is so well "knotted" that nothing remains to be said: "The detail is its own solution." The twigs for example, suggest both an upward movement (*top* is the final word of the poem) and a return to earth in their horn-like bend. Like the ornament and the steeple or the contrast between a squat edifice and the moon in "To a Solitary Disciple" (*CEP* 167–68), the image of the two twigs moves Williams's readers in two directions simultaneously. Similarly, the poem both is and is about a unique object even as it suggests that all objects, once subjected to lively attention, can be made to release a creative energy that necessarily transcends the discrete structure of individual objects.[12]

Finally, the result of the creative energy alluded to in the poem is the revelation of a structure. As the life of the poem is parallel to the life of the tree, creativity is itself another version of the structure imaged by the entire movement of the poem from the poet's presence, insisted upon in the first line, which roots the poem in a creative, human, speaker, to the final equation of the formal essence of the poem and the bare architecture of the leafless tree.

Williams often described the force or energy of poems as an essence or rare presence (*A* 362). These images occur quite early in his writing. A 1921 editorial in *Contact*, discussing Burke's article on Laforgue, describes the search for a "milligram of radium" (*SE* 36), while the essay on Marianne

Moore published in *A Novelette and Other Prose* speaks of the "white light that is the background of all good work" (*SE* 122). In the Rasles section of *In the American Grain*, Williams isolates within himself a "core of nature" (*IAG* 105) analogous to "the strange phosphorus of the life" (*IAG* v) that he seeks throughout the book. At all stages of his career, Williams refers to an incandescent universal presence that informs and perhaps is in all art and all natural objects, but the status of this essence varies. In "Young Sycamore," at least, it is presented as a structure, and finally as impersonal, and this reading is reinforced by the poem's use of language. That is, the visual regularity of the quatrains and the sparse, unembellished lines and vocabulary, like the imagistic progression of the poem, add to this effect. [13]

Descriptions of such poetry as impersonal, or at least as objective, are commonplace in modernist poetics, and the link between this style of poetry and science is widely noted. [14] Moore identified Louise Bogan's terse pronouncements as being "rendered with laboratory detachment" (*R* 230). And Eliot, to choose a poet with whom Williams generally took issue, suggested that it is in "depersonalization that art may be said to approach the condition of science." [15] Williams's own descriptions of the use of language in poems such as "Young Sycamore" similarly invoke science, as when he approvingly says in his 1931 review of Moore's poetry that words are "separated out by science, treated with acid to remove the smudges, washed, dried and placed right side up on a clean surface" (*SE* 128). [16] Here Williams praises removing the emotional and conventional associations of words, and sees the poet's cleansing activity as akin to the laboratory or assembly line worker's. [17]

Williams thus recognizes that his insistence upon words as objects or structures, central to the style and content of "Young Sycamore," might be linked to science, to technology, and ultimately to the products of technology. The link, indeed, is subtle. The poem not only appeals to a taste for the clean lines and efficiency associated with industrial technology, but it is defined as a discrete structure, a "machine made of words" that does not need to refer outside of itself for its effect since "its movement is intrinsic" (*SE* 256).

Williams describes the need to reclaim the essence of poems, trees, and other objects "nameless under an old misappellation" (*IAG* v) with a new, cleaner language to be provided by the poet. What the poet reclaims then, in "Young Sycamore," is not a particular tree, but a method of reclamation and an essential structure that is in one aspect purely formal. In fact, "Young Sycamore" 's reference to the poet's process of creation recasts creativity itself not only within but also as a formal structure.

To force Williams's poetic to one possible conclusion, it is not that poems, more self-consciously than machines, reveal human inventiveness, but that knowledge, language, poems, plants, and men are structurally similar, and their structural essence is best described by analogy to machines or technological products. Indeed, in 1919 Williams wrote in an article for the magazine, *Others*, with which he was involved: "Poets have written of the big leaves and the little leaves, leaves that are red, green, yellow and the one thing they have never seen about a leaf is that it is a little engine. It is one of the things that make a plant GO."[18] Similarly in "Young Sycamore," the human mind, another example of a biological design, is reenvisioned as a mechanism, analogous to the formal structure of the poem.[19]

Williams, however, was not fully comfortable with this view to which his acceptance of a certain style seemed to commit him.[20] In the 1937 dialogue on poetry and architecture, for example, he tries to explain why he rejects the " 'back to humanity, back to the soil' business" about the organic production of art while still believing that people are the "origin of every bit of life that can possibly inhabit any structure" (*SE* 178). His prose reflects his difficulties with the vocabulary he had available to him. People, he continues, "represent, in themselves, the structure which art . . . Put it this way: If we don't cling to the warmth which breathes into a house or a poem alike from human need . . . the whole matter has nothing to hold it together and becomes structurally weak" (*SE* 178).

The first ellipsis in the above quotation is Williams's, and seems to indicate his unwillingness or inability to say what the structure of art has to do with the structure of people. The logical way to complete the sentence would be to suggest, as "Young Sycamore" suggests, that art also represents, or repeats, the structure found in human beings. Such a conclusion, however, does not locate people as the origin of the life that inhabits structures like plants as well as poems and buildings. And Williams usually wanted to insist, as an essay from around 1926 entitled "What is the Use of Poetry" put it, that poetry "returns authority to man."[21] Hence he stops and proposes instead that all inventions arise from human need. This proposal avoids the more radical implications of adopting a machine aesthetic, but still it does not fully answer the question of how, in the practical American context Williams set for himself, one might show that poetry is important and necessary. Indeed, moments such as this in Williams's prose underline why he felt the need to find a more convincing way of defining poetry and its importance.

In 1944, Williams cautioned that the "arts have a *complex* relation to society" (*SE* 256). Exploring one aspect of his attempts to define this relationship illuminates the development of Williams's poetry and poetics. More importantly, in adopting a modern style commonly associated with the rise of technology and in simultaneously attempting an analysis of American modernity generally, Williams reveals the difficulties involved in sustaining a defense of modern poetry or in describing its importance given the values of modern America and the Americans for and to whom Williams wanted his poetry to speak.

Notes

1. Parenthetical citations are as follows: A: *Autobiography* (1951; New York: New Directions, 1967). CEP: *Collected Earlier Poems* (1951; New York: New Directions, 1966). I: *Imaginations* (New York: New Directions, 1970). IAG: *In the American Grain* (1925; New York: New Directions, 1966). SE: *Selected Essays* (1954; New York: New Directions, 1969). SSA: *Interviews*, ed. Linda Wagner (New York: New Directions, 1976).

2. *The Hieroglyphics of a New Speech: Cubism, Stieglitz, and the Early Poetry of William Carlos Williams* (Princeton: Princeton University Press, 1969), pp. 190–91.

3. "Introduction," *William Carlos Williams: A Collection of Critical Essays*, ed. J. Hillis Miller (Englewood Cliffs, New Jersey: Prentice-Hall, 1966), p. 12.

4. In *William Carlos Williams: A Collection of Critical Essays*, pp. 3 and 8, Miller describes the tree as nonsymbolic, but he goes on to note that "Young Sycamore" exemplifies Williams's most characteristic mode of describing motion. See also Richard A. Macksey, " 'A Certainty of Music': Williams' Changes," in *William Carlos Williams: A Collection of Critical Essays*, pp. 132–47, and J. Hillis Miller, *Poets of Reality: Six Twentieth-Century Writers* (New York: Atheneum, 1969), pp. 328–55, on Williams's *cycles*.

5. Indeed, the trunk's "undulant / thrust" is recalled by Williams's description of the undulant character of both poems and machines in the 1944 introduction to *The Wedge* (SE 256).

6. *Critic As Scientist*, pp. 244–46, contains an insightful critique of this side of Williams's poetics, as does *The Meanings of Measure*, p. 137, which proposes that Williams may draw on Emerson for such ideas.

7. *A Recognizable Image*, p. 137.

8. *The Hieroglyphics of a New Speech*, pp. 164–65; *Poets of Reality*, pp. 306–07.

9. *The Visual Text of William Carlos Williams*, pp. 21 and 14, n. 7. Although I agree with Sayre's reservations about those who accept Williams's prose statements without noticing how the poems work, I maintain that Williams's prose disclaimers grow out of his attraction to a poetics that did not fully satisfy him.

10. Williams describes Sheeler's later art as "subtler particularization, the abstract if you will" (SE 233).

11. In a 1950 interview with John W. Gerber, transcribed by Emily Mitchell Wallace, Williams noted: "Off center, that's what eccentric means" (SSA 15).

12. See *The Meanings of Measure*, especially pp. 106–12, on Williams's exploration of expressive and mimetic theories of art. J. Hillis Miller, in "Williams' *Spring and All* and the Progress of Poetry," *Daedalus* 99 (1970):415–29, also discusses Williams's early simultaneous attraction to theories of the imagination as mimesis, revelation, and creation *ex nihilo*. Finally, see David Walker's suggestion in *The Transparent Lyric: Reading and Meaning in the Poetry of Stevens and Williams* (Princeton: Princeton University Press, 1984), p. 23, that Williams's poems deliberately refuse to let his readers "rest secure in any fixed, comfortable pattern of seeing or thinking." In view of Cushman's suggestions about how the poems express "antagonistic cooperation" (p. 112) and in view of the double status, as metaphor and as objective description, of the concluding image of "Young Sycamore," there may well be a subdued pun on the phrase "the horns of a dilemma" in the image of the horned twigs.

13. See Cushman's arguments on stanzaic patterns and Williams's use of measure as both scheme and trope, as well as Sayre's description of how Williams's understanding of Cubism and Objectivism informs his shorter, stanzaically patterned poems that consist of apparently objective description (*The Meanings of Measure*, pp. 3, 93–99; *The Visual Text of Williams Carlos Williams*, pp. 71–73).

14. In *The Transparent Lyric*, p. 20, David Walker notes a possible source of this idea of impersonality in the writings of Cubist and Precisionist artists and further discusses how

impersonality did not necessarily mean lack of emotion. My argument is not that Williams equated the impersonal with the unemotional, but that he at times had other definitions of emotion—as *loosening* and as rooted in a person—which were not as easily reconciled with the aesthetic under discussion, given the American audience for whom he wrote.

15. *Selected Prose of T. S. Eliot*, ed. Frank Kermode (New York: Farrar, Straus and Giroux, 1975), p. 40. Obviously, I have ignored the complexity of Eliot's discussion of the artist's extinction of personality in order to make my point about the common association between impersonality and science. I could equally have invoked others; for example, Auden rebukes Spender for his love of classical music by saying that "the poet's attitude must be absolutely detached, like that of a surgeon or scientist" (cited by Julian Symons, *The Thirties: A Dream Revolved* [London: Cresset Press, 1960], p. 13).

16. The image may be borrowed from Moore, who reviewed Roget's *Thesaurus*, defining it, typically, in more biological terms as "analogous to the laboratory scientist's classification of species" ("Briefer Mention," *Dial* 80 [May 1926]:431); she also called Williams "our Audubon" in her speech presenting him with the Russell Loines Memorial Award in 1951 (YALC), again borrowing from other scientific disciplines.

17. Cecilia Tischi has pointed out that Williams's descriptions of poems as machines and of words cleansed in acid baths may draw on the image of words as precision parts, which the poet then creatively assembles ("Medicine and Machines Made of Words"). [Reprinted in part in this volume.]

18. "Belly Music," *Others* 5 (July 1919):26.

19. Tischi describes how Williams's training, among other things, would have made him see plants as well as human beings as machines or structures, that is, "to see the material world virtually as an engineer would" ("Medicine and Machines Made of Words").

20. Henry Sayre agrees that "Precisionism, Objectivism and the aesthetics of the machine . . . were finally antagonistic to at least a part of [Williams's] sensibility" ("After *The Descent of Winter*," p. 24).

21. "What is the Use of Poetry," p. 10.

Paterson and Epic Tradition

PETER SCHMIDT

In the traditional epic, the action begins *in medias res*, with the hero and his companions farthest from their goal. The narrative approaches its end as the hero approaches his home: Odysseus' reformed Ithaca, mankind's Christian paradise regained, William Wordsworth's mature retrospection, Whitman's transference of his quest for the union of body and soul to the reader. Conventionally, epic narrative also has two points of view. One is prospective and dramatic, recreating the past adventures of the book's hero. The other is retrospective and (relatively) static, magisterially framing the action to let us know not only that its events have previously occurred but also that their meaning and their part in the larger story of the hero's race have already been defined. This retrospective point of view can be said to operate even in epics like Vergil's *Aeneid* or John Milton's *Paradise Lost*, which seem at first glance to end still in the middle of their stories. In both cases, the endings allude by their self-conscious incompleteness to the larger story of which they are a part. For Vergil, this story is the rise of Augustan Rome, which had already occurred when he composed the *Aeneid*; for Milton, it is God's judgment of man, which will occur at the end of time. From Augustus Caesar's point of view in history or God's point of view above history, the epics are retrospective. In the romantic period, the epic's prospective and retrospective points of view began to dissolve into one, creating an epic without a frame in which the poet's developing consciousness became the one subject in romantic art that had the nobility and universality traditional epic narratives required. Some indication of this redefinition of epic retrospection by romanticism can be seen in Wordsworth, who planned a four-part epic describing his growth as a poet but was able to finish only its prelude. As the opening lines of *The Prelude* make clear, however, the poem is narrated retrospectively, from the vantage point of the poet's mature consciousness. It is English romanticism's version of the retrospective epic. American romanticism was more radical. Whitman's egotistically sublime "Song of Myself" is also a poem about the poet's developing consciousness, but unlike Wordsworth's it is brazenly ahistorical and open-ended and thus carries to an extreme the process of conflating the twin points of view that had been begun by Wordsworth. Whitman's poet-protagonist does not have a past and a present identity so much as two selves perpetually in flux, the natural "Me myself" and the artificial (or social) "the other I am." And as is well known, the last sentence of the poem in the 1855 edition did not end with a period. This was because Whitman's quest itself could not end; it was *periodic*, to be continued by each reader who takes Whitman up on his challenge to make himself the hero of his own life. Twentieth-century epics, most notably Pound's, have now generally made these unfinished and unfinishable histories of the growth of the poet's mind the norm for the epic, so that any firm separation between retrospective and prospective points of view becomes impossible. Eliot's *Four Quartets* and James Merrill's *The Changing Light at Sandover* are calculated exceptions to this generalization; they both pointedly try to reestablish the extratemporal perspective and formal closure of Dante's long poem as a model.

Recently several critics have tied *Paterson* firmly to romantic epic tradition by stressing that the protagonist, Dr. Paterson, gradually matures during the course of the poem. In their account, Dr. Paterson possesses an idealized, mythic vision of the Beautiful Thing at the opening of the poem, but he loses it and then slowly learns to search instead for a humbler, more time-bound vision that concedes that in modern Paterson beauty will necessarily be imperfect and impermanent. James Breslin in particular has drawn our attention to the implications of the scene involving Dr. Paterson and a poor black woman that follows the fire storm in Book Three. Dr. Paterson encounters the woman in a basement and suddenly recognizes in her all the primal power that the library lacked—power for which he has been searching since the beginning of the poem. The woman becomes a battered Kora or Persephone figure, imperfect and even filthy but carrying within her all of nature's powers of renewal. "I can't be half gentle enough, / half tender enough / toward you," he says, humbled and awed, and then sings,

> BRIGHTen
>
>   the cor
>
>   ner
>
> where   you   are!
>
> (*P*, 128)[1]

("Corner" is split by a line break here to emphasize the parallel with "core" and "Kora.") As Breslin has shown, Dr. Paterson in this scene has changed markedly since the previous section of Book Three. When he encountered the same woman then, he first turned her into a virgin in a "white lace dress," and then when she did not conform to his idealized fantasy self-righteously treated her as if she were a whore:

> (Then, my anger rising) TAKE OFF YOUR
> CLOTHES! I didn't ask you
> to take off your skin   .   I said your
> clothes, your clothes. You smell
> like a whore. I ask you to bathe in my
> opinions, the astonishing virtue of your
> lost body (I said)
>
> (P, 104–105)

Williams here unflinchingly records Dr. Paterson's brutal treatment of the woman but also includes key phrases in parentheses that separate Williams the narrator from Dr. Paterson the protagonist, therefore encouraging us to criticize Dr. Paterson's actions and rhetoric. Such ironic asides in parentheses are absent from the later lyric rhapsody sung by the contrite Dr. Paterson to the woman (P, 128) and help to portray Dr. Paterson's partial regeneration, his new willingness to find beauty in this world, not an ideal one of his own making. Much of the drama of *Paterson* can therefore be uncovered if we attend to Dr. Paterson's own struggle to change and the many successes and reversals he undergoes.[2]

Despite many instances of Dr. Paterson's growing self-knowledge, however, the examples of anger, despair, and divorce that surround Dr. Paterson at the start of the poem become dominant in Books Three and Four, thereby changing the overall mood of Books One through Four from celebratory to satiric. Book One began in prehistory, with Dr. Paterson witnessing the male and female principles of the poem interpenetrating perfectly.

> Paterson lies in the valley under the Passaic Falls
> its spent waters forming the outline of his back. He
> lies on his right side, head near the thunder
> of the waters filling his dreams!
> . . . .
> And there, against him, stretches the low mountain.
> The Park's her head, carved, above the Falls, by the quiet
> river; Colored crystals the secret of those rocks
>
> (P, 6, 8)

This mythic and timeless union is immediately counterpointed by a vision of modern spiritual, sexual, and intellectual dysfunction, as represented by "automatons" living in the cities,

> Who because they
> neither know their sources nor the sills of their
> disappointments walk outside their bodies aimlessly

for the most part,
locked and forgot in their desires—unroused.

(P, 6)

At the start of *Paterson*, the theme of marriage predominates, and
the passages introducing the poem's examples of divorce are kept clearly
subordinate. The later books shift their focus downstream from the Falls
(first to the park by the Falls, then to the areas of Paterson below the Falls
such as the library, then to New York City and the Atlantic Ocean), and
examples of spiritual and physical divorce play an increasingly prominent
part in the poem. The economy is shown to be more usurious, the language
more corrupt, the communication between people—especially between lovers—more sterile. In Book Four, Section II, admittedly, Madame Curie
emerges as a heroine, and as such represents an advance beyond the grim
frustration of the lesbian Corydon in the poem's previous section. But viewing
Madame Curie in the context of all of Book Four, we see that she is surrounded
by figures representing self-destruction rather than self-discovery: Corydon,
the murderer Jack Johnson, the "blood-red" Atlantic, and the shark that
snaps at his own guts (P, 200), among others. Even Curie's own important
discovery of how to split the uranium atom and release energy (P, 175–78)
is parodied in the same section of the poem by another kind of splitting,
in which a corrupt evangelist accepts "27 Grand" for his efforts to divide
striking Paterson mill workers by "calling them to God" instead (P,
172–73). Book Four, Section II, in other words, is not a "visionary" answer
to Corydon's mock pastoral in the first section; its hopeful vision glows
strongly at times, but most often in this particular section and in Book Four
as a whole we feel the leaden oppressiveness of history.[3] In general, Book
Four reads like a long mock pastoral with few truly pastoral or visionary
interludes. It is dominated by figures in historical and modern Paterson who
distort pastoral's traditional celebration of love, fertility, labor, and honor,
and by beasts like the shark, which eats its own guts and thus is a grotesque
parody of the interpenetrating River and Mountain at the beginning of Book
One.

Book Four also represents the sharpest reversal in the poem of Dr.
Paterson's epic quest to discover the Beautiful Thing. At the end of Book
Three, he was hoping to make a fresh start. And, indeed, the homage he
paid to the black Kora figure had suggested that he might succeed. But by
the opening of Book Four, Dr. Paterson seems as far as he has ever been
from his goals of reforming society, language, and himself. The liberating
clearing of the ground accomplished by the flood and the fire in Book Three
has been lost; Book Four is set in the most congested locale of the entire
poem, the shores and the mouth of the polluted Passaic River as it enters
the Hudson and then the Atlantic. As Corydon says at the start of the book,
the three guano-stained rocks in the East River that she sees out of her window

are "all that's left of the elemental, the primitive / in this environment" (P, 152). Even Dr. Paterson himself is apparently not immune from this corruption. At one point the poem's narrative comments sardonically,

> Oh Paterson! Oh married man!
> He is the city of cheap hotels and private
> entrances . of taxis at the door, the car
> standing in the rain . . .
> . . . .
> Goodbye, dear . I had a wonderful time.
> Wait! There's something . but I've forgotten.
>   (P, 154)

"He is the city": Dr. Paterson as a sleazy city is much closer to the "automatons" in Book One or to the exhausted Tiresias of *The Waste Land* who imitated the clichés of conversation ("Goodnight ladies, goodnight, sweet ladies") than he is to the mythic giant Paterson in the poem's opening pages or to the humble but resolute poet at the end of Book Three. Moreover, despite Dr. Paterson's discovery of Madame Curie, Social Credit, and so on, in the later episodes of Book Four, he is largely reduced to satirizing stale literary conventions rather than finding ways to make those conventions new: like Corydon, his alter ego, he writes a long mock-pastoral poem. Compared with his deliriously successful obliteration of tradition in Book Three, this attack on tradition in Four seems labored and ineffectual. The "white-hot man" (P, 123) of Book Three reshapes and invents; the exhausted man of Book Four largely resigns himself to parody, documentary, and nostalgia.

Dr. Paterson's tragic descent seems consistent both with the topography of the Passaic River valley, which descends toward the sea, and with certain general principles of Dada that appear to have influenced the structure of *Paterson*. The Dadaists believed that art and ideas petrify and therefore have to be discarded soon after they are invented. This is why they urged artists to forget everything they learned; the memory of what they and others have done would impede their efforts to do new things. Dada thus made artists martyrs to the impossible ideal of perpetual self-renewal. As J. Hillis Miller has noted, Williams consistently discriminated between creative shaping energy and the passive forms created by that force and then left to congeal as the force passes on.[4] In Book Four of *Paterson*, Williams calls this shaping force "the radiant gist," while the stale forms of beauty that congeal after the creative force passes on are called both "the final crystallization" and "lead" (P, 109, 178). In Williams' earlier volume *Kora in Hell*, he imagined creativity and decadence as a wheel cycling between upturn and downturn: "When the wheel's just at the up turn it glimpses horizon, zenith, all in a burst, the pull of the earth shaken off, a scatter of fragments, significance in a burst of water striking up from the base of a fountain. Then at the sickening turn toward death the pieces are joined into a pretty thing, a bouquet frozen in an icecake" (*I*, 71). The beginning of *Paterson* draws on this passage from *Kora in Hell* to represent the buoyant creativity of the Falls. Its waterdrops, Williams shows us, are suspended against gravity and against time: "fall, fall in air! as if / floating, relieved of their weight" (*P*, 8). But this energy gradually succumbs to its natural fate, to gravity and time; *Paterson* becomes dominated by references to blockage, divorce, decay, murder, and "pretty things" such as the stale literary parody used by Corydon in her *Corydon, a Pastoral* (*P*, 159–62). The shift in the epic's overall tone from sweet to sour is thus emphatic. All we need do is compare the first few pages of Books One and Four to see that the pure, spontaneous energy of the Falls has run its course. The free water of the Falls is now, Williams puns, "sea-bound" (*P*, 200).

At the conclusion of Book Four, Dr. Paterson awakens from this suicidal nightmare of modern history: "Waken from a dream, this dream of / the whole poem . sea-bound" (*P*, 200). If the descent of Dr. Paterson imitates the fate of creativity in time (inevitably declining into decadence, parody, death), at the very end of Book Four Williams' hero eludes such a fate by refusing to be either sea-bound or tradition-bound. He audaciously stands the traditional conclusion of the epic on its head:

> I say to you, Put wax rather in your
> ears against the hungry sea
> it is not our home!
>
> .   draws us in to drown, of losses
> and regrets   .
>
> (*P*, 201)

Books One through Four do not conclude as a traditional epic does, when the hero arrives home, but when the hero realizes that he is *farthest* from home, from the Passaic Falls and their unending creative power. And when Williams wittily alludes to Odysseus' blocking his sailors' ears from the Sirens' song, he reminds us that as the wily pilot of his own epic craft he hears the beautiful music of epic precedent, the temptation to follow the "correct" way of ending an epic, but refuses to give in to it.

For Dr. Paterson, discovering how far he is from home is the first step toward a successful Odyssean escape from the forces that entrap him. During the very last pages of Book Four images of cleanliness and fertility dominate the poem once more. After swimming in the sea, Dr. Paterson is greeted joyfully by his dog (one of his alter egos throughout the epic), spits the seed from a beach plum out onto the dunes, and then heads inland with the "steady roar, as of a distant / waterfall" on his mind (*P*, 203). In doing so, he reverses the direction of the entire poem and begins a new quest to recover the creative powers he has gradually lost. Williams, of course, originally planned to have his epic be only four books long. He thus intended to conclude the poem at the moment that his hero, after a pause, renews his quest. Such an ending is a prospective or "open" one, despite Williams' references to "the eternal close" and "the end" on the book's last page. We leave Dr. Paterson as he stands on the dunes contemplating an endless series of other Odyssean descents into history—and, consequently, an endless series of further losses and self-defeats. Williams emphasizes this pessimistic, Dadaist truth by interrupting Dr. Paterson's lyrical meditation on rebirth with a reference to the eternal violence of history: "John Johnson, from Liverpool, England, was convicted after 20 minutes conference by the Jury. On April 30th, 1850, he was hung in full view of thousands who had gathered on Garrett Mountain and adjacent house tops to witness the spectacle" (*P*, 203). This juxtaposition of a rebirth and an execution contains in miniature the entire descent of Books One through Four.

When Book Four was published in 1951, Williams thought he was done. But after recovering from several strokes, he conceived and wrote Book Five, inspired by his harrowing of death. By adding it to the first four books of *Paterson* in 1958, he makes us read the ending of Book Four differently from how we read it when considering Books One through Four alone. The ending of Book Four implies that a sequel to the epic does not need to be written because any further adventures of Dr. Paterson would inevitably be other descents made up of gradually increasing despairs and diminishing awakenings. But if Books One through Five are taken as a unit, it seems that when Dr. Paterson walks on the dunes at the end of Book Four he meditates not just on another descent but on Book Five, which thoroughly revises the role played by descent in Williams' poem.

In Book Five the destructive and creative principles that had been at war throughout the previous books are wrested at last into equilibrium, so that each creative "upturn" and the decadent "downturn" are fiercely held in balance. If the mythical nature-goddess the Mountain dominated the opening of Book One and the decadent Corydon the opening of Book Four, in Book Five Williams introduces a paired or doubled image of women: "The moral / / proclaimed by the whorehouse / could not be better proclaimed / by the virgin" (*P*, 208). This doubling continues throughout the book as Williams counterpoints references to powerful women (including Mary in Brueghel's Nativity painting, the Virgin in the Unicorn tapestries, Sappho, and the anonymous passerby on pages 219–20 to whom Williams impulsively dedicates all his poems) with those to barren or self-destructive women (such as the whores in Gilbert Sorrentino's letters on pages 214–15, or the poignant old woman on the penultimate page of the poem who wore "a china doorknob / in her vagina to hold her womb up"). Similarly, if Dr. Paterson migrates in Books One through Four from expressing the comic realm of mythic creative power free from time (the Falls and the Mountain) to the tragic, degenerative fate of all that is born into history (Paterson the city), in Book Five fallen history and the eternal world of art are interwoven into a harmonious, tragicomic design. The descent motif no longer controls the poem: its powers are continually counteracted by motifs of ascent and recovery.

In Book Five, moreover, Williams gives Dr. Paterson the homecoming denied him in Book Four:

> Paterson, from the air
>   above the low range of its hills
>   across the river
> on a rock-ridge
>   has returned to the old scenes
>   to witness
>
> What has happened
>   since Soupault gave him the novel
>   the Dadaist novel
> to translate—
>   *The Last Nights of Paris.*
>   "What has happened to Paris
> since that time?
>   and to myself?"
>
>   A WORLD OF ART
>   THAT THROUGH THE YEARS HAS
>   *SURVIVED!*
>   (P, 209)

Dada's principles guided Dr. Paterson during his descent into decadence in Books One through Four. But in Book Five Williams puts Dada in its place, satirizing it and carefully restricting its destructive energy. The movement that was to end all art has survived, as have the works it meant to destroy. The apocalyptic Surrealist novel *Last Nights of Paris* (written in 1929 by Philippe Soupault, who coauthored *Les Champs magnétiques* with André Breton) has been translated into another language, and Paris itself has survived two European wars. Dada's pessimistic view of the fate of art is now counterpointed by a faith that creative power is perpetually able to escape from the forces that try to destroy it. As Williams caustically says near the very end of Book Five, alluding to Duchamp's celebrated announcement (which later proved untrue) that he was rejecting art for chess: "Equally laughable / is to assume to know nothing, a / chess game" (P, 239). Book Five of *Paterson* thus restores the traditional epic conclusion that Williams excluded from his earlier ending for the poem. That is, if we take Books One through Four as a unit, we find that the epic ends with the hero realizing that he is farthest from home. But if we consider Books One through Five together, the poem ends classically, with the hero symbolically returning to the Falls, to a world where the eternal and the time-bound, the creative and the decadent, may be held in balance.

Williams acknowledges in the last lines of *Paterson* that this balancing act characterizes Book Five as it does no other book in the poem. The lines describe a satyr's dance. The "tragic" beat of the satyr's foot represents history as a tragedy in which creativity is lost and the artist is inevitably reduced to Dadaist satire and erasure ("We know nothing" [*P*, 239]). Because the satyr is half-man, half-goat, he can be seen as an emblem of a grotesque degeneration from the norm of what man should be, and is thus connected etymologically for Williams with satire, the mode of literature, including Dada, that criticizes such deviations. As Williams had said at the end of Book One, quoting J. A. Symonds, "The Greeks displayed their acute aesthetic sense of propriety, recognizing the harmony which subsists between crabbed verses and the distorted subjects with which they dealt—the vices and perversions of humanity—as well as their agreement with the snarling spirit of the satirist. Deformed verse was suited to deformed morality" (*P*, 40). But throughout Book Five Williams also syncopates this tragic, "deformed" beat with what he calls a "pre-tragic" or comic one.[5] It, too, is associated with the satyr, but in this case the satyr represents man's sexual and spiritual potency, his ability to create.

> the Satyrs, a
> pre-tragic play,
> a satyric play!
> All plays
> were satyric when they were most devout.
> Ribald as a Satyr!
>
> Satyrs dance!
> all the deformities take wing
> (*P*, 221)

The complementary meanings of Williams' references to satyrs thus contain in miniature the contrapuntal, tragicomic structure of Book Five itself.

We know that in the late 1950s Williams decided that *Paterson* was to have been an open-ended epic, for drafts for a sixth book survive. As the poem now stands (or dances, rather), it is an epic documenting the history of a locality, Paterson, New Jersey, in which its hero, Dr. Paterson, succeeds when he discovers that local history is both his proper home and his place of exile. He must journey downriver and face the failures of his city and his self—he must, in his own words, look "death / in the eye" (*P*, 106). But by the end of Book Four he is also freed to somersault upstream, aware that his decline into satire, Dadaist disgust, and violence is merely part of an inexorable creative dance that will soon counter its own rhythms. If the first four books of Williams' epic seem to descend from their early poetic heights (as most contemporary critics, comparing the poem to the other epics they knew, saw and protested), Williams would perhaps answer that that is the way time, rivers, and modern epic poems naturally flow. But Book Five countered Dadaist pessimism by describing the fate of art and the body in time without despairing of the mind's ability to rediscover its creative heights. Books Four and Five thus construct two endings for *Paterson*. The first is an open ending, with the poet beginning a new journey. The second is a truly closed ending in which the poet concludes an old journey: as Williams says near the end of Book Five,

> The (self) direction has been changed
>   the serpent
>   its tail in its mouth
> "the river has returned to its beginnings"
>   (*P*, 233)

In creating two endings for his long poem, Williams fashioned an agitated equilibrium between the impulses toward closure and exposure, retrospection and progression, that have informed epics from the *Iliad* on.

Notes

1. *Paterson* (New York: New Directions, 1969).

2. James Breslin, *William Carlos Williams: An American Artist* (New York: Oxford UP, 1970), pp. 192–95; for a more general discussion of the significance of "reversal" in the poem, see pp. 178–82. Paul Mariani first pointed out the core / Kore pun in *William Carlos Williams: A New World Naked* (New York: McGraw-Hill, 1981), pp. 581–82. [Both books are reprinted in part in this volume.]

3. Breslin, p. 201.

4. Miller, *Poets of Reality* (Cambridge: Harvard UP, 1965), pp. 328–44. [Reprinted in part in this volume.]

5. See also Margaret Lloyd, *William Carlos Williams' "Paterson"* (Cranbury, N. J.: Associated UP), pp. 267–71.

Attitudes Toward History

Brian A. Bremen

Williams "moves in on" historical texts such as Cotton Mather's *The Wonders of the Invisible World*, Kip's *The Early Jesuit Missions in North America*, Olson and Bourne's *The Northmen, Columbus, and Cabot, 985–1503* and the *Narratives of the Career of Hernando De Soto, Conquest: Dispatches of Cortez from the New World*, Franklin's *Poor Richard's Almanac* and *Autobiography*, along with the papers and memoirs of Burr, Hamilton, Washington, and Poe. And in doing so, Williams performs a complicated act of "ideological analysis" in *In the American Grain* that is at the same time a re-formation of American "history" and "tradition."[1] Williams's project here is to "rewrite" historical texts in order both to expose what history *is* by revealing a Puritan tradition of domination and subversion at the textual level, and to suggest what history *should be* by including those voices that tradition has repressed or silenced. In doing so, Williams's "history lesson" re-presents "the task of effective-historical consciousness" in an effort to enlarge that discursive space in which self-creation can occur.

Williams dramatically re-presents what Gadamer called "the task of effective-historical consciousness" in the conversation he re-creates in "The Virtue of History." The two "voices" Williams uses bring out that "tension" between the "horizon of a particular present" that sees Burr in his generally received historical position of being a "dangerous man, one who ought not to be trusted with the reins of government" (*IAG* 190) and the "text" made vocal by Burr's defender. In presenting this section in the form of a conversation, literally the "conversation of history," Williams makes clear several of Gadamer's points about the "fusion of horizons." First, and perhaps most readily visible in this "conversation," are the "prejudices" that Gadamer says are brought out in this tension between historical horizons, along with the "otherness" of "historical consciousness." In this way, the two voices are both "something laid over a continuing tradition" and act dialectically to "recombine what . . . [is] distinguished" in the "unity of the historical horizon" thus acquired.[2]

This final "fusion of horizons"—what Gadamer calls the "task of effective-historical consciousness"—is finally left up to the reader, however, as Williams ends this section with the two "voices" in disagreement:

> But passion will obscure our sense so that we eat sad stuff and call it nectar. Burr was heavily censured by his time, immoral, traitorous and irregular. What they say of him, I still believe.
>
> Believe it if you will but listen to this story: Near the end of his life a lady said to him: "Colonel, I wonder if you were ever the gay Lothario they say you were." The old man turned his eyes, the lustre still undiminished, toward the lady—and lifting his trembling finger said in his quiet, impressive whisper: "They say, they say, they say. Ah, my child, how long are you going to continue to use those dreadful words? Those two little words have done more harm than all others. Never use them, my dear, never use them."
>
> (*IAG* 207)

While Williams's "conversation" is admittedly weighted against the "swing of the pendulum" in favor of Burr's "textual" defender, it is important to note that the disagreement itself is still recorded. What "they say" is still a part of history, shaping the "tradition." What's added here is Burr's own voice, which has always been apart from that tradition. Moreover, Burr (and Williams) only admonish against the unquestioned acceptance of what "they say," and this notion of interrogating both the "facts" as well as the very consciousness with which we interrogate those facts is acted out in Williams's text. We need to be aware of both voices in the conversation. Moreover, this interrogation is grounded neither in foundationalist thinking, nor in some "hermeneutics of suspicion." Williams gives us instead the voices of two suspicious hermeneuticists. Finally, by forcing the reader to mediate between these "voices," Williams also forces an empathic act of the imagination analogous to the one he creates in his prose / poetry sequences by creating the opportunity for our own "identification" of and within the conversation. "The Virtue of History" (both as a title and as a quality) is an act of "engaged diagnosis" like the ones we discussed in Chapter 3. Here, a fluid exchange needs to be maintained between the nomothetic law—what "they say"—and the idiographic—the unique case of Aaron Burr—in an act of empathic "identification" that enlarges the tradition of American "identity" by leaving "a vantage open (in tradition) for that which Burr possessed in such remarkable degree" (*IAG* 197).

The "history" that Williams wants us to "identify" here marks an important corrective to what Williams sees are the dominant "symbols of authority"—the workings of Washington, Hamilton, Jefferson, and the rest of the "Virginia Junto" (*IAG* 202)—just as . . . the "virtues" that Williams "coaches" in this "history" mark an important adjustment of Pound's more metaphysical notion of "virtú." In particular, Williams enlarges the notion of "the individual" from the pursuit of "self-interest" as embodied in Hamiltonian Federalism to Burr's "sense of the individual"—"the basis on which the war was fought, instantly the war was over began to be debauched" (*IAG* 194). The "individual" is the cornerstone of Williams's "history lesson," though Williams's notion of the individual shares almost nothing with the bourgeois ideal of autonomous, rugged individualism. This notion, we will see below, relies on an act of forgetting that is antithetical to Williams's project. Rather, Williams's "individual" is a "humanity, his own, free and independent, unyielding to the herd, practical, direct" (*IAG* 204). As such, the "individual" constructs his "identity" within the discursive space of what *should be* history from a firmly cathected set of values. These values grow out of the "transformation of narcissistic energies" in their sense of "identifying with" others but maintaining an integrity between self and other. A crucial part of these values is a near-Stoic notion of "servitude" that, Williams says, is "foreign to us: a trick for foreigners, a servant's trick. We are afraid that we couldn't do it and retain our self-esteem. . . . Thus we see of what our self-esteem is made" (*IAG* 176). This sense of "self-esteem" is constructed on "self-interest" and depends on structures of domination for its sense of "identity." Consequently it rejects "servitude" out of fear and replaces it with "service," which Williams explains as "Sending supplies to relieve the cyclone sufferers in Indiana" (*IAG* 176). This "self-esteem" also relies wholly on notions of difference, and so structures of racial, sexual, and ethnic prejudice all become a vital part of this structure and its need to reject "servitude." As Williams puts it, "Do not serve another for you might have to TOUCH him and he might be a JEW or a NIGGER" (*IAG* 177, Williams's emphases).

Williams's notion of self-creation is neither unrestrained nor reliant upon a stable notion of self. Self-creation always takes place for Williams within the discursive space of a tradition. As Williams says of Samuel de Champlain, "Is it merely in a book? So am I then, merely in a book" (*IAG* 69), and the "textual act" of self-creation depends on those "books" that make up the tradition in which we "find" ourselves. The American "identity" is made up of that "Babel of voices," that "corporate we" that Burke "identifies" in *Attitudes Toward History*. Consequently, Williams's struggle with Eliot over the the demarcation of tradition—over the "symbols of authority"—is a very real struggle for political power. We will examine Eliot's tradition more fully in the next chapter; for now it should be clear that a tradition that rigorously excludes the voices of women and minorities effectively relegates these groups to a subordinate silence, while it also denies them both active subjectivity and the possibility of "identifying" themselves with their own voices within its "conversations."

Williams asserts early on in *In the American Grain* that we are like

the Caribs whom The Great Maker had dropped through a hole in the sky among their islands; they whose souls lived in their bodies, many souls in one body. . . .

> Fierce and implacable we kill them but their souls dominate us. Our men, our blood, but their spirit is master. It enters us, it defeats us, it imposes itself. . . .

> If men inherit souls this is the color of mine. We are, too, the others. Think of them! The main islands were thickly populated with a peaceful folk when Christ-over found them. But the orgy of blood which followed, no man has written. We are the slaughterers.

> *(IAG 39–41)*

"We are, too, the others," and this "recognition" of both the self in the other and the other in the self may be the most vital part of Williams's notion of self-creation. As such, no one individual or group is either wholly valorized or condemned in this work. Christopher Columbus is both the discoverer of the "beautiful thing" that is the New World (*IAG* 26) and "Christ-over," the bringer of "an orgy of blood." Williams's discursive space of tradition and self-creation operates within the larger textual realm of history, whose narrative is one of power and domination: "History, history! We fools, what do we know or care? History begins for us with murder and enslavement, not with discovery. No, we are not Indians but we are men of their world. The blood means nothing; the spirit, the ghost of the land moves in the blood, moves the blood. It is we who ran to the shore naked, we who cried, 'Heavenly Man!' These are the inhabitants of our souls, our murdered souls that lie . . . agh" (*IAG* 39). Even Montezuma, generally valorized in critical descriptions, explains that "his people were not the aborigines of the land but that they had emigrated there in times past and ended by accepting the Spanish Monarch as his rightful and hereditary master" (*IAG* 31–32).

Williams's notions of "self" and of the "individual" follow along closely with the notion of "mutuality" and "narcissistic transformation" that we looked at in the first two chapters, and we can see them operate "dramatically" here in Burr's relationship to women. One of the charges "they say" against Burr was that he was "immoral," and Williams sees this charge as the "only defense" against the kind of "liberating force" that Burr's relationship to women possessed. Burr's "defender" argues that "He was perhaps the only one of the time who saw women, in the flesh, as serious, and they hailed and welcomed with deep gratitude and profound joy his serious knowledge and regard and liberating force—for them" (*IAG* 204–05). While Williams is guilty of idealizing the feminine as the embodiment of the imaginative and sensual "spirit" of the land, particularly in the De Soto section, we need to remember that for Williams the "feminine psychology" was "grounded" in an empirical relation to the "real," and unlike a "male psychology" of abstraction, it remained firm in its relationship to the concrete. Consequently, we need to "read" Williams's valorization of the feminine against the Puritan's "unofficial sexual indulgence and the plight of [their] women" (*IAG* 119).

Burr is praised in his regard for women because

> he kept their secrets; no man has a better record. Asked his opinion he could say of women: all seriousness, yet you must speak light nothings to them. The rest were frivolous with women. The rest denied them, condoned the female flesh, found them helpmates at the best and at the worst, horses, cattle, provincial accessories, useful workers to make coffee and doughnuts— and to be left to go crazy on the farms for five generations after—that's New England, or they'd hide the bull behind the barn, so that the women would not think it knew the cows were—Bah, feudal dolls gone wrong, that's Virginia. Women? necessary but not noble, not the highest, not deliciously a free thing, apart, *feminine*, a heaven;—afraid to delve in it save like so much dough. Burr found the spirit living there, free and equal, independent, springing with life. Or did he? I say if he did he was before his time. Surely they drank of him like water.
>
> (*IAG* 205)

Williams's own "identification with" Burr is nearly as complete as his "identifications with" Père Rasles and Poe, and in all three cases Williams's "exaggerations" are attempts to "swing back the pendulum" of commonly held opinion. But even Williams's idealization of the feminine here avoids the "aestheticization" of women into lifeless objects. Instead, the feminine is valued as "free and equal, independent, springing with life." Williams's greatest avatar of the feminine in this work—Jacataqua (who briefly meets Burr)—is valued for her active role as "Sachem" and as "poetically" giving "form" to "the positives that . . . give character and dignity to the damp mass of the overpowering but characterless resistance" (*IAG* 186).

Burr's relationship with women is an act of empathic identification that maintains the identity of "spirit" along with both the difference of sexuality and a relationship to the "real" that was immediate and open. This second difference is also, paradoxically, an "identity" for both Williams and Burr, as it forms the "ground" of both men's ideal of "creative democracy." It is here in his notion of "democracy" that Williams's own "frame of acceptance" approaches the "transcendental," marking the site where Williams's notions of writing coincide with his relations to women and the "common people." As Williams continues his "conversation," he explains,

> Burr knew what a democracy must liberate.
> What then?
> Men intact—with all their senses waking. He had, raised to a different level, the directness of "common people" which reformers, that is to say, schemers, commonly neglect, misname, misapprehend as if it were anything but to touch, to hear, to see, to smell, to taste.

Transcendental theory, my dear countryman.

What is; the delicious sincerity of pioneer people? In Burr this aristocratic strain, straight out of the ground, was *seeing* its own ground belied. To maintain the truth up through the scale is the hard thing.

(*IAG* 206, Williams's emphasis)

Williams's "other" openly questions the "transcendental" nature of his own belief both in his ideal of "contact" and in his romantically locating this "quality" in the "common people." It is this same quality that Williams will "quote" in "The Advent of the Slaves" as the only way that blacks— who are socially determined as *"nothing"* and "NOBODY"—come to be " 'ME' . . . That's SOMETHIN'. . . . There is a racial solidity, a racial irreducible minimum, which gives them poise in a world where they have no authority—" (*IAG* 209). And it is vital to note that Williams not only gives blacks the authority of having voiced their own language in this section, but also respects the integrity of that authority in voicing a desire to "write a play in collaboration with" a black man in his town (*IAG* 211). Most significantly, though, he records these African-American "voices" in his "conversation of history," making them a crucial part of his "tradition." This tradition is allied with Burr in the above section as Williams links Burr's valuation of the "common people" with the very source of Williams's poetry:

A while ago, just here, I heard a Polish woman saying to her daughter: "you bust your coat with your fifty sweaters."

What's that: You bust your coat with your fifty sweaters?

Its immediacy, its sensual quality, a pure observation, its lack of irritation, its lack of pretense, its playful exaggeration, its repose, its sense of design, its openness, its gayety, its unconstraint. It frees, it creates relief. In the great it is the same, or would be if it ever existed, a delicious sincerity (in greater things of course) not a scheme, nor a system of procedure—but careless truth.

(*IAG* 206)

Williams's poetics are his politics, and just as, as Williams himself once said, his poetry comes from "the mouths of Polish mothers" (*Autobiography*), his politics includes the voices that other writers either omit, repress, or seek to silence. But Williams's politics, like his poetics, are not a sentimental over-valuation of some "transcendental" ideals. Williams's matrix of "history" and "tradition" operates in a fluid realm of power, domination, and resistance, though Williams retains the possibility of human agency in the determination of that matrix. In this same way, Williams's poetry operates in a similarly textual realm of dominant traditions that can likewise be resisted and re-formed. To remain with the political, however, Williams's understanding of the forces of "history" and "tradition" demonstrates the complicated ways in which—while we can never exist outside of either one—we can influence both. In this way, Williams combines the "task of effective-historical consciousness" with Jameson's notion of "ideological analysis" by "the rewriting of the literary text in such a way that it may itself be grasped as the rewriting or restructuration of a prior ideological or historical subtext."[3] In particular, by exposing the ways in which the dominant Puritan tradition subsumes alternate traditions in its own rewriting of history, Williams can effectively create his own historical subtext of buried voices, making those alternate traditions once again available in order to enlarge the "corporate we" of American "identity."

But just as Burr was "the essence of the schemes the others made" (*IAG* 207), Williams himself embodies those "qualities" that make up part of the Puritan's contribution to the "American Grain," though it takes a Frenchman, Valéry Larbaud, to point this out to Williams in yet another "conversation of history" in the "Père Sebastian Rasles" section:

> This interests me greatly because I see you brimming—you, yourself—with those three things of which you speak: a puritanical sense of order, a practical mysticism as of the Jesuits, and the sum of all those qualities defeated in the savage men of your country by the first two. These three things I see still battling in your heart. This interests me greatly—and it pleases me still more that you show a taste for books. Does this indicate, I say to myself, a new force in your country? Are you today presenting me with a new spectacle, a man, no matter what his qualities may be, who has *begun* to reach a height but who still retains his warmth; that moment when all greatness is conceived. It is no more than a moment, it is the birth of a civilized interest in the world.
>
> No, no, no, I cried. I speak only of sources. I wish only to disentangle the obscurities that oppress me, to track them to the root and to uproot them—
>
> Continue, he said. Adding with a smile, You wish to uproot history, like those young men of the Sorbonne.
>
> No, I seek the support of history but I wish to understand it aright, to make it SHOW itself.
>
> Continue, continue.
>
> (*IAG* 116, Williams's emphases)

Larbaud is "a student" while Williams is "a block . . . the brutal thing itself" (*IAG* 107), and the "history lesson" he gets from Larbaud is a sense of his own "otherness"—a "recognition" of the other in the self. Again, both sides of the "conversation" make up the "lesson": "By the strength of religion alone, [the Puritans] surmounted all difficulties in which science has degraded us again today; all things they explain, with clarity and distinction. It is firm, it is solid, it holds the understanding in its true position, not beneath the surface of the facts, where it will drown, but up, fearlessly into a clear air, like science at its best, in a certain few minds. For our taste, it is perhaps a little grotesque, this explanation—but firm. There is vigor there—and by that a beauty" (*IAG* 110). As Williams will later say, "If history could be that which annihilated all memory of past things from our minds it would be a useful tyranny. But since it lives in us practically day by day we should fear it" (*IAG* 189). What Williams recognizes here is the inescapability of history. Williams, as the "brutal thing itself," is as much orderly Puritan as he is mystical French Jesuit, and sensual Indian. As Larbaud says in his conversation with Williams, "As with all histories, it begins with giants—cruel but enormous, who eat flesh. They were giants" (*IAG* 113), and the three giants of English Puritans, French Jesuits, and American Indians all stake their claim in the discursive space of Williams's own identity.

The Puritans were "the first American democracy," but it was also "they, in the end, who would succeed in making everything like themselves" (*IAG* 63), and their determination to make the new world over in their own likeness is anathema to Williams's notion of self-creation. This distinction is analogous to those differences between an oedipal model of domination and a narcissistic model of mutuality . . . , where the oedipal model divides the world into active self—modeled after the dominant father—and passive (m)other. The narcissistic model allows for both identification and difference with mother and father, holding this paradoxical relationship in tension.[4] All people, then, become potentially both self and other while, strictly defined, they are also always other. In this way notions of "identification" and "empathy" maintain this paradox of identity and difference by moving beyond power relations to achieve greater intersubjective understanding.

This ideal is embodied in the "Père Rasles" section in the example of Père Rasles himself, who sees the Indians as "his children" and yet respects the integrity of both their language and their ways. He shares with Burr the quality of being a "great listener," and "his generous spirit" is the "moral source" that Williams wants to "make Americans see" (*IAG* 122–23). But Williams admits that "much the Puritans complained of in the Jesuits was justified"—just as "much that Père Rasles might have said against the Puritan-English was also true"—leaving us with "two flaming doctrines" (*IAG* 127–28). Both Puritans and Jesuits are figured in the section using religion as a means of dominating and exploiting the Indian, and Puritanism and Catholicism both act as kinds of grammars for interpretation. The Puritan "grammar" is in effect a "grammar of transference"—like the one developed in Chapter 1—that remains within its own set "lines of projection" in order to read signs. Williams elsewhere calls it "this pale negative to usurp the place of that which really they were destined to continue" (*IAG* 66). Consequently, Williams says, "the Puritan, finding one thing like another in a world destined for blossom only in 'Eternity,' all soul, all 'emptiness' then here, was precluded from SEEING the Indian. They never realized the Indian in the least save as an unformed PURITAN. The *immoral-*

ity of such a concept, the inhumanity, the brutalizing effect upon their own minds, on their SPIRITS—they never suspected" (*IAG* 113, Williams's emphases). Catholicism is equally a "grammar of transference," but, Williams argues, it at least offers "ALLEVIATION" from "lack of sensual application, removed from without by an authority that represents mystery itself" (*IAG* 129) in its emphasis on ritual and the mystical.

Père Rasles combines this mystery and ritual within his own "grammar of translation" that seeks to maintain and appreciate the integrity of the other. As such, Rasles is described in terms of an empathic identification with the Indian—"In Rasles one feels THE INDIAN emerging from within the pod of his isolation from eastern understanding, he is released AN INDIAN. He exists, he is—it is an AFFIRMATION, it is alive" (*IAG* 121, Williams's emphases). But a "grammar of translation" is nonetheless a "grammar"—one that relies on the subjectivity of the translator to give as "true" a translation as possible by eliminating "prejudices" from his act. It is for this reason that the ideals of translation, mutuality, and identification all rely on the vehicle of conversation if they are to avoid becoming "grammars of transference." Only by recognizing the "otherness" of historical consciousness, as well as the subjectivity of the other itself, can we ensure against having translation or identification become forms of domination.

Consequently, an even more vital way the "Père Rasles" section embodies Williams's ideals of intersubjectivity and mutuality, which are intimately allied to his ideals of both democracy and the individual, is in the very act of conversing with Valéry Larbaud about books. Larbaud and Williams reveal each other's "prejudices" during the course of their talk, with Williams noting Larbaud's relatively detached, analytical appreciation of American history—"Cotton Mather's books, to you an enchanting diversion, a curious study" (*IAG* 116)—and Larbaud bringing out not only the three forces within Williams, but also an awareness of Williams's own "theoretical interests":

> It is good that you struggle to appreciate it. Proceed. Mather. *What* a force, still to interest you; it is admirable. But I find your interest "très théorique."
> What! I cried. Wait a bit. These men are not the only ones of these times.
> It is of books that we were speaking.
> It is of books that I wish to tell you.
> Then they live still, those books?
> I could not assure him that they did, those books of Mather's. As books, no, I said to him. But what is in them lives and there hides, as in a lair from whence it sallies now and then to strike terror through the land.
> And you would be the St. George? Are they then in such a bad state in America, in such a swamp? I thought—
> As always, I answered him. This fiery breath, as of a dragon, is to us a living thing. Our resistance to the wilderness has been too strong. It has

turned us anti-American, anti-literature. As a violent "puritanism" it breathes still. In these books is its seed.

(IAG 115–16)

Williams "cannot merely talk of books" here, and his "wish to drag this THING out by itself to annihilate it" (*IAG* 115) is the part of his "theory" of history that needs most to be reconsidered. Williams claims in this section that he speaks "only of sources. I wish only to disentangle the obscurities that oppress me, to track them to the root and to uproot them—" and that he seeks "the support of history but I wish to understand it aright, to make it SHOW itself." Williams knows that the American construction of identity most often takes place in an act of forgetting—"the fools do not believe that they have sprung from anything: bone, thought and action. They will not see that what they are is growing on these roots. . . . Their history is to them an enigma" (*IAG* 113). But the mere exposure of these "roots" will not alter that textual matrix of tradition in which self-creation occurs. Only by effectively "moving in on" these texts—by rewriting them in such a way that their own historical subtext of domination is revealed in an attempt to enlarge that tradition—can Williams get beyond his "theoretical interests" in them and effectively alter that matrix of history, making audible those voices that these texts would leave silent. Consequently, a section like "Cotton Mather's Wonders of the Invisible World" both reveals the effaced voice of Mather himself in a supposedly "neutral" account of the facts of witchcraft and makes visible the property squabbles and sexual jealousies beneath the accusations. "The May-Pole at Merry Mount" compares various accounts of the "incident of the May-pole at Merry Mount" to reveal the conscious burying of Thomas Morton's punning, sexual story beneath both Bradford's limited understanding of the forces at work in the incident and A. C. Adams's modern preface to Morton's *The New English Canaan*, which describes Morton as "a vulgar, loyalist libertine" (*IAG* 75).

But Williams's story here also embodies his historical project in an even more significant way by re-producing Williams's own historical conditions around the time of the work's production. The section begins with a string of names of artists that Williams met during his six week stay in Paris in 1924, the year before *In the American Grain* was published. The similarities between this opening and Williams's 1926 "Poem"—a list of figures from American history—makes clear the kinds of conflations between poetics and politics that we discussed above, as it also hints at Williams's differences with other modernists. Williams describes them as "*warily* conscious of a newcomer, but wholly without inquisitiveness—No wish to know; they were served" (*IAG* 105–06, original emphasis), and Williams's own "servitude" combines here with his desire to articulate an American tradition to begin to suggest both political and aesthetic distinctions between himself and writers like Pound and Eliot. . . . By incorporating his own history within the dialectic of his conversation with Larbaud, Williams embodies that paradoxical tension between identity and difference with an equally complicated tension between the living and the dead. Larbaud, a Frenchman, lives at "the bottom of an alley which opened out into a court, as of a decayed cloister" (*IAG* 107). Williams, "the brutal thing itself," would also "be the St. George" (*IAG* 107 & 115). In this way, Williams makes clear both what history *is* and what history *should be* through the textual construction of his own "identity" in a fusion of historical horizons that involves both the texts of the past and the text of Williams's present.

Notes

1. *IAG: In the American Grain* (New York: New Directions, 1956).
2. See Hans-Georg Gadamer, *Truth and Method* (New York: Crossroads, 1985), pp. 267–74, 305–41.
3. Fredric Jameson, "The Symbolic Inference," *Critical Inquiry* (Spring 1978): 511.
4. See Jessica Benjamin, *The Bonds of Love* (New York: Pantheon, 1988), pp. 159–81.

"Witness the Words Being Born":
The Miscarriage of Language
in Williams's Stecher Trilogy

SHERYL A. MYLAN

Williams's career as a pediatrician immersed him in ordinary life. His close-up view of children provided material for his stories and novels as well as a language to speak about artistic creation. In his *Autobiography*, he calls writers the "words' very parents";[1] sometimes he goes so far as to refer to his work as his children.[2] He also considered childbirth—an event he witnessed as a doctor over 2,000 times—as analogous to literary creation, even using the word "physician" when he meant "writer": "The physician enjoys a wonderful opportunity actually to witness the words being born. Their actual colors and shapes are laid before him carrying their tiny burdens which he is privileged to take into his care with their unspoiled newness" (*Autobiography*, 361). In such comments, Williams sees the writer as guardian of language's newness and purity, implicitly controlling, molding, and guiding language to preserve its innocence, and to restore that innocence when needed.

Although Williams was concerned throughout his career with safeguarding and recovering the original purity of words, in practice, he recognized the impossibility of this task, and at times lamented the uncontrollability of language. In a letter to his wife Flossie he says, "The damned words keep jumping and slipping, until before long we've said just the opposite of what was intended" (*Letters*, 82). He was speaking of love in this letter, which was certainly not intended as a public pronouncement on language, but elsewhere he writes of the failure of language. In *Paterson*, for example, he writes, "the language, the language / fails them."[3] In a 1951 letter to Marianne Moore, he said "at times there is no other way to assert the truth than by stating our failure to achieve it" (*Letters*, 304).

In other words, language, like an unruly child, sometimes defeats attempts to control and keep it pure. Yet Williams seemed reluctant to let go of his idealized view of language and writers. Images of purification by

This essay was written specifically for this volume and is published here for the first time.

fire and breakage and images of the poet as purifier are found in *Paterson*. And only three years after Williams's lament in his letter to Marianne Moore, he praised her for "wiping soiled words or cutting them clean out, removing the aureoles that have been pasted around them or taking them bodily from greasy contexts."[4]

Nevertheless, as James Breslin has observed, Williams's art is more honest than his pronouncements.[5] As a theorist, Williams saw language as a way of getting at the essence of life, "that essence which is hidden in the very words which are going in at our ears and from which we must recover underlying meaning as realistically as we recover metal out of ore" (*Autobiography*, 362). Although Williams believed that redemption, or the recovery of essence, is possible, in his novels (especially in the Stecher trilogy) he demonstrates how the contamination of language—the chief mediator between people—inevitably complicates and hinders human relationships.

Williams's de-idealizing tendencies as a poet and novelist were evident from fairly early in his career. In *A Voyage to Pagany*, for example, he comes down squarely in favor of the messiness of actual life when Dr. Evans rejects a life devoted exclusively to art in Europe in favor of a life that includes both medicine and art in America.[6]

Williams himself chose the life of medicine and art, stating that it allowed him to observe the essence of humanity: "Was I not interested in man? There the thing was, right in front of me. I could touch it, smell it. It was myself, naked, just as it was, without a lie telling itself to me in its own terms" (*Autobiography*, 357). He goes on to defend the compatibility of medicine and art: "one occupation complements the other, . . . they are two parts of a whole, . . . it is not two jobs at all, . . . one rests the man when the other fatigues him" (359). From this statement we can see Williams's nearly complete merging of the identities of physician and writer, just as when he said that it is the *physician* who is able to "witness the words being born" (361). These statements reflect a similar ambivalence for both his pediatric practice and language and literary creation. Nevertheless, when he discusses the day-to-day problems of his patients and his practice, Williams often finds them to be at best a distraction from his work as a writer and, at worst, a waste of time.

Given Williams's conflicting views about language and his medical practice, it is difficult to accept his seemingly naive equation of child with word. This romantic analogy is false to both Williams's experience with language and the knowledge of children he gained from his years as a pediatrician. Women writers have used this trope more authentically to contest the pen / penis metaphor (discussed fully by Gilbert and Gubar), and the accompanying notion that writers "father" texts.[7]

Although Williams frequently declared his admiration for women, there ∴ nothing but patriarchal appropriation in his discussion of the artistry of *White Mule*, the first novel in his trilogy of the immigrant Stecher family.

He begins innocently enough: "I take care of babies and try to make them grow . . . Nothing is more appropriate to a man than an interest in babies."[8] But when he displaces the woman and begins his discussion of the artist, the appropriation is obvious: "He should today substitute his interest for that of the obsolete mother. Women today merely have babies. It takes a man to bring them up. And it had better be a man with an interest in good style in order that we don't load up the little composition with "lies" (244).

Like Williams's analogy between child and word, this statement minimizes the woman's role and casts the male / artist as sole protector of the child and of language, sheltering them from a contaminating world. Once again, Williams makes an odd conflation, not between physician and writer, but between baby and composition. The identification of baby and composition is total—and totally staggering is Williams's nonchalant movement from discussion of medicine to writing.

This passage also moves the physician / writer away from his role as mere "witness" of the child / word's birth to a more active, parental role as protector and guide of the innocent. Yet he makes this remark about a novel that utterly undermines the ideas that the child or word is pure, and that either can be controlled.

Williams's dazzling portrait of the baby in *White Mule* (1937) deconstructs his analogy about the purity of word and child by demonstrating that no baby is a *tabula rasa*. From the outset, the baby, Flossie, has a distinctively strong and willful nature. She is by no means an idealized baby—sweet, beautiful, and docile. Williams begins by reminding us of Botticelli's *Birth of Venus*: Flossie "entered as Venus from the sea, dripping."[9] But he quickly undercuts this image of calm beauty. Flossie enters life "flinging out her arms . . . and screwing up her tiny smeared face . . . twisting and flinging up [her] toes and fingers into the way—free" (1). Nor is her birth idealized: "Stop that crying," the midwife says to the newborn, "you should be glad to get outa that hole" (1). The birth scene is far from pretty; the baby, yelling convulsively, lies near the "smeared triple mountain of its mother's disgusted thighs and toppled belly" (2).

Similarly, Williams de-idealizes motherhood. When Gurlie Stecher learns that her baby is a girl, she tells the nurse, "Take it away. I don't want it. All this trouble for another girl" (1). She thinks of the baby as a "miserable scrawny little brat" (7) and is even angered by its inability to nurse: "It fumbled, did not close its jaws but panted eagerly without taking hold, rubbing its face back and forth on the breast aimlessly, then screwing up its face again and squawking feebly" (42). Gurlie is so enraged that she flings the baby across the bed and leaves the room.

Williams's realistic portraits of childhood, infancy, and motherhood are far from the romanticized analogy he presents to describe literary creation. They are, in fact, much closer to what he actually shows us about language in the trilogy. Not surprisingly, the focus on language often centers on

Flossie's linguistic development, as James Guimond has observed.[10] Through the insights about language in these novels, we begin to see the flaws in Williams's critical assertions about the purity and controllability of language.

At the end of *White Mule*, Flossie has developed linguistically to the stage where she can say single words like "mama," "papa," "book," "hat," and "hot." The most important of Flossie's new words is "no." It gives her a measure of linguistic control over her environment and especially over her mother. But Gurlie takes no pride in Flossie's new words. She speaks of Flossie's development only when prodded and then only in the most dismissive way. When the woman with whom Gurlie and the children are staying in the country admires Flossie and asks how many words she knows, Gurlie tells her, and then adds, "But she talks a lot of foolishness too that nobody can understand" (245). Given most parents' enthusiasm about their children's first words, Gurlie's lack of pride is not only surprising; it also calls our attention to the issue of linguistic development and control.

Until Flossie learns to say "no," her rebellion has been entirely nonverbal. Now language begins to form a powerful barrier between her and her mother, just as it is a barrier for all of the other characters in the novel.

Gurlie and her mother, for example, often speak at cross-purposes. When her mother first comes to live with the family, she takes Gurlie to task for her treatment of the baby. Interestingly enough, the grandmother chastises Gurlie in Norwegian, since, like a baby, she knows only a few words of English. Gurlie, however, as if to take linguistic control, answers her in English. But no one wins in this conversation. Neither can control the other because the grandmother's ignorance of English and Gurlie's willful refusal to speak Norwegian result in an utter failure of language.

In an early scene with the grandmother, Gurlie, and Flossie, we see three generations for whom language misfires. The grandmother is distressed that Gurlie pays no attention to Flossie's cries. Those cries, of course, are the only sounds Flossie has to communicate with. The grandmother, attempting to jump a generation and speak for the granddaughter, interprets the cries as a need for attention and care. Gurlie, on the other hand, sees them as her daughter's nascent attempts at domination and ignores the sounds. She may, in fact, be right. For even at this stage, the cries, which constitute the baby's language, are overpowering: "It sobbed and forced its piercing little voice so small yet so disturbing in its penetrating puniness, mastering its whole surroundings till it seemed to madden them" (9). The baby's cries are meaning and content without actual words.

These cries are truly pregnant with multiple and, very likely, conflicting meanings. They signal need and dependence, but also serve as a weapon and sign of defiance. The melding of sound and meaning into the creation of a strong new voice in this scene seems admirable. Yet this is the very opposite of Williams's wish to purify the word, to use it "without smear[ing] it again with thinking (the attachments of thought) but in such a way that it will remain scrupulously itself, clean perfect, unnicked beside other words in parade" (*Essays* 128–29).

The baby's new voice increasingly undermines Williams's conscious aesthetic in several ways. Flossie's physical growth is as significant as her linguistic growth. She is not a "disembodied" voice. Williams is a careful observer of each stage of the child's development, and as we measure her physical changes, we are also aware of the power of the body, with its own desires and will to mastery. At each stage of her life, from infancy through childhood to young womanhood, Flossie's needs and individuality increasingly assert themselves. Her language, then, is not pure vocalization unsmeared with thought; it is sound in service of the body's growing demands.

Flossie also becomes aware that silences are part of language as she witnesses her mother's and grandmother's increasing alienation. By the second novel, *In the Money*,[11] as Flossie's language develops, her mother and grandmother paradoxically stop speaking to each other, but not before each has accused the other of acting like a child. These mutual accusations are ironic, given Flossie's struggles to attain linguistic control. As Flossie watches them fight, she feels the significance of their tense silence; although she is too young to comprehend their words, nevertheless, she "seemed to know that there was lightning in the air" (*Money*, 214).

Flossie, although still linguistically unsophisticated, is attuned to nonverbal clues. In fact, language is such a failure in these novels that only nonverbal relationships seem to hold much power. Verbal communication, far from being an asset, is a barrier to understanding. Gurlie, who shares a language with her mother, loathes her, while Joe, who does not speak their language, actively likes his mother-in-law, "and she, while not understanding him, always treated him with respect" (211).

Throughout the first two books of the trilogy, verbal communication and linguistic development are more often than not sources of frustration. By the second novel, for example, Flossie and her grandmother share the same level of mastery of English. Both know a few nouns, the names of some common things, but they are unable to make the connections out of which meaning is forged. In an effort to make meaning, the grandmother resorts to her own language, which is as incomprehensible to most of her family as baby talk is to the adults. When, for example, Flossie's older sister, Lottie, asks for a pair of scissors, her request results in a mystifying conversation: "Scissors? No, no," she said. "Not for little girls," but that part of it was in a strange language and Lottie looked at her as she had been doing for the past few days, very much puzzled (*Money*, 208). The grandmother, having exhausted her knowledge of English with the noun and repeated negation, continues speaking to Lottie in Norwegian, with the girl looking at her "as if she were crazy" (208).

The failure of communication between parents / caretakers and children breeds not only bewilderment but also anger and frustration. Like the grand-mother, the children's maid, Elsa, has language skills no better than Flossie's. She takes Flossie to the park not only for the baby's sake, but to listen to other maids and children speak in an attempt to learn English. But listening to them is "like hearing people from the moon" (*Money*, 299). Although Elsa is terrified of displaying her ignorance of English to anyone, and thus avoids contact with adults in the park, she does allow small children to approach her. When a little girl asks Elsa and Flossie if they'd like to see her new knickers, Elsa forces herself to ask, "What is knickers?" while Flossie tries to repeat the word "knickers" (306). Elsa's adult interest in learning the meaning of the word so that she can use it contrasts strikingly with Flossie's childlike interest and delight in mere sound. Rather than answering her, the girl asks, "Can't you speak English?" (306). This innocent question shames Elsa because her linguistic skills have been bested by a small child. It's little wonder then that she panics whenever adults try to talk to her. When a woman asks if she may sit next to her, Elsa is reduced to shaking her head to say no—revealing a nonverbal state of powerlessness, weaker than even Flossie's. A baby's language includes a variety of meaningful cries that are unavailable to an adult. Elsa's linguistic deficiencies leave her virtually alienated and totally without the ability to communicate verbally. "Ashamed of herself and her broken way of talking" (309), Elsa is rendered mute. She "felt like a stupid little peasant . . . and that made her mad. So she got up and went away furious" (309).

These episodes suggest that without language—for all its hopeless imprecision—an adult, who does not have recourse to the cries and nonverbal demands of a baby, is powerless. These portraits of frustration and help-lessness stand in powerful opposition to one of Williams's best known state-ments about the source of his poetic language. At a speaking engagement at City College in New York, a British instructor asked Williams about the source of his language. Williams replied, "From the mouths of Polish moth-ers" (*Autobiography*, 311). Throughout his career, Williams argued for the importance of an American idiom to revitalize literary language. He felt that Eliot's language, for example, "returned us to the classroom" (*Autobiogra-phy*, 174) and that language should take its strength from the local and the ordinary. He said that beyond this prosaic language lies a poetic essence to be extracted: "By listening to the minutest variations of the speech we begin to detect that today as always, the essence is also to be found hidden under the verbiage, seeking to be realized" (362). But the episodes showing the grandmother and Elsa don't suggest such an underlying essence or power. If these two women are in some sense like the Polish mothers in whose language Williams finds the possibility of redemption, then it seems odd that the reader is given no sense of this power. Rather than a transparent medium of truth (once any contamination is wiped clean), the language of these "Polish mothers" is incomprehensible. As a result, Williams's apparent affirmation of such language and the traditional privileging of speech in Western metaphysics are undercut in his trilogy.

Communication fails not only for those who do not understand the language or for the very young, but also for adults who have supposedly achieved linguistic mastery. Gurlie and her husband Joe, for example, bicker their way through the three novels. Gurlie is constantly asserting her superiority over Joe. When he tells her his problems, she says his difficulties arise from not listening to her. When he tells her about his successes, she claims that it is all due to her influence and that he would be nothing without her. At their best, their conversations are exchanges of information rather than the verbal intimacies one would expect of a married couple. Even these conversations quickly degenerate into a series of non sequiturs, sabotaging even such simple exchanges. At worst, their conversations are verbal assaults, an admixture of defensiveness, self-justification, and blame. Sharp attacks are typical: " 'Do you want to tell me something I don't know myself?'. . . . 'Why don't you answer? Now pout like a spoiled child and say I did it.' 'Did what?' said Joe. 'YOU did it. I didn't want to argue. Well, why don't you speak? Did you hear what I said? Go to hell!' " (*Money*, 82–83). Joe momentarily retreats in silence. When she taunts him to act like her master if he dare, he answers by saying, "I wonder if it's worth it," adding, "Look what a beautiful night it is out there" (83). His refuge is in the preverbal and visual worlds. In this respect, he is much like Flossie, for whom he holds a special affection.

At one point, after another peevish exchange with Gurlie again ends in silence, Joe gives Flossie and Lottie a bath. The task pleases him immensely. In contrast to his highly verbal relationship with Gurlie, Joe's relationship with the children is largely tactile and visual. He derives great pleasure from holding and watching them. As they splash in the bath in absolute delight, Joe is "sad, somehow. He didn't know why" (105). We can surmise, though, the cause of his sadness. As an adult, he belongs to a world where words never hit their mark.

It almost seems as though Joe wishes he could return to the world of a small child because it is a world of sensations rather than abstractions. Joe has learned that words don't lead to truth. In business, he has seen that one's word has no value, in marriage that words too often bring pain rather than intimacy. The world of a child is the world readily called to mind in Williams's often-quoted dictum, "no ideas but in things."[12] It is a world of pure experience unmediated by language. Perhaps this is what gives this scene its poignancy. Joe longs for Flossie's world, but there is no return to pure origins either in language or in life.

Unlike Joe, Gurlie takes no delight in Flossie's world; instead she is convinced that in this world of words, she holds the power. Despite the challenges to her power posed by Flossie (through the child's increasing linguistic mastery), and by her own mother (in their verbal sparring), for the most part, Gurlie holds the power in her largely female-centered home. Adopting a sharp parental tone, Gurlie often accuses Joe of acting like a baby, whom she tries to dominate through words. Although Joe has proven himself to be a hard-working, tough, and well-respected businessman, Gurlie insists on accompanying him to see his former employers, who are angry that he has taken a government printing contract away from them. Gurlie talks about Joe as if she were his mother and he a small child who cannot handle the situation. Gurlie's mother cautions her against going, but Gurlie says, "I'd like to see anybody keep me away. Joe needs me. Those people are crooks and they might hurt him" (*Money*, 198). When her mother reluctantly agrees, saying that it's all right if Joe wants her to go, Gurlie says, "he has nothing to say about it" (198).

At the meeting, Joe's former boss greets Gurlie with initial surprise and a patronizing air that places Gurlie in the role of a child. He acknowledges her wish to stay with the utmost condescension: " 'Well. All right. I suppose you know your husband's business as well as he does, Mrs. Stecher,' he laughed. 'You look it' " (201). Gurlie, who seemed so dominant before the meeting, sits wide-eyed and silent—surrounded by men during the meeting—save for one plea to allow Joe to finish his comment. She can barely take her eyes off Joe, who is commanding and articulate in this male setting. As they walk home, both are silent. Since conversations for Gurlie and Joe are a vehicle for either insults or information, there is nothing more to say.

For his part, Joe is quiet because, after the bitter accusations in the meeting, he is left not with words but with action—filling the government printing order. He knows that in the male-dominated world of business, words are easily broken. The man of action, rather than the man of words, is the one who garners respect.

Gurlie is silent because she has witnessed the entire meeting, and since she is interested in information rather than Joe's feelings, she has nothing to ask or to add. In addition, Gurlie has not only seen a new, powerful, and articulate side of Joe, which leaves her dumbfounded; she has also made her first entry into the male-controlled world of business, where her naturally blunt and outspoken manner is silenced merely because she is a woman. Joe's former boss has remarked, albeit sarcastically, that Gurlie probably knows Joe's business as well as Joe, but the verbal dominance that she exhibits in her home is nowhere evident in this scene. This incident marks the first time that Gurlie is dismissed merely because of her gender. Yet it seems that she has known and unconsciously subscribed to society's devaluation of women all along. When Flossie was born, Gurlie was deeply disappointed that the baby was just "another girl" (*Mule*, 1). And despite being rendered almost mute and invisible during this meeting, Gurlie still maintains the same attitudes. When she gets pregnant again, Gurlie hopes for a

boy and is overjoyed when she finally has one. Perhaps her continued desire
for a son suggests her awareness that one's voice—particularly if it is a
woman's voice—may be silenced no matter what its power, and that not
all things are possible through willpower and language.

If, as we see in these first two novels, no genuine communication is
possible (even for two adults like Joe and Gurlie, whose relationship is highly
verbal), then this revelation undercuts the conventional concept of progressive
linguistic mastery. In the third novel, *The Build Up*,[13] Flossie and Lottie
grow to adulthood, but neither is able to overcome the failures in communication that characterized their parents' relationship. The new generation is no
more successful with language than was the old.

Lottie learns to use language in a way that mystifies rather than clarifies.
While Flossie as a baby uses "no" as a symbol of defiance and a show of
independence, as a young woman Lottie uses "yes" to guard her privacy.
"It didn't matter what it was, her answer was yes" (*Build Up*, 44). In
addition, language is a way of getting what she desires. Lottie thinks: "I
won't ask for too much—not at first. Until then no one shall know what
I'm thinking. No one" (45).

And indeed, no one ever really does know what she is thinking. When
Lottie, whose real language is music, pleads to go to Germany to pursue
her career as a pianist, Joe is exasperated. He tells Flossie, "Your sister's
crazy" and then adds in complete frustration, "She needs to learn to speak
English" (167). Lottie has succeeded in using language to hide her thoughts
as she wished, but she has succeeded so well that her father fails to understand
the intensity of her artistic desires. Even using language as she had planned
leads to defeat.

Flossie's linguistic evolution is a failure as well; it is really less a
development than merely an accumulation of words that fail to communicate.
As an adult she rarely speaks, perhaps underscoring the futility of this
accumulation. All of her development, shown in *White Mule* and *In the
Money*, leads to silence.

When Flossie reaches young womanhood and is courted by Charlie
Bishop, the poet-doctor, her speech virtually ends. This is an astonishing
conclusion for a character who has been defined primarily through her linguistic growth. As a baby, she cried—deafening, agonized, and desperate cries—
"to hear herself again—to know that she was there" (*Money*, 223). Now as
an adult the person who was defined by her voice is mute.

Charlie Bishop, who loved Lottie, only turns to Flossie after his brother
Fred tells Lottie that both of them love her and that she must choose. Lottie
chooses Fred. In a "passion founded on despair" (*Build Up*, 262), Charlie
asks Flossie to marry him, almost without preamble. Until the proposal, he
had barely spoken to her. But immediately after learning that Lottie has
accepted Fred, Charlie calls Flossie, asks to visit her, arrives at her house,

suggests that they sit outside, and then proposes, never saying that he loves her—only saying that he doesn't love Lottie.

Flossie and Charlie's relationship seems to be Williams's plea for a new type of pure understanding—"not an adulteration . . . [but] a vivid, living thing—of a new sort" (*Build Up*, 263). Perhaps this is why Charlie will not falsify his proposal with declarations of love that he does not feel. He prefers the "uncompromising cruelty" (263) of honest language or, perhaps more accurately, of honest silence, to fake sentimentality. He believes that they can be happy and says so but will say no more.

Flossie wrestles with her decision, knowing that "if she said yes, it would be the end for her" (264). "Finally, at the far side of a field, in the darkness she paused and, hanging her head, said very doubtfully to him, 'Yes, I'll marry you' " (264). Perhaps Williams hoped that Flossie and Charlie's relationship would be a "living thing—of a new sort"; instead it seems to be a deathly thing of the old sort, for her tentative and joyless acceptance marks the beginning of the end of Flossie's fiercely independent voice. Apart from a few remarks, Flossie is basically silent for the remainder of the novel.[14] At her wedding, "Floss, pale as a ghost, walked up the aisle on her father's arm" (307). This spectral vision is our final view of Flossie. The last line we hear her utter—"A boy?" (318)—at the birth of her son brings us back to the beginning of the trilogy, to Flossie's own birth—her strong wails, her mother's disregard simply because of her gender, and the linguistic development that has come to nothing.

Williams's trilogy demonstrates that adults have a larger repertoire of words that they often hurl at each other. But these words are no more effective than the cries or "mysterious sign language" of a baby (*Mule*, 66). These novels show further that language is a system of signs that point only to other signs rather than to an essence, and that recovering linguistic purity and achieving control, which Williams desired, are forever deferred.

Perhaps it is most telling that *The Build Up* begins with the very topics of deferral, lies, and purity. This curious opening, a chapter about the Stechers' move to a new house, once again directs our focus to language, and indicates that Williams's interest in language and recovering its purity was so profound that these concerns burst through the surface of the narrative:

> Waiting, that's the most terrible word in the language.
> Flossie was waiting to grow up. All the happiness of childhood is bordered in black by that crushing weight . . . Falsehood is the natural flower of such a vine. Children lie naturally. Flossie did. To keep, to keep the "thing," the nameless thing that never waits, never intact (3).

Waiting—endless deferral—is the "most terrible word" to a writer who seeks to redeem the language. Unlike the analogy through which Williams compares words, literary creation, and the purity of the infant, here he conjoins language, falsehood, and children. Set against his romanticized, idealistic pronouncements on language, this passage accords with the views of language shown in Williams's trilogy. The falsehood that he calls the "natural flower" of waiting is a slippage between word and thing that is inescapable. Language fails, not because writers are poor parents who fail in their guardianship of words, but because words, like children, have an independence that we can never claim to own.

Notes

1. William Carlos Williams, *Autobiography* (New York: Random House, 1948), 361.

2. In a letter to his wife Flossie about *A Voyage to Pagany*, for example, he said "I have to confess that I am not altogether disgusted with my newest child." *Selected Letters* (New York: McDowell, Obolensky, 1957), 98.

3. William Carlos Williams, *Paterson* (New York: New Directions, 1946), 11.

4. William Carlos Williams, *Selected Essays* (New York: Random House, 1954), 128.

5. James E. B. Breslin, *William Carlos Williams: An American Artist* (New York: Oxford University Press, 1970); (Chicago: University of Chicago Press, 1985). [Reprinted in part in this volume.]

6. William Carlos Williams, *A Voyage to Pagany* (New York: Macaulay, 1928).

7. Sandra M. Gilbert and Susan Gubar, *The Madwoman in the Attic: The Woman Writer and the Nineteenth-Century Imagination* (New Haven: Yale University Press, 1979).

8. William Carlos Williams, *"White Mule* Versus Poetry," *Writer* (August 1937): 244.

9. William Carlos Williams, *White Mule* (New York: Random House, 1937), 1.

10. James Guimond, *The Art of William Carlos Williams: A Discovery and Possession of America* (Urbana: University of Illinois Press, 1968).

11. William Carlos Williams, *In the Money* (New York: Random House, 1954).

12. Of course, in *Paterson* this aphorism concerns the world of art, not the world of children. John Dewey's statement, "the local is the only universal, upon that all art builds," which Williams had read, states the idea more fully. Nonetheless, Williams's statement can also reflect a longing for the world of experience shown in this scene.

13. William Carlos Williams, *The Build-Up* (New York: Random House, 1946).

14. Flossie's silence is particularly disturbing in view of the autobiographical foundation of the three novels. Williams's own marriage occupied a special place throughout his writings, and he said his wife Flossie was indispensable to him. Although he often praised women for their power and insight, he also felt they were beyond man's control. Perhaps Flossie's silence at the end of the novel reflects Williams's ambivalence towards women, his desire to praise and his impulse to control.

Can "Beautiful Thing" Speak?:
Race and Gender in *Paterson*

SERGIO RIZZO

William Carlos Williams's effort in *Paterson* to create various female characters has recently received important scholarly attention.[1] For example, Williams's relationship to the poet Marcia Nardi has been reexamined in ways
that shed new light on the pair's representation within the poem as Paterson
and Cress. As valuable as these efforts to read *Paterson* in light of gender
relations have been, we also need to pay more attention to the way Williams's
experience of racial difference underwrites and informs his effort to create a
woman in *Paterson*.

It has long been a truism that the central female protagonist in *Paterson*
is "Beautiful Thing" (96)—an African-American who appears in book 3.[2]
Any study that looks at Williams's interconnected understanding of race
and gender must therefore take her into account. Furthermore, if "Beautiful
Thing"'s black feminity is central to *Paterson*, then the poem is governed
by Williams's effort to represent racial difference. Her role in *Paterson* is
doubly critical. She is crucial to the white fictions that support the author
as man and poet. Yet her presence within *Paterson* also reveals Williams
valiantly attempting to criticize and revise those fictions.

As Williams introduces "Beautiful Thing" in book 3, he appears to be
aware and ashamed of his angry desire to put down and control her inexplicably frustrating black femininity:

> (Then, my anger rising) TAKE OFF YOUR
> CLOTHES! I didn't ask you
> to take off your skin   .   I said your
> clothes, your clothes. You smell
> like a whore. I ask you to bathe in my
> opinions, the astonishing virtue of your
> lost body (I said)   .
>
> (*Paterson*, 105)

Williams's revealing denial, "I didn't ask you / to take off your skin,"
indicates "Beautiful Thing"'s veiled significance. Despite his denial, it is

This essay was written specifically for this volume and is published here for the first time.

her black skin and not her clothes that frustrates the author's desire to know her. The "astonishing virtue" of her "lost body" is highly cathected for Williams. It recalls his youthful astonishment before the spectacle of Georgie, the family maid, at her bath and his later observation of the stiff beauty of a black cadaver.[3]

In addition, "Beautiful Thing"'s "astonishing virtue" makes a deliberate contrast with the library's men of stone who exist by a "DEFECT OF VIRTUE" (122) since they cannot contain the likes of "Beautiful Thing." *Paterson*'s effort to contain "Beautiful Thing" will save Williams, he hopes, from becoming yet another man of stone like his father and the other librarians. Williams's search for a usable past discovers "Beautiful Thing"'s native silence, which provides him with a tabula rasa for his art.

Nevertheless, as *Paterson*'s ultimate attempt to locate the origin of "Beautiful Thing" suggests, Williams and his poetry cannot exploit her stony silence with impunity. In book 4—well after her first appearance in book 3—*Paterson* associates her name with Columbus's journal entry describing his discovery of the New World:

> On Friday, the twelfth of October, we anchored before the
> land and made ready to go ashore . There I sent the people
> for water, some with arms, and others with casks: and as it
>   was
> some little distance, I waited two hours for them.
> During that time I walked among the trees which was the
> most beautiful thing which I had ever known.
>
> (178)[4]

If the explorer's discovery of the New World empowers him to speak, his words seem tied to a moment of his own speechless astonishment. Consequently, Columbus's discovery speaks of his inability to speak. Williams's identification with Columbus is revealed by the fact that Williams appropriated the passage for his *In the American Grain* from Columbus's *Journals*. By quoting himself quoting Columbus, Williams may be exhibiting his anxiety over "Beautiful Thing"'s silent origins and the New World she represents. At another level, the recognition of "Beautiful Thing"'s colonial (dis)inheritance forces Williams to confront Gayatri Spivak's postcolonial question, "Can the Subaltern Speak?"[5]

There are only two places in *Paterson* where an African-American woman does speak. Their rare appearances draw "Beautiful Thing," the poem's most prominent African-American, toward them like a magnet. The first African-American voice in the poem occurs in book 1 and appears to be a prefiguration of "Beautiful Thing."

> Will you give me a baby? asked the young colored woman in
> a small voice standing naked by the bed. Refused

she shrank within herself. She too refused. It makes me
too nervous, she said, and pulled the covers round her.

(33)

It seems that Paterson approaches the woman as he does "Beautiful Thing,"
in his capacity as a doctor. In both cases, the African-American women have
needs which expose not only the ineffectiveness of his medicine but also the
sexual / poetic failure of Paterson as a man.

Of the various flower women in book 1 who are missed by the poet's
pollinating "tongue of the bee" (11), it is the African-American woman—
along with Cress—who comes closest to finding her tongue and criticizing
the poet's sexual / poetic efforts. Her "small voice" (33) puts Williams into
an ambiguous relationship with his material. Paterson's refusal of the woman
would seem fundamentally to call the poem's celebration of the New World's
racial hybridity, as epitomized by the Jackson Whites, into question. Her
comments suggest that the man-poet Paterson cannot perform the racial
integration which Williams unabashedly embraces as the driving force behind
America's New World preeminence on the stage of world history.[6]

The other point at which an African-American woman speaks occurs
in Book Three (*The Library*). If the speaker isn't "Beautiful Thing" herself,
Williams seems to intend this character to represent the way "Beautiful
Thing" *would* speak, if she could. Furthermore, the letter written in Black
English by an uncertain "D J B" (124) to an equally uncertain "Kid" (123)
serves as a transition between the two major manifestations of "Beautiful
Thing" in Book Three, part II.[7] Preceding the letter, "Beautiful Thing"
appears as the disembodied spirit of the fire that engulfs Paterson. After the
letter, she is incarnated as the beaten and bruised survivor of a gang rape
to whom Paterson attends in the basement of someone's house. A smoldering
remnant of the previous fire goddess still remains, which Paterson tries to
nurture and sustain.

On the surface, the letter seems plagued by the problems that Williams
has in many of his other attempts to represent African-American life.[8] The
letter writer's childlike exuberance in recounting tales of drinking, partying,
and sexual promiscuity perpetuates a popular stereotype that Williams often
employs. But the letter also presents a sensitive recognition of African-
Americans and their attempts to represent and understand themselves that
goes beyond anything else in Williams's writing.

The letter's ambiguous authority, as it does and does not speak for
"Beautiful Thing," illustrates her subaltern dilemma. Furthermore, if the
letter's Black English lacks the authority to speak for "Beautiful Thing,"
Paterson's poetic attempts to represent her before and after the letter seem
no more authoritative. Between her disembodied appearance as revenging
fire goddess and her incarnation as victimized "love" object, the letter appears, and something *like* "Beautiful Thing"'s voice tries to emerge.

Black English alone cannot empower "Beautiful Thing" to speak. Rather, it is the subversive creativity evident in speakers of Black English, who attempt to break through the conventional impositions of a language which is, in fundamental ways, not their own.[9] The letter's redemptive core lies not in its content—the speaker's descriptions of African-American sexuality. Instead, it is the speaker's "new way of talking" (124) which is the redemptive kernel. In the letter's final paragraph, the speaker says: "Tell Raymond I said I bubetut hatche isus cashutute / Just a new way of talking kid. It is called (Tut) maybe you heard / of it. Well here hoping you can read it" (124).

What Williams appreciates in Black English and the game of Tut is the aesthetic validity of emerging voices and their subversive creativity as they struggle to represent themselves within their American idiom(s). Williams acknowledges his debt to such "foreign" speakers of English in his *Autobiography* when he recounts an exchange with a hostile critic, "a Britisher," who asked Williams where " 'this language of [his]' " came from; Williams shot back, " 'From the mouths of Polish mothers' " (311).[10]

The creative challenge contained within D J B's "new way of talking" goes beyond a merely aesthetic appreciation of her speech. The letter's uncertain authority does not only alert the reader to the idea that "Beautiful Thing" both does and does not speak; it also seems part of a larger project of self-examination that Williams carries out with regard to his poetic authority over her. In effect, *Paterson* attempts to deconstruct an earlier version of "Beautiful Thing" and her author found in "Paterson: Episode 17."[11]

The different versions of "Beautiful Thing" found in "Episode 17" and *Paterson*, represent in miniature larger formal tensions in Williams's construction of the long poem. *Paterson*'s disseminating dismemberment of "Episode 17" carries out what Mikhail Bakhtin, in *The Dialogic Imagination*, terms a "novelization of other genres."[12] Bakhtin explains the process as follows: "[Other genres] become more free and flexible, their language renews itself by incorporating extraliterary heteroglossia and the 'novelistic' layers of literary language, they become dialogized, permeated with laughter, irony, humor, elements of self-parody and finally—this is the most important thing—the novel inserts into these other genres an indeterminacy, a certain semantic openendedness, a living contact with unfinished, still-evolving contemporary reality (the openended present)" (7). *Paterson*'s novelization of the lyric is a concept that could be applied to many of Williams's modernist contemporaries and post-modernist followers.[13] In this light, Williams and *Paterson* can be seen as part of a general crisis in representation that requires the "indeterminacy" of novel forms.

If, as Paul Mariani and others maintain,[14] "Beautiful Thing" is the core of *Paterson*, then it follows that the poem is determined by the crisis of representing racial difference. The text of *Paterson* may be better able to articulate this crisis in racial representation than the author himself.

Nonetheless, *Paterson*'s revision of "Episode 17" registers an important dissatisfaction with the author's earlier attempt to represent "Beautiful Thing," which calls both his past and present authority into question.

Using Bakhtin's terms, *Paterson* has dialogized "Beautiful Thing" and her author. The letter written in Black English, for example, provides some of the "extraliterary heteroglossia" (7) that invites humor and laughter to enter the relationship between Paterson and "Beautiful Thing." The very act of revision implies a level of authorial self-parody, which is explicitly reinforced in many of the scenes placed between the dispersed fragments of "Episode 17."

This self-parody may be humorous, as in the description of various doubles for Paterson: for example, the tight rope walker, Harry Leslie, who attempts to cross the falls in drag, or the grimy old man in a "Volunteers of America" cap who wants to marry his own "beautiful thing" (102). But the self-parody can also convey a more devastating critique: "Give it up. Quit it. Stop writing. / 'Saintlike' you will never / separate that stain of sense" (108). Or, there is the scene in which Paterson bullies "Beautiful Thing" into undressing herself and then sheds pathetic tears. One of the consequences of *Paterson*'s extraliterary heteroglossia is that Paterson, unlike the narrator of "Episode 17," can say that the poet "along with the rest" is only "squirting / at the fire" (120).

Paterson's retextualization of "Episode 17" inserts the novel into the poem through its novelistic protagonist, Paterson. Paterson's interaction with "Beautiful Thing," while not a dialogue, is dialogic. His interactions with her not only allow for elements of irony, humor, and self-parody, but they also—for better or for worse—may change him. These elements of change and interaction are absent from "Episode 17." Throughout the earlier lyric, the anonymous first person narrator is moved by "Beautiful Thing" through observation rather than interaction. Neither the narrator nor the object of his meditative gaze seems capable of change or even to desire change.

Williams's revision of his earlier sighting of "Beautiful Thing" creates what Bakhtin calls, "a certain semantic openendedness" (7). Consequently, "Beautiful Thing" becomes something more than an object of fetishistic scopophilia or a residuum of African primitivism. Her claim to an openended present begins to be enunciated by the letter from D J B—that transgressive message, sent from the fires of hell in a language that is and is not "Beautiful Thing"'s. Existing within the gap provided by her apotheosis as fire goddess and her incarnation as victim, the letter indicates a living contact that works against either of these roles.

Considering some of the feminine prefigurations of "Beautiful Thing" in Williams's youth—the scopophilia associated with Georgie and the corpse of the "young Negress" (see note 3)—"Episode 17" can be seen as a masculine effort to contain the anxieties of difference (black) femininity provokes by a process Laura Mulvey describes in her essay, "Visual Pleasure and Narrative Cinema."[15] The male observer attempts to overcome the anxiety that the spectacle of woman presents by building up "the physical beauty of the object, transforming it into something satisfying in itself" (421). In "Episode 17," Williams avails himself of the lyric, a genre he conceives primarily as a visual force, to comprehend the essentially spectacular significance "Beautiful Thing" holds for him. The logic of fetishistic scopophilia is further demonstrated in "Episode 17" by its removal of "Beautiful Thing" to a place outside linear time where, as Mulvey says, "the erotic instinct [can be] focused on the look alone" (422).

If *Paterson*'s desire to refashion the earlier spectacle of "Beautiful Thing" exhibits elements of what Mulvey describes as narrative's sadistic impulses, deriving pleasure from "ascertaining guilt, . . . asserting control, and subjecting the guilty person [to] punishment or forgiveness" (421), *Paterson*'s textual struggle has its masochistic turn. Furthermore, *Paterson*'s novelization of "Episode 17" signifies something more than the author's entrapment within the sadomasochism of a master-slave opposition. Surely, Williams's effort to revise "Episode 17" is not just an attempt to revise "Beautiful Thing" but also a painful effort to revise himself. Behind this process of revision lies the desire to move beyond the relationship's sadomasochistic understanding. *Paterson*'s linear reworking of the spectacular "Beautiful Thing," while not free of voyeurism, tries to locate a site where "beauty is," or at least could be, "a defiance of authority" (119).

Mariani suggests that "Episode 17" contains an element of Williams's guilty self-recognition. He maintains that the gang rape of "Beautiful Thing" seems "a confession of guilt on Williams's part for too often wanting to tear into the women around him whom he genuinely loved and cared for and yet by whom he was driven to distraction" (415). Mariani's insight is indeed compelling. Nevertheless, *Paterson*'s revision of "Episode 17" admits the insufficiency of both the form and content of the author's earlier confession. Perhaps the weakness of "Episode 17" as a vehicle for either confession or self-recognition can be seen more clearly by considering the deeper sources of guilty self-recognition that the rape of black femininity would provoke in Williams.

As a metaphor, sexual violence may stand for the rape of the Americas and Africa that engendered the West Indies, and for the American history that Williams wants to make "usable." It also speaks to the Williams family's domestication of one of the offspring of that rape—their maid, Georgie. She was part of the northward migrations of African-Americans who competed with European and Asian immigrants to provide rapidly developing suburbs like Rutherford with an army of wage slaves. It also speaks to the "corpse of a young negress" which provided medical students with cheap instruction (see note 3). Last but not least, the rape of "Beautiful Thing" speaks to Williams's aesthetic appropriation of African-American femininity.

Paterson's return to "Paterson: Episode 17" could be read as Williams's attempt to grapple with the criticism of his aesthetic leveled by Fred Miller in the process of their collaboration on *Man Orchid*, one of Williams's most extensive efforts to represent and understand African-Americans.[16] In *Man Orchid*, Miller indirectly charges Williams with a "patronizing attitude" and the "snobbish literary assumption that the Negro in America is an exotic bloom. Negro equals jungle" (111). Clearly, this criticism has implications for Williams's writing beyond *Man Orchid*. At the time, however, Williams seemed unable to respond or even to hear Miller. Perhaps three years later, while composing *Paterson* 3 and reconsidering "Beautiful Thing," Williams was in a better position to appreciate Miller's critique.

In *Paterson's* revision of "Beautiful Thing," Williams does not entirely give up the idea that "Negro equals jungle." Among the four pieces from "Episode 17" interspersed throughout parts 1 and 2 of *Paterson* 3, Williams retains an important fragment of the third stanza from "Episode 17."

> The incredible
> nose straight from the brow
>   the empurpled lips
> and dazzled half-sleepy eyes
>   Beautiful Thing
> of some trusting animal
>   makes a temple
> of its place of savage slaughter
>   revealing
> the damaged will incites still
>   to violence
> consummately beautiful thing
> and falls about your resting
>   shoulders—
>
> (*Poems I* 440)

Shearing away the poem's first two stanzas and most of its third, *Paterson* retains "Beautiful Thing"'s "half sleepy eyes," which are like those "of some trusting animal" (109). But *Paterson's* faceless reconstruction of her eyes erases her aestheticization in "Episode 17" as the "consummately beautiful thing."

In *Paterson's* recontextualization of "Beautiful Thing," the disembodied eyes reject their original taxonomy of facial beauty. Gone, along with the "incredible / nose" and "empurpled lips," are the erotic connotations of the original first two stanzas:

> Lift the stick
> above that easy head
> where you sit by the ivied

> church, one arm
>   buttressing you
> long fingers spread out
> among the clear grass prongs—
>   and drive it down
>   Beautiful Thing
> that your caressing body kiss
>   and kiss again
> that holy lawn—
>
>   (*Poems I* 439–40)

In "Episode 17" Williams, from some invisible vantage point, voyeuristically eroticizes "Beautiful Thing"'s work. Of course, part of the scene's eroticism is that her "sexual performance" is carried out under the nose of the church. Williams's poetic tries to reconcile the scene's profane and sacred elements, lifting "Beautiful Thing" out of harm's way, protecting her from those who would repress her on the one hand, and rape her on the other.

Through the aesthetic appreciation of "Beautiful Thing"'s erotic nature, "Episode 17" tries, both figuratively and literally, to comprehend her rape. The last 19 lines return from the rape scene to the themes of the first stanzas:

> It would take
> a Dominie to be patient
>   Beautiful Thing
> with you—
>
> The stroke begins again—
>   regularly
> automatic
>   contrapuntal to
> the flogging
> like the beat of famous lines
> in the few excellent poems
>   woven to make you
>   gracious
> and on frequent occasions
>   foul drunk
>   Beautiful Thing
> pulse of release
>   to the attentive
> and obedient mind.
>
>   (*Poems I*, 442–43)

"To be patient" with "Beautiful Thing" requires the austere celibacy of a monk, a patience few men apparently have. Indeed, true union with "Beautiful Thing" does not lie in the sexual realm, but in the aesthetic domain. As Williams's mind returns from his imaginary reenactment of "Beautiful Thing"'s rape he hears her "flogging" the rug. Her "savage" rhythms are answered by a poet whose "attentive / and obedient mind" captures these rhythms, making their source "gracious" or "foul drunk" as the occasion warrants—or, both together, as Williams does in "Episode 17."

In *Paterson*, however, all that remains of the aesthetic and erotic framework surrounding "Beautiful Thing"'s rape in "Episode 17" is her eyes. Compare Williams's contextualization of those eyes in "Episode 17" with *Paterson*.

> Certainly there is no mystery to the fact
> that COSTS SPIRAL ACCORDING TO A REBUS—known
> or unknown, plotted or automatic. The fact
> of poverty is not a matter of argument. Language
> is not a vague province. There is a poetry
> of the movements of cost, known or unknown .
>
> The cost. The cost
>
> and dazzled half sleepy eyes
>   Beautiful thing
> of some trusting animal
>   makes a temple
> of its place of savage slaughter
> . . . .
> Try another book. Break through
> the dry air of the place

> *(Paterson*, 109)

Paterson's recontextualization of "Beautiful Thing"'s eyes disembodies them, giving them a surreal dislocation. These new eyes emerge not out of a beautiful face, but out of place where "The fact / of poverty is not a matter of argument." Instead of some aesthetic transport over the benefits of poverty, there must be "a poetry / of the movements of cost, known or unknown." By borrowing "Beautiful Thing"'s eyes, attempting to see as she sees, Williams tries to recognize "the cost" of poverty.

Gone is the assertion found in the last stanza of "Episode 17" that Williams will be able to escape with her through a "few excellent poems." Instead, he attempts to *identify* with her. Like "Beautiful Thing"'s eyes, *Paterson*'s "dazzled half sleepy eyes" struggle groggily against insensitive and, essentially, dead men. Their different forms of victimization represent that double cost of poverty that introduces "Beautiful Thing"'s faceless eyes. Nevertheless, despite the resemblances, these costs are separate, as indicated by the line of dots separating "Beautiful Thing"'s "place of savage slaughter" from Paterson's place in the library.

The attempt to identify a mutual violation carries with it a deeper recognition of difference. Paterson's effort to "Break through / the dry air of the place" by trying another book amounts to a critique of writing's impotence that could easily be extended beyond the confines of the library. It would seem to implicate Williams's own efforts to rewrite "Beautiful Thing." For no matter what he does to revive her from the operating table of aesthetics, in the end she will always be another book. "Beautiful Thing"'s "place of savage slaughter," as Bakhtin would say, has "a certain semantic openendedness" (7): is it located in Paterson the city, Paterson the man, *Paterson* the text, or one of *Paterson*'s pre-texts?

Rather than mirroring the redemptive savior of "Episode 17," the poet Paterson reveals the impotent frustration behind the artist's fetishistic preoccupation with the feminine ideal. The new Paterson confronts his brutality and confesses that he, too, is one of those "guys from Paterson," as the narrator of "Episode 17" refers to them (*Poems I* 441). In the scene where he orders "Beautiful Thing" to undress, *Paterson* reveals how the poet, who sees so much and so well, has trouble feeling. *Paterson* suggests that, like Othello's mad need for "ocular proof," the poet's quest for "Beautiful Thing" includes a sadomasochistic preoccupation with guilt and redemption: "And let me purify myself / —to look at you, / to look at you (I said)" (104). Furthermore, unlike "Episode 17," *Paterson* has tried to imagine the fires of "Beautiful Thing"'s silent rage. Passing through those flames, the poet's earlier poetic hubris is chastened—"I along with the rest, squirting / at the fire" (120).

Paterson's recontextualization of "Beautiful Thing"'s rape attempts to realize her beauty in a new way. Most notably, *Paterson* frames her rape with the rape's aftermath. In "Episode 17," the rape is framed by the poet's tranquil reflection upon the unconventional beauty of an African-American maid at her work. Despite the effort of "Episode 17" at an overlap, the rape victim and the maid seem to be separate individuals as indicated by the contrast of the former's "busted nose" (*Poems I* 442) and the latter's "incredible nose / straight from the brow" (440). The bifurcation of "Beautiful Thing" in "Episode 17" helps Williams maintain an aesthetic distance from the violence done to her.

In contrast, *Paterson* focuses on "Beautiful Thing" as the survivor of the rape and tries to erase the author's prior distance. In Paterson's descent into the basement in order to attend to "Beautiful Thing," Williams attempts their mutual recovery, bringing the two of them both figuratively and literally closer. In his return to "Episode 17," Williams recognizes a level of contact and responsibility missing from the previous poem's postscript to the rape. Paterson does not approach "Beautiful Thing" merely as a poet who wants to apostrophize her as "gracious." He approaches her as a man who recognizes she has wounds that need healing.

Paterson's effort at recovery immediately follows D J B's letter, which carries over into his new interactions with "Beautiful Thing." She is still presented through the sound of silence, but her "quietness" does not "haunt" (104) Paterson and evoke the fury it did previously:

> For I was overcome
> by amazement and could do nothing but admire
> and lean to care for you in your quietness—
>
> who looked at me, smiling, and we remained
> thus looking, each at the other . in silence .
> *(Paterson* 125)

In contrast to the scene where he shouts at her to take off her clothes, this time Paterson shares her quiet. They have become silent partners, indicated by the fact they look "each at the other"—holding each other in a mutual regard. Paterson is no longer exploiting "Beautiful Thing"'s quiet in order to assert the master's gaze or voice. Most importantly, he tries to "care" for her. In his "leaning" to care for "Beautiful Thing," there is an alliterative association with the idea of Paterson *learning* to care as well.

The idea of a new opening engendered by Paterson's contact with "Beautiful Thing" is conveyed by the last lines of Book Three, part II, which immediately follow *Paterson*'s incorporation of the rape scene from "Episode 17."

> I can't be half gentle enough
> half tender enough
> toward you, toward you,
> inarticulate, not half loving enough
>
> BRIGHTen
> the cor
> ner
> where   you   are!
>
> —a flame,
> black plush, a dark flame.
> *(Paterson* 128)

Approaching "Beautiful Thing," the narrator recognizes division and lack. Paterson sees that even he is not half gentle, tender, or loving enough. Because of his self-recognition, he does not presume, as does the narrator of

"Episode 17," to aesthetically transform "Beautiful Thing"'s victimization. To help signify Paterson's incapacity, the adjective "inarticulate" is left indeterminate. It could apply to both "Beautiful Thing" *and* Paterson who, for vastly different reasons, have both been unable to articulate her story.

Despite their failure to communicate, there has been a movement "toward" one another. Williams takes the words of the preacher Billy Sunday in a new direction. He moves against the hierarchical downward and upward motions of the poem and strikes out laterally. This lateral movement "opens the field" of poetic and human understanding, recognizing the integral significance of simple acts of human compassion that exceed efforts to contain them within either ethical schemes, such as Christianity, or aesthetic schemes, such as those "few excellent poems" mentioned by the narrator of "Episode 17."

In the process of trying to represent or speak for "Beautiful Thing," *Paterson* reveals the limits of its language. It is through *Paterson*'s process of self-examination that the reader begins to hear "Beautiful Thing"'s voice as well as her silence. Of course her voice is uncertain and incomplete, as the voice of her author has become. That is because—as in any dialogical relationship—neither party can afford to have the last word. *Paterson*'s tendency to undermine its poetic authority—which earlier critics often condemned—moves *Paterson*'s representation of race away from a monolithic and exploitive modernist symbol of The Primitive. Instead, Williams's ability to leave himself and his poetry open to revision moves *Paterson* towards a postmodern appreciation of race—where the significance of race lies between the fault lines of difference.

Notes

1. For studies that look at *Paterson* in terms of William's relations with women, see Sandra M. Gilbert, "Purloined Letters: William Carlos Williams and 'Cress,' " *William Carlos Williams Review* (Fall 1985): 5–15; and Theodora R. Graham, " 'Her Heigh Compleynte': The Cress Letters of William Carlos Williams' *Paterson*," *Ezra Pound and William Carlos Williams*, ed. Daniel Hoffman (Philadelphia: Pennsylvania University Press, 1983), 164–93. For more general studies of the influence of women on Williams's art, see: Kerry Driscoll, *William Carlos Williams and the Maternal Muse* (Ann Arbor: UMI Research Press, 1987) [reprinted in part in this volume]; Ann W. Fisher-Wirth, " 'A Rose to the End of Time': William Carlos Williams and Marriage," *Twentieth Century Literature* 36 (1990): 155–72; and Theodora R. Graham, "Williams, Flossie, and the Others: The Aesthetics of Sexuality," *Contemporary Literature* 28 (1987): 163–86.

2. William Carlos Williams, *Paterson* (New York: New Directions, 1963). All quotations are from this edition.

3. In his *Autobiography*, published the year after "Beautiful Thing"'s appearance in *Paterson III*, Williams remembers spying on the family's African-American servant, Georgie, while she was at her bath (*Autobiography*, New York: New Directions, 1951). Georgie had earlier appeared in Williams's story, "The Colored Girls of Passenack—Old and New" (*The*

Farmer's Daughters, New York: New Directions, 1961: 50–57). Williams also recalls Georgie, in a confrontation with Williams's father, in *Yes, Mrs. Williams* (New York: McDowell, Obolensky, 1959). It would be hard to overlook Georgie as a significant precursor to "Beautiful Thing." Another episode of voyeuristic fascination with black femininity appears in the chapter of the *Autobiography* entitled "Medicine," in which Williams recalls "falling in love with the corpse of a young negress" (55). Although it's unlikely Williams would trace "Beautiful Thing" back to the domestic voyeurism of his father's patriarchal household or to the professional voyeurism of medicine, he nonetheless had both a fetishistic fascination with women like Georgie and a genuine sympathy and wish to care for them.

4.   My understanding of "Beautiful Thing" 's New World significance owes much to Bryce Conrad, "Engendering History: The Sexual Structure of William Carlos Williams's *In the American Grain*," *Twentieth Century Literature* 35 (Fall 1989): 254–77.

5.   Gayatri C. Spivak, "Can the Subaltern Speak?," *Marxism and the Interpretation of Culture*, ed. Cary Nelson and Lawrence Grossberg (Urbana: University of Illinois Press, 1988), 271–313.

6.   In *Yes, Mrs. Williams*, where he traces his own mixed ancestry, Williams reveals how romantic his view of racial mixing could sometimes be: "It is precisely the racial solidarity, the traditional aloofness of the nomadic tribe, the ancient, the classic 'purity of the race' which forms the basis for Nazi action. It is precisely this that the West Indian tradition abhorred also and tended to break down" (137).

7.   For more details about the letter, see Christopher MacGowan, ed., *Paterson* (New York: New Directions, 1992), 283. MacGowan uncovers an annotation by Kathleen Hoagland on one of the *Paterson* typescripts that identifies the letter as "a letter to my maid Gladys [Enalls] from her girlfriend [Dolly]" (283). Hoagland was a friend of Williams and typist of the *Paterson* drafts.

8.   See Aldon Nielsen, "Whose Blues?," *William Carlos Williams Review* 15 (Fall 1989): 1–8.

9.   Two instances of recognizing Black English as an aid to Williams's own artistic creativity appear in the *Autobiography*, where he briefly mentions enjoying his father's readings of Paul Lawrence Dunbar (15), and in Van Wyck Brooks's introduction to *The Farmer's Daughters*. Brooks says that Williams had "ingrained in his very bones a love of the Negroes, 'furnaces of emotional power.' A Negro soldier, whom he was doctoring for a venereal disease, gave him the courage to persist in the use of his native language—it was 'always a treat to hear him'; and this new language, live and immediate, accounts very largely for the spell of these crisp sketches and stories" (xii).

10.   The political analogue Williams has in mind for the subversive parody and language games of Black English is clarified in an important sister text to *Paterson III*: his libretto, *Tituba's Children* (in *Many Loves and Other Plays*, [New York: New Directions, 1961], 225–300). *Tituba's Children*, written not long before Arthur Miller's *The Crucible*, takes place between the McCarthy witch hunts of Washington, D. C. and the Puritan witch trials of Salem, Massachusetts. At one point, the McCarthyite Senator Yokell and an F. B. I. agent named Fred respond with befuddled disapproval to a group of African American waitresses who are playing Tut (247–48).

11.   William Carlos Williams, *Collected Poems, Vol. I*, ed. Christopher MacGowan and A. Walton Litz (New York: New Directions, 1986), 439–43. Quotations of "Episode 17" are from this edition.

12.   Mikhail M. Bakhtin, *The Dialogic Imagination*, ed. Michael Holquist, trans. Caryl Emerson and Michael Holquist (Austin: University of Texas Press, 1981), 7.

13.   See Michael André Bernstein, *Tale of the Tribe: Ezra Pound and the Modern Verse Epic* (Princeton: Princeton University Press, 1980); and Steven Gould Axelrod, "Starting Over: Learning from Williams," *Robert Lowell: Life and Art* (Princeton: Princeton University Press, 1978).

14. Paul Mariani, *William Carlos Williams: A New World Naked* (New York: McGraw-Hill, 1981). [Reprinted in part in this volume.]

15. Laura Mulvey, "Visual Pleasure and Narrative Cinema," *Women and the Cinema* (New York: Dutton, 1977), 412–28.

16. William Carlos Williams, Fred Miller, and Lydia Carlin, *Man Orchid, Massachusetts Review* 14 (Winter 1973): 77–117.

Williams's Drama: From Expressionism to Postmodernism in *Many Loves,* *A Dream of Love,* and *Paterson IV*

Elizabeth Klaver

At the height of his poetic experimentation, William Carlos Williams was also exploring his playwrighting impulse. Traces of dramatic form can be sensed throughout the long poem, *Paterson*, most particularly in "An Idyl," the embedded playlet which opens Book Four. Indeed, throughout the 1940s and 1950s Williams often turned from the composition of *Paterson* to write and revise two plays, *Many Loves* and *A Dream of Love*.[1] It should not be surprising, then, if similar concerns about the status of the text, its generation and self-assessment, occur as the poet-playwright crosses genres. On the one hand, Williams's experiments with the literary work as an assemblage of linguistic forces, visible in *Paterson*, appear in the dramatic constructs as a form of expressionism. In keeping with early twentieth-century drama by playwrights such as August Strindberg and Eugene O'Neill, theatrical space is emotionalized, and the mind and / or its contents are displayed for viewing. On the other hand, the expressionistic treatment in Williams's plays anticipates postmodernism, being considerably more language-bound and textually playful than expressionism. Entangled in semiotic processes, the plays pose questions concerning the constitution and effects of the expressionistic subject and, consequently, of the text as well.

Although it is tempting to place Williams's drama purely within a modernist framework, there is clearly an identifiable postmodern thrust.[2] As Thomas Kilroy suggests, *Many Loves* and *A Dream of Love* use a mixture of styles,[3] a formal technique undoubtedly operating in *Paterson* as well. Though all three are works conceived as an assemblage of discourses, critics do not forgive Williams's drama as easily as they do his poetry; for instance, Kilroy also remarks that *A Dream of Love* "fails to provide a coherent unity of disparate styles" (85). Nevertheless, from a postmodern perspective, one could say that the disparate styles present a problematic that specifically works to undermine coherence, subverting the modernist desire for formal

This essay was written specifically for this volume and is published here for the first time.

213

integrity. As in many postmodern plays, such as Beckett's *Waiting for Godot*, the critique of dramatic forms and conventions is itself a major concern, so that the idea of "playing well" begins to take on a different significance from the usual theatrical meaning.

Nevertheless, the fact that Williams's drama is situated at a crossroads between modernism and postmodernism makes it one of those curious transitional experiments. The drama includes the expressionistic overtones of Strindberg's and O'Neill's work, particularly in features such as the dream sequence in *A Dream of Love*, or the farm playlet in *Many Loves*, which, Hubert remarks, is "something suggestive of the Greek theater" (*Many Loves* 35), also suggestive of the classical elements in *Desire Under the Elms*. Even though *Many Loves* and *A Dream of Love* express in various contexts the workings of the mind and/or its unconscious depths, the plays' treatment tends to be language-bound, projecting the mind into fields that are increasingly revealed as sign systems. Rather than suggest the transparent dream or visionary worlds of Strindberg's plays, Williams's drama tends to evoke a textualized expressionism, an expressionism making the transition to postmodernity.

Many Loves is a case in point. Consisting of three embedded playlets, which are in rehearsal for an onstage audience of Director-Playwright (Hubert) and Producer (Peter), the play presents itself as written and theatrical. The stage directions for act 1, scene 1 expose the processes behind dramatic illusion by placing the audience in the position of witnessing a play as if it were in preparation for production. Ignored by the cast and "stagehands," the audience "finds itself in a darkening, menaced space" (stage direction, 4). During the first few minutes a cacophony of fragmented scenes and lines occurs as various actors practice different, decontextualized portions of the play, while stagehands adjust the lighting and sets. In other words, the opening of act 1, scene 1 presents the play first as an estranged, defamiliarized sequences of signs and only much later, "[when] the lighting is brought under control" (5), as contextualized dramatic discourses. From this point on, the play will continuously blur the borders between encompassing structure and embedded playlets, causing the signs of one to collide with the signs of the other, causing each universe to disrupt the cohesiveness, unity, and theatrical mystification of all the others. For instance, the audience not only sees the same actress play Hubert's fiancée in the frame play, but also sees her as three different characters in the playlets. At least one passage of the second playlet requires practice and is played twice over on Hubert's command, enforcing a collision between structures:

HUBERT: Hold it! We'll cut out the business of the flowers. Just "Good-bye, sucker!" and a slow curtain. Pick it up from "For Christ's sake . . ."

(29)

In being specifically semiotic, the numerous play universes not only mediate any effect of transparency through their textual webs, but also enact the disruption of content and form associated with postmodernism.

Initially, the most striking aspect of *Many Loves* is an opacity of textual forces as the play moves within and along the margins of its various structures. There is nevertheless an expressionistic relationship developing among the embedded playlets and the encompassing structure of Hubert, Peter, cast and stagehands. The text clearly encodes a clue in the following exchange:

PETER: What's this?

HUBERT: Picnickers at a public park in the neighborhood.

PETER: What! On the same scene?

HUBERT: The mind's the scene.

PETER: Whose mind?

HUBERT: Let them continue.

(45–46)

Juxtaposing incongruent images "on the same scene" makes sense if the scene acts as the expression (and has the facility) of the mind. The three embedded playlets embody the vision of Hubert's creative imagination, the contents of his daydreaming mind projected outwards as a mediated scene or landscape. The audience of *Many Loves*, both onstage and offstage, experiences Hubert's mind as display, but in the semiotic terms of performance text.

While *A Dream of Love* works toward a similar project as *Many Loves*, it does so in a modified, almost contrary way. As the techniques of expressionism becomes more evident in this play, so does textuality. When *A Dream of Love* initiates the onset of its dream sequence, it signals the imminent display of Myra's mind by having the unconscious begin to perforate the waking state. Twice, Myra hears the voice of Doc, her husband, but only as his poetry:

> the Voice:
>   —a dream
> we dreamed
>   a little false
> of love . . .
>   (161)

This poem is recognizable as a slightly different version of the lyric occurring earlier in the play, which was delivered as one of Doc's published pieces. To present the earliest indicators of a dream state in such mediated terms is to call attention to the textual network, to prepare a linguistically-charged setting for the dream itself. As expected, when Myra's dream is fully under-way (in scene 3) it is presented in the form of an embedded playlet, complete with an onstage audience consisting of the maid, the butcher boy, the milkman and Myra herself. Like Hubert's, the contents of Myra's imagination are ultimately projected outward into a visual and linguistic field, where even she becomes a member of its audience.

This expressionistic treatment brings out several important points. Wil-liams's drama can be seen as addressing a problematic similar to the one Beckett approaches in his 1950s novel trilogy, *Molloy, Malone Dies* and *The Unnamable*. The mind and / or the self are presented as accessible only through mediation and in the nonhumanistic terms of a fragmented subject. Well into the postmodern project, Adrienne Kennedy's 1976 play, *A Movie Star Has to Star in Black and White*, continues to exemplify this situation in dramatic form, for Clara, Kennedy's main character, both writes the land-scape of this play as her imagination goes along and displays the vision as mediated on the "big screen." The idea of transparent access to a unified self comes undone, rendering in Lacanian terms a split subject. In Kennedy's play, for instance, the split is dramatized as a distinction between writer and written images.

Similarly, a playfulness with or questioning of the constitution of the subject allows *Many Loves* and *A Dream of Love* to present a character on stage and to project the character's vision at the same time. As with Kennedy's Clara, Hubert and Myra also dramatize the dis-integrated self to a similar postmodern effect, for when they project their visions into the field of the other, a domain quite specifically ordered as semiotic appears. Hubert and Myra manage to maintain a ruptured "presence" both in the onstage character and in its dispersal into a recessed network of signifiers. Interestingly, though, this textualizing of the displayed self ends up reverberating back on to the status of the characters as seen in the frame plays.

While the self-aware, intertextual collisions occurring in both plays have already revealed the frames as, in Kilroy's words, "self-consciously artificial" (81), the constant interweaving of linguistic commentary into the fabric of the frames finally disrupts the presentation of the subject. When Peter in *Many Loves* complains that verse is inappropriate for a Broadway show while speaking throughout in verse, the text is generating him as nontransparent, ironic self-reflection. The alliterative parallel of Peter / Hu-bert / Alise in the frame play and Peter / Horace / Ann in the second playlet foregrounds the expressionistic displacement from one semiotic universe to another as a kind of Saussurian "difference." In addition, the Doc character in both plays encodes in a Derridian signature the trace of Williams himself as writer. Consequently, any subject in these plays will rebound through the signifier and through the play of texts. Hubert and Myra especially, because they are so clearly designated as part of the signifying structure, are therefore never able to locate an integrated self or grounded play universe in any of the various texts involved.

It is interesting that in a dramatic piece the dispersal of the self suggests that semiotically constructed subjects such as Hubert and Myra cannot only watch the effects of their fragmentation on the screen of the embedded landscape, but also can experience a divided form of vision. Although Hubert and Myra are viewing aspects of their own minds, they do not gain the capacity to see themselves seeing themselves, a phenomenon which would present the illusion of integrated self-reflection and sustain the privilege of the subject.[4] Rather, standing back to view themselves as other, both characters are placed in the vacillating position of voyeur and exhibitionist.

This condition is especially clear in *A Dream of Love*. Myra cannot come to terms with Doc's death until she fantasizes, displaying and watching it as expressionistic monodrama, a kind of "dream-script." Earlier in the play, she had begged Dotty, Doc's mistress, to describe the death, which had occurred during one of the lovers' meetings. Myra wants to be placed in the position of voyeur. When refused, she writes the death scene herself and this fictionalization becomes the embedded playlet of her dream. Sitting with the onstage audience, Myra projects Doc's love affair. As a form of exhibitionism, her scenario locates itself as a seen object in the field of the other and depends on Myra in the position of voyeur. Toward the end of the scene, however, the Lacanian gaze comes into play.

According to Jacques Lacan in *The Four Fundamental Concepts of Psychoanalysis*, there is a preexistent gaze of the other which he associates with the object *a*. Each individual is under the permanent possibility of being seen by the other, of being placed under this gaze. Unable to remain merely a watcher, Myra perforates her own display, provoking a manifestation of the gaze by confronting the image of Doc: "How can you be so thoughtlessly indifferent? So cruel?" And he responds: "You asked for it. I'll stop if you'll let me" (219). By breaking into the landscape of the vision, Myra situates herself as given-to-be-seen by the other as exhibitionist turned "seer." Myra enacts Lacan's formulation, "the gaze is outside, I am looked at, that is to say, I am a picture" (Lacan, 106).

The metaphor of the picture that Lacan uses at this juncture in his discussion suggests that the self is always a representation, always alienated from a sense of wholeness and reminded once again of its fragmented status even while being subjectified by the gaze. Of course, this scene of *A Dream of Love* also addresses the idea of the gaze as imagined because the field of the other is Myra's fantasy, text, or fantasy-as-text. Myra as other ends up placing herself under her own imagined gaze, producing a sort of self-reflection, not because she watches herself watching herself and is integrated as a whole entity, but because the already alienated self, further split between seen and seer, circulates between the two. The seen becomes the seer, and the seer becomes the seen.[5]

In a similar way, *Many Loves* evokes this form of self-reflection, an awareness of the subject as alienated and subjectified through a function of the gaze. Like Myra, Hubert also engages in voyeurism, studying the contents of his mind as written across the display of his playlets. And like Myra's dream scenario, the playlets as exhibitionistic material are not only dependent upon the voyeur, but are also vulnerable to his interruptions. Consequently, at several points in the play, the gaze appears. The most prominent example occurs at the end of the final playlet during the flirtation between Doc and Clara, in which Peter, as part of the onstage audience, perforates the dramatic illusion. This derisive interruption reverses the perspective from voyeur to exhibitionist and places Hubert and the onstage audience under the empowered, scrutinizing gaze of the other, in this case the playlet. Hubert "hangs his head," while Clara and Doc (the *characters*, not the actors) "stand back, disapproving and disturbed" (stage direction, 87)

Voyeurism and exhibitionism are therefore two activities that indicate in *Many Loves* and *A Dream of Love* a decentered and split subject in the visual field. Since Lacan describes the eye as an erogenous zone in the context of the scopic drive, it should not be surprising to find that, because William's plays are so sexually charged, voyeurism and exhibitionism become key factors in a sexuality that permeates the texts. Both plays, in fact, constitute erotic landscapes. Every playlet in *Many Loves*, for instance, involves striking sexual subtexts, from Serafina's unhappy marriage and affairs to Ann and Horace's relationship to Doc and Clara's extramarital flirtation. Furthermore, the enclosing dramatic structure of Hubert, Peter, and cast includes a homosexual relationship between Hubert and Peter and a heterosexual one between Hubert and Alise. As Linda Wagner notes, *Many Loves* presents a range of unconventional sexual topics: bisexuality, male homosexuality, lesbianism, illicit and multiple sex, unwanted pregnancy, and abortion.[6] Similarly, *A Dream of Love* is replete with discussions of Doc and Myra's sexual problems, Doc's compulsive infidelities, and his death while involved in sexual intercourse, which, of course, Myra writes as her playlet.

Still, because of the play's postmodern expressionism, sexuality is presented in a self-reflective textual mode, in a self-voyeurism of the subject that produces a semiotic eroticism. Since Hubert's and Myra's playlets are fragments of their selves projected outwards into the other, the two characters are in effect dispersed sexually as well, experiencing their own desire as reverberating through the playlets as other. The characters are located in a kind of sexual "differance," where the eroticized subject can both display and watch, exhibit and study itself.

In other words, the sexuality of the displayed self is studied as a semiotically structured "body" and is already experienced as fragmented and as part of the signifying process. Separable among signifiers in the embedded fields, this "body" is divided among Serafina, Boyfriend, Laddie, Horace, Ann, Doc, Clara, and Doc and Dotty. In trying to maneuver among these sexual

markers, the self as writer finds that it cannot fully realize the "body." In
Many Loves, for instance, each playlet ends on the verge of closure: contrary
to our expectations, Serafina does not run off with either Boyfriend or Laddie;
instead of Horace taking Ann in his arms, Miss Breen embraces the young
woman; Doc and Clara kiss, but as Peter remarks, "it's unresolved, / floating,
too silly. The old goat / gets nowhere" (87–88). In addition, the ambiguous
ending of the frame play leaves the Hubert / Peter and Hubert / Alise
relationships unresolved. And even though Myra fantasizes Doc's final moments in *A Dream of Love* as machine gun fire, we can't be sure if these
pyrotechnics suggest sexual climax, heart attack, or both. In other words,
the inability to complete sexual acts becomes equivalent to an inability to
achieve textual closure.

Sexuality and semiosis are thus intimately entwined in these two plays.
The sexual unions implied but not consummated in *Many Loves* and *A Dream
of Love* remain as unresolved as any signifying process in a textual matrix.
The plays not only present the object of desire as unobtainable within the
sexual web; they also structure desire as existent specifically in language, in
the written fabric of expressionistic dream, vision, or fantasy. Doc and
Dotty's encounter within Myra's "dream-script," for instance, explicitly foregrounds the merging of the sexual signifiers with the textual. Their lovemak-
ing is all talk—talk of art, aesthetics, and texts, at that. Foreplay consists
of a tirade by Doc on the status of Greek poetry. Dotty, refusing to let Doc
touch her, undresses instead to the increasing excitement of his language.
Responding to Doc's penultimate point in which he refers to James Joyce,
Dotty cries, "Yes, yes, yes, yes," echoing Molly Bloom (222). As Dotty's
slip falls to the floor, Doc dies in a semiotic explosion while the onstage
audience takes up the chant, "yes, yes, yes, yes." Sexual encounter thus
becomes expressed as textual encounter, and desire as incompleteness circulates through and eradicates the boundaries of the sexual and textual bodies.[7]
Myra, as writer of this scene, ends up presenting a dramatization of the
mediation of the body through her own projected fictionalization or fantasy.
If there is no access to the mind except through sign systems, her "dream-
script" implies that access to the sexual self is also problematized by an
eroticized, semiotic machinery.

The intertwining of sexuality and semiosis occurs in other sites in *A
Dream of Love* as well, indicating that outside of the embedded playlet
sexuality and textuality also conjoin. Trying to justify his infidelities, Doc
claims that "[a man] must create a woman of some sort out of his imagination. . . . A woman out of his imagination to match the best. All right, a
poem. I mean a woman . . ." (200). To which Myra, recognizing the sexism
in his defense, retorts "the rape of the imagination." Clearly, Doc places
poetry in the same register as woman and, according to David Fedo, sees
them as passions that become one.[8] Corresponding to this woman-poem,
Dotty becomes the body of the other upon whom Doc experiences his sexual

and textual urges. Myra says to Dotty, "He told you you were beautiful—the most *beautiful thing* in the world" (my emphasis, 174), reminding us of "Beautiful Thing" in *Paterson*, "a dark flame, / a wind, a flood," "the flame's lover" (*Paterson* 100, 123). "Beautiful Thing" in *Paterson* functions in much the same way as Dotty in *A Dream of Love*, as a woman or a text endowed with sexual power which is played upon by the male imaginer's creative forces.

In fact, the sexual and textual interconnections suggested by "Beautiful Thing" in *Paterson* III appear again in "An Idyl" in *Paterson* IV. Dramatic in its presentation of interwoven scenes and dialogues between Corydon and Phyllis and Mr. Paterson and Phyllis, as well as letters from Phyllis to her father and remarks by The Poet, "An Idyl" also delivers an erotic landscape. Corydon, the woman-poet to whom Phyllis gives massages, is in love with the young woman, calls her "darling," shows a jealous interest in her boy-friends, and writes pastoral poetry in celebration of their relationship. Juxta-posed against this homoerotic relationship is Phyllis's affair with Mr. Paterson. Although Phyllis's encounters with both characters involve physical contact, sexual intercourse never seems to occur. Phyllis indicates several times that she and Mr. Paterson do not complete the coital act; for instance, she says to him, "I don't know why I can't give myself to you" (159). As in the plays, the sex act is not consummated and desire is not assuaged.

At the same time, as in Myra's erotic fabrication in *A Dream of Love*, sexual encounters in *Paterson* are entangled with textual ones. Like Dotty's affair with Doc, Phyllis's affair with Mr. Paterson is as much a linguistic event as anything else. "And what do you do together?" Corydon asks Phyllis. "Just talk," she replies. Phyllis and Mr. Paterson make love "on the couch, kissing and talking while his / hands [explore] her body . . ." (153,155). Rather than leading to a sexual climax, though, the lovers are soon deep in the discourse of fishing. The body of language and the body of sexuality thus become virtually indistinguishable.

In a similar way, Corydon feels compelled to transpose her sexual passion into the textual terms of pastoral poetry. She writes:

> Come with me to Anticosti, where the salmon
> lie spawning in the sun in the shallow water
>   I think that's Yeats   .
> —and we shall fish for the salmon fish
>   No, I think *that's* the Yeats   .
>
> (167)

In this case, the discourse of fishing is not only tied intratextually as metaphor to sexual activity, but is also imprecisely attributed to Yeats.[9] Corydon's poem momentarily interrupts itself to wonder about its textual intersections while at the same time exploring sexual intersections in the trope of spawning salmon. Unsure even of genre, Corydon works in a self-interruption, ex-claiming "This is a POEM!" (165). Such doubts suggest an uncertainty on the part of both Corydon and the embedded poem over the capacity of either to complete the seduction of Phyllis or the assemblage of text. Without the attainment of sexual or textual closure, desire is situated as deferral, weaving itself throughout the written and sexual fabrics. Corydon's poem becomes the locus for both sexual and textual problematics, suffusing each with the other.

There is another player in *Paterson* IV who participates in the self-reflective nature of the poem and who also acts in a capacity similar to Hubert and Myra: The Poet. This figure has also been encoded into the web of *Paterson* as a split subject, both as the "presence" of a writing self and as the projector of the poetic imagination into the landscape of "An Idyl." Like Hubert and Myra, he is not only a part of the juxtaposition of scenes and texts that make up *Paterson*'s embedded playlet; he is also placed in the position of voyeur. In particular, The Poet keeps an eye on Mr. Paterson:

> Oh Paterson! Oh married man!
> He is the city of cheap hotels and private
> entrances .   . . .
> Good-bye, dear. I had a wonderful time.
>   (154)

At first, The Poet is concerned with witnessing the shabby sexuality of both Mr. Paterson and the dramatic construct. Through his intrusion into "An Idyl," though, we can soon follow a dramatization of the fragmentation of the subject. The Poet starts as voyeur, seeing Mr. Paterson as object, but turns into the object of discourse and eye himself. The phrase, "*I* had a wonderful time" (my emphasis), suggests the internalization of Mr. Pater-son's language in The Poet's, as well as the displacement of The Poet as subject into the other. Paterson is a poem, but also, as Williams states in his Author's note, a man and a city. It is, furthermore, a poet, a landscape and a text; it is, like *Paterson*'s "Sunday in the Park," a display to be exhibited for watching. In other words, The Poet not only meets the poem in the field of the other, but in being part of the textual assemblage, experiences his dissolution as subject. In addition, his self-voyeurism as exhibiting, constructing, and looking at the semiotic self within the textual landscape, becomes equivalent to the self-reflection of the text. In this way, the encoun-ter between The Poet's words as an embedded structure and the poem as a textual site indicates that the text itself is experiencing something like a self-scrutiny, a kind of self-voyeurism on a semiotic scale.

Metadramatic theory has shown us that the relation among intratexts or embedded structures does have a self-scrutinizing quality. This theory may suggest, however, that texts are capable of watching themselves watch themselves and therefore privilege the text as an integrated subject. Such a condition could hardly be acceptable given the ontological problematic involved in all semiotic structures which, because of "differance" in language, eradicates the possibility of a self-same presence.[10] In *The Pleasure of the Text* Roland Barthes provides a theory that offers a useful angle on the relations of embedded texts to each other or to the encompassing frame in his explanation of the effects undergone by a reader in the process of reading criticism. He describes this kind of reading as voyeurism because the reader enjoys clandestine pleasure from reading about another reader's pleasure in a text.[11] And, as Lacan points out, voyeurism can provoke the gaze (Lacan, 84).

I think a similar condition arises when a text includes embedded structures, for one text is virtually in a process of "reading"—watching or allegorizing—another text which is in the position of exhibitionist. The text of The Poet in *Paterson*, for example, watches and "reads" the text of Mr. Paterson as well as those of Corydon and Phyllis and the other linguistic domains. But because the text of The Poet is also a part of "An Idyl" and under the vacillating gaze of a self-voyeurism, the scrutinizing nature of the structure thoroughly entangles the exhibitionistic and voyeuristic domains. The semiotic fields "read" each other. Given the erotic landscape characteristic of "An Idyl," this section of *Paterson* becomes as much an entangled textual and sexual construct as Phyllis, an exhibited body shaped and explored both linguistically (by the poem *Paterson*) and sexually (by the man Paterson).

The self-voyeurism in "An Idyl" is also clearly at work in *Many Loves* and *A Dream of Love*. In the two dramas, the play among texts constitutes an assemblage of scenes that watch each other, distort each other's reflections, and "read" each other as erotic, semiotic bodies; and the vacillation between seer and seen, between voyeur and exhibitionist, also bleeds eroticism over boundaries and is partly responsible for the ravelling of both plays throughout with the sexual and textual problematic of desire discussed earlier. As a result of the vacillations and collisions, the structures of the two plays do not deliver integrated, cohesive texts in any way. *Many Loves* and *A Dream of Love* as subjects are themselves disseminated among embedded structures and played across fragmented, semiotic fields.

The dispersal of the text as subject helps explain why *Many Loves* and *A Dream of Love* do not work as unified, modernist forms. The relative transparency of early twentieth-century expressionism is undermined by Williams's concern with language and the ways in which semiotic forces entangle, complicate, and generate textual material. Like *Paterson*, Williams's plays are frustratingly complex, in part because the poet-playwright is not only experimenting with the elements used to assemble texts, but is examining philosophical issues about the structure of and relations among subject, text, and body. The plays discover that textualization takes place throughout the dramatic structure, affecting the subject in its body and sexuality as well as in its mind and unconscious. Inevitably, this realization problematizes the shape of the text itself. Such a self-deconstructive project places works like *Many Loves, A Dream of Love*, and *Paterson* IV on a postmodern trajectory, pointing toward later literary projects that investigate the textualization of the mind, the ravelling of textual and sexual desire, and the demystification of discourse and gender by writers such as Samuel Beckett, Robert Coover, and Joanna Russ. Viewed in this company, Williams's drama appears to "play well."

Notes

1. In about 1940, Williams combined three one-act plays, written in 1939, into *Many Loves*, which opened at the Living Theatre in New York in 1959. During the early 1940s, he worked on *A Dream of Love*, first performed at the Hudson Playhouse in New York in 1949. These plays may be found in *Many Loves and Other Plays: The Collected Plays of William Carlos Williams* (New York: New Directions, 1961). *Paterson*, books 1 through 5, was published between 1946 and 1958 and collected in *Paterson* (New York: New Directions, 1963).

2. Because the differences between modernism and postmodernism are many and controversial, I include here only those pertinent to my discussion. Modernism is generally concerned with a unity of form, whereas postmodernism disrupts form, challenging the attempts of systems such as language to totalize the literary project. Modernism is self-conscious about self-expression, whereas postmodernism is self-conscious about the construction of self-expression. Finally, modernism tends to foster a transparency of language to content whereas postmodernism focuses on the linguistic functions of the text and, thereby, textualizes content.

3. Thomas Kilroy, "Brecht, Beckett and Williams," *Sagetrieb* 3 (1984): 86.

4. See Jacques Lacan, *The Four Fundamental Concepts of Psychoanalysis*, ed. Jacques-Alain Miller, trans. Alan Sheridan (New York: W. W. Norton, 1981), 80–81.

5. This scene is also interesting in terms of feminism, for the gaze that Myra imagines is male.

6. Linda Wagner, "The Outrage of *Many Loves*," *Sagetrieb* 3 (1984): 66–67.

7. In *Returning Words to Flesh: Feminism, Psychoanalysis, and the Resurrection of the Body* (Boston: Beacon, 1990), Naomi Goldenberg offers a discussion of the confluence of language and the body from a feminist and psychological perspective, arguing for a resurrection of the body. In reference to Hélène Cixous's and Catherine Clement's text, *The Newly-Born Woman*, Goldenberg states that "now [women] can write out those [past hysterical] visions and bring that turbulent energy into the bodies of our texts. Sexualized experience becomes textualized" (40).

8. David Fedo, "The Meaning of Love in William Carlos Williams' *A Dream of Love*," *Contemporary Literature* 13 (1982): 176.

9. The lines may obliquely refer to the "salmon-falls" of "Sailing to Byzantium." The exact lines do not occur in Yeats.

10. As Jacques Derrida explains in *Positions*, trans. Alan Bass (Chicago: University of Chicago Press, 1981), "the play of differences supposes, in effect, syntheses and referrals which forbid at any moment, or in any sense, that a simple element be *present* in and of itself, referring only to itself" (26).

11. Roland Barthes, *The Pleasure of the Text*, trans. Richard Miller (New York: Hill and Wang, 1975), 17.

Index